NEW
CUTTING
EDGE

INTERMEDIATE

STUDENTS' BOOK

sarah cunningham   peter moor

Longman

CONTENTS

Task	Further skills	Study Practise Remember
Task: Find things in common *Preparation: listening* *Task: speaking* *Follow up: writing*	**Writing**: E-mail an old friend	**Study tip**: Using English in class *Pronunciation spot: Stress and the /ə/ sound*
Task: Test your memory *Preparation: reading* *Task: speaking*	**Real life**: Showing interest *Pronunciation: Sounding polite*	**Study tip**: Using the mini-dictionary *Pronunciation spot: The sound /w/*
Task: Design a tour *Preparation: listening* *Task: speaking* *Follow up: writing*	**Real life**: Booking a flight	**Study tip**: Keeping notes *Pronunciation spot: The sounds /ɪ/ and /iː/*
Task: Talk about someone you admire *Preparation: listening* *Task: speaking* *Follow up: writing*	**Writing**: A curriculum vitae	
Task: Choose the best candidate *Preparation: reading* *Task: speaking*	**Writing**: A covering letter **Real life**: A formal telephone call *Pronunciation: Sounding polite*	**Study tip**: Improving your spoken fluency *Pronunciation spot: The sounds /ɒ/, /ɔː/ and /əʊ/*
Task: Review a book/concert/CD *Preparation: listening* *Task: speaking*	**Writing**: A consumer review	**Study tip**: English outside the classroom (1): Using the media *Pronunciation spot: The sounds /æ/ and /ʌ/*

Task	Further skills	Study Practise Remember
Task: Give tips on how to behave *Preparation: listening* *Task : speaking*	**Real life:** Making a social arrangement	**Study tip:** Using revision techniques *Pronunciation spot: The sounds /θ/ and /ð/*
Task: Make a list of things you'd hate to be without *Preparation: listening* *Task : speaking*	**Real life:** Buying things **Writing:** Saying thank you	
Task: Decide how to spend lottery money *Preparation: listening* *Task : speaking*	**Real life:** Ways of saying numbers	**Study tip:** English outside the classroom (1): Using the Internet *Pronunciation spot: The sounds /b/ and /v/*
Task: Tell a ghost story *Preparation: speaking* *Task : speaking and listening*	**Writing:** A narrative	**Study tip:** Making the most of graded readers *Pronunciation spot: Pronouncing 'h'*
Task: Present your opinions *Preparation: vocabulary* *Task : speaking*	**Writing:** Linking words	**Study tip:** Checking your written work *Pronunciation spot: Review*
Task: Find solutions to problems *Preparation: reading and vocabulary* *Task : speaking* *Follow up: writing*	**Real life:** Saying goodbye	

Irregular verbs page 155   **Mini-checks** pages 156–158   **Tapescripts** pages 159–175

All about you

- ▶ Asking and answering questions
- ▶ Present simple and continuous
- ▶ **Vocabulary**: Everyday activities, People around you
- ▶ **Reading and speaking**: *How we really spend our time*
- ▶ **Wordspot**: *have* (and *have got*)
- ▶ **Pronunciation**: Auxiliary verbs
- ▶ **Task**: Find things in common
- ▶ **Writing**: E-mail an old friend

Language focus 1
Asking and answering questions

1 Look at the photographs of people meeting. Which photo shows the following?

a   a businesswoman meeting a colleague from abroad for the first time
b   a person answering questions for an application form
c   two old friends chatting about their news
d   some students on an English course getting to know each other during a break

Think of two questions the people in each photo might ask each other.

2   **T1.1**   Listen to ten questions you might hear in these situations. Write brief answers for yourself.

Analysis

1   Asking questions
How many of the questions from exercise 2 can you remember? Use the verbs below to write them.

> are   is   do   does   have   was   were   did

Listen again and check. Then ask and answer the questions with a partner.

2   Auxiliaries in answers
Can you shorten these long answers using auxiliary verbs?
a   Have you got any brothers and sisters?
   No, I haven't got any brothers and sisters.
b   Does all your family live round here?
   My parents live round here, but my sister doesn't live round here.

▶ Read Language summary A on page 144.

Practice

1 a Add the correct verbs to the following questions.

      are
1 How ∧ things with you?
2 How you do?
3 What your full name and address?
4 How your flight?
5 When you get here?
6 You have a good journey to school this morning?
7 Where you staying while you're here?
8 You got any special reason for learning English?
9 You speak any other languages?
10 How your job going?
11 You got any brothers and sisters?
12 You have a nice holiday?
13 This your first visit to New York?
14 How all your family?

b **T1.2** Listen and check. Which questions belong with each photo?

Pronunciation

1 Listen again and notice how we stress the important words in the questions in exercise 1a. What happens to the pronunciation of the auxiliary verbs?

How are things with you?

How do you do?

2 Listen again and underline the stressed words in exercise 1a. Practise saying the questions.

2 Work in pairs. Act out two of the conversations in the photos, using questions from exercise 2 on page 6 and from Practice exercise 1.

3 *Either* Work with two new partners. Think of four questions to ask each person. Ask and answer.

Or Think of some questions to ask your teacher, depending on how well you already know him/her.

4 a Work in pairs. Discuss what questions you would ask in the following situations.

Example:
You don't know what 'pensioner' means.
What does 'pensioner' mean?

1 You want to know the English word for ⬭.
2 You don't know how to pronounce a word.
3 You don't know how to spell a word.
4 You don't know which page to look at.
5 You want to know what tonight's homework is.
6 You didn't hear what the teacher said.
7 You want your teacher to write a word on the board.
8 You didn't understand something.

b **T1.3** Listen and check.

Vocabulary 1
Everyday activities

1 **a** Match the phrases in A with their opposites in B.

A	B
1 I spend a lot of time	I'm not interested in
2 I really love	I don't have enough time for
3 I spend too much time	I'm not very good at
4 I'm quite good at	I absolutely hate
5 I'm really into	I don't spend much time

b What verb form is used after all of these expressions?

2 Use the phrases in exercise 1 to make eight true sentences about the activities in the box.

chatting on the phone	listening to music	doing exercise
hanging out with your friends	doing your homework	doing housework
shopping	playing computer games	reading
relaxing and doing nothing	texting your friends	walking
watching TV	(on/using) the Internet	cooking

Examples:
I'm not very good at cooking.
I spend a lot of time chatting on the phone.

3 Choose four activities from the box to ask a partner about. Then choose four more activities to ask a new partner about.

> Do you like playing computer games?

> Do you spend much time doing exercise?

Reading and speaking

1 Read the following statements, checking the phrases in bold in your mini-dictionary. Which do you think are true for your country? Compare your ideas in groups.

a People are **working longer hours** than in the past.
b Watching TV is the most popular **leisure time activity**.
c Most people read a newspaper regularly.
d The majority of women **work full-time**.
e Women do **the main share of the housework**.
f People are eating more and more **ready meals** and **takeaways**.
g The majority of young people have a **full-time job** by the time they are twenty.
h Young people these days spend more time **socialising** than doing homework.
i Pensioners are more **physically active** than teenagers.
j **Regular Internet users** are often keen on sport as well.
k The majority of people take part in a sport at least once a week.
l People **waste a lot of time** at work.

How we really spend our time

Time, it seems, is what we're all short of these days. One reason perhaps, why there are thousands of studies every year into how we spend our time and how we could spend it better. Some of the results are startling. Did you know for example ...?

* Although people all over the world are working longer and longer hours, we also have more leisure time than ever before.

* After sleeping and working, watching TV is by far the most popular leisure activity the world over. The British watch more TV than any other nation in Europe, but they also read more. The vast majority, eighty-five percent, regularly read newspapers, and fifty-four percent regularly read books.

* Although up to two thirds of modern European women work full-time, they still do the main share of the housework, too. Husbands help in the house more than they did in the past, but in the UK for example, men do an average of just six hours a week compared to their wives, who do over eighteen hours. No wonder that the vast majority of working women in the UK say they are stressed and exhausted!

* According to the latest research by supermarkets, the average British family spends just eleven minutes preparing the main evening meal, and prefers 'ready meals' and takeaways to home-cooked food. Almost half of all families in the UK eat together only once a month or less.

* More than half of young people in the UK have a full-time job by the age of nineteen, but the majority of young Spanish and Italian people do not start full-time work until they are twenty-four.

* The average American fourteen-year-old spends only half an hour a day doing homework, and less than a fifth of young people participate in sports, clubs, music or other traditional hobbies. Instead, sixty-five percent say they spend their time chatting on their mobiles and hanging out with their friends in shopping malls.

* In the UK, pensioners are almost twice as active as teenagers, according to recent research. People over sixty-five spend nearly two hours a day doing physical activities such as walking, cycling, gardening or sport, while teenagers spend only seventy-five minutes. However, surprisingly, people who use the Internet regularly do more sport than people who never use it.

* The Swedes and Finns are the sportiest nationalities in Europe. Seventy-three percent do some kind of sport at least once or twice a week.

* People may spend more time at work these days, but are they always working? The latest research reveals that each day the average British employee spends fifty-five minutes chatting, sixteen minutes flirting, fourteen minutes surfing the Internet and nine minutes sending e-mails to friends!

2 Read the text quickly. Which country (or countries) does each of the statements in exercise 1 refer to? Which are true 'all over the world'?

3 Underline four things in the text that you think are surprising or interesting. Compare with your partner.

4 Mark the following phrases S (if they both mean the same) and D (if they are different).

a two thirds / sixty-six percent   S
b the main share of the work / most of the work
c an average of six hours / exactly six hours
d over eighteen hours / less than eighteen hours
e the vast majority / ninety percent
f almost half / fifty-two percent
g more than half / forty-five percent
h a fifth / twenty percent
i at least twice a week / two times a week or more

5 What was the significance of the following numbers in what you read? Look back at the text, if necessary.

a eighty-five percent   *Eighty-five percent of British people regularly read newspapers.*
b six hours   *The average British husband does six hours of housework a week.*
c eighteen hours
d eleven minutes
e twenty-four
f half an hour a day
g seventy-five minutes
h seventy-three
i fifty-five minutes

6 Are you happy with the way you use your time? What would you like to spend more/less time doing? Discuss in groups.

Vocabulary 2
People around you

1 a Check the meaning of the words in the box in your mini-dictionary. Then write the words in the table below.

acquaintance	aunt	best friend
boss	classmate	colleague
cousin	ex-girlfriend	flatmate
headteacher	husband	mother-in-law
neighbour	niece	parent
relative	stepmother	stranger

family	
friends	
work	
school	
other	

b Can you add any other words to each category?

2 `T1.4` You will hear eight instructions. Listen and write your answers in the squares below.

3 Exchange books with your partner. Look at what your partner has written and ask questions to find out the meaning of the names and numbers.

Who's Alain?

Why did you write 'nine'?

Language focus 2
Present simple and continuous

1 `T1.5` Karina is showing a colleague the photos from her twenty-first birthday party. Listen and write her relationship to each person.

a _____   d _____
b _____   e _____
c _____

Karina   **a** Danny   **b** Nikita

2 Can you complete the sentences? Compare your answers with a partner. Then listen again and check.

a Karina is showing her colleague some photos of her <u>birthday party</u>.
b Nikita lives _____ from Karina. She is also Karina's brother's _____ .
c Danny usually lives _____ , but at the moment he's staying with his _____ in Edinburgh. He _____ a design course at Edinburgh College of Art.
d Danny _____ the course, but he _____ what he wants to do.
e Holly looks _____ Karina, but she's actually her _____ .
f Karina's grandmother is getting _____ so she _____ more help these days. She stays with Karina's family at the _____ .
g Richard looks so _____ . He's getting really _____ .

c Holly

d Jean   e Richard

Analysis

1 Underline the Present simple verbs in exercise 2 like this ____, and Present continuous verbs like this ~~~~ .

2 Match the examples in A with the explanations in B.

A	B
They're looking at photos.	a habit
She stays with us every weekend.	an action happening at this moment
She lives upstairs.	a permanent situation
He's staying with his aunt.	a changing situation
Holly looks like Karina.	a temporary situation
He's getting really tall.	a 'state'

3 Verbs that describe states are not used in the continuous form. Find more examples of 'state' verbs in exercise 2 on page 10.

▶ Read Language summary B on page 144.

Practice

1 Choose the correct tense.

a Ben doesn't smoke / isn't smoking – he hates cigarettes.

b Raoul wears / is wearing a tie today – he looks very smart.

c I stay / I'm staying with my uncle while my parents are away.

d Eva is a fantastic musician. She plays / is playing the piano, the guitar and the violin.

e 'Is that you? Hi, it's me. I sit / I'm sitting on the train, but it doesn't move / isn't moving.'

2 a Complete the questions (in the *you* form) in the Present simple or continuous.

1 _____ (like) meeting new people?
2 _____ (read) a good book at the moment?
3 _____ (read) a daily newspaper?
4 _____ (study) for any exams at the moment?
5 _____ (listen) to the radio in the morning?
6 _____ (prefer) smart or casual clothes?
7 _____ (usually get up) late at the weekend?
8 _____ (find) English grammar difficult?
9 _____ (enjoy) the course so far?
10 _____ (get) better at English?

b Ask other students the questions. Try to find one person who answers 'yes' to each question.

3 Discuss in pairs which of the following are true for you.

a I'm getting taller.
b I'm losing weight.
c My hair's going grey.
d My hair's getting long.
e It's getting colder.
f I'm getting hungry.

4 a Write the names of six important people in your life on a piece of paper.

> Andreas
> Gabby   Bruno
> Peter   Lucia   Anna

b Work in groups. Ask and explain who the people are, what they do and what they are doing at the moment.

> Bruno's my boyfriend. He's working in a restaurant at the moment, but he really hates it.

Wordspot
have (and *have got*)

1 [T1.6] Complete the gaps to make phrases with *have*. Then listen and check.

a In some countries it's common to have _____ at twelve o'clock, but we usually eat around two.

b A: I can't find my socks anywhere, Mum!
   B: Have a _____ in the basket by the washing machine.

c I've got a terrible _____ . Is there any aspirin?

d James really makes me laugh. He's really got a great sense of _____ .

e I'm afraid we've got a serious _____ . We've run out of petrol.

f I was tired after walking so far, so I stopped to have a _____ .

g I've got a very large _____ – five brothers and three sisters!

2 The diagram below shows some common uses of *have*. Add the phrases from exercise 1 to the correct section.

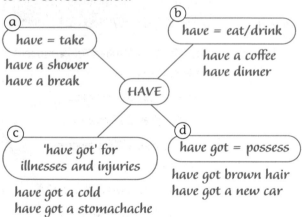

ⓐ have = take
have a shower
have a break

ⓑ have = eat/drink
have a coffee
have dinner

HAVE

ⓒ 'have got' for illnesses and injuries
have got a cold
have got a stomachache

ⓓ have got = possess
have got brown hair
have got a new car

3 Add the words and phrases below to the correct section of the diagram.

a bad back	blue eyes	breakfast	a walk
flu	a holiday	an ice cream	blond hair

4 Discuss the following questions in pairs.

• How often do you do the things in the 'take' part of the diagram?
• What time do you have the things in the 'eat and drink' section?
• Which of the illnesses and injuries have you had?
• Which of the things in the 'possess' part of the diagram have you got?

Task: Find things in common
Preparation: listening

1 [T1.7] Listen to two conversations at a party. Which people already know each other and which have just met? Which topics on page 13 did they discuss? Complete the table.

	Do they know each other?	Which topics did they talk about?
Conversation 1	No,	hobbit football children
Conversation 2	yes.	job. language

2 Listen again. What have the people got in common in each conversation?

Examples:
Conversation 1: *They both like football.*
Conversation 2: *Neither of them like their job.*

3 Read the tapescript of the conversation between Phillip and Petra on page 159. Underline the questions that they ask to find out more about each other, and the phrases that they use to talk about similarities, e.g. *Me too.*

What have you got in common?

Family and home

People you live with?
Married or single?
Brothers and sisters?
Extended family?
Area you live in?
Type of home?

Interests and tastes

Sport, etc?
Reading books/newspapers?
TV/Radio?
Computers/Internet?
Shopping?
Cinema/Theatre/Concerts?
Music?
Food?
Travelling?
Things you especially love/hate?

Work/Studies

Previous jobs/studies?
Aims and ambitions?
Work or study?

Daily Life

Get up / Go to bed?
Mealtimes?
Go out a lot?
Evenings/Weekends?
Housework?
Transport?
Childcare?

Task: speaking

1 Work with a partner you don't normally work with. You are going to find what you have got in common and what differences there are between you. Choose at least six topics on the left to ask about. Think of relevant questions to ask. Ask your teacher for any words or phrases you need.

2 Interview your partner for about ten minutes. Keep brief notes about the things you have got in common and the differences.

▶ Useful language a and b

3 Tell the class briefly what you discovered. Which pairs have got the most/least in common?

▶ Useful language c

Useful language

a Finding things in common
Me too/neither.
That's the same for me.
So/Neither do/have I.

b Finding differences
Oh, I'm the opposite!
Really? I (get up really early).
Oh, that's interesting!

c Telling other people
We both (like jazz).
Neither of us (have breakfast).
I (go to bed really late), but he/she …

Follow up: writing

Write a paragraph or two about your partner, but do not include his/her name. Your teacher will give the paragraphs to other students to read. Can they guess who it is?

Writing
E-mail an old friend

1 **a** Charlotte is getting in touch with an old school friend, Laura, via the 'Friends Reunited' website. Read the e-mail she wrote. What do you learn about Laura and Charlotte?

A voice from the past!! - Message

🔁 Reply 🔁 Reply All 📧 Forward   🖨 📧 ✖ ⬆ ⬇   📎 Follow Up 🅰 ▾

From:	charlotte.b@totalserve.com
To:	ljjkeyes@bsm.com
cc:	
Sent:	Tuesday, April 8, 2003 4:18 pm
Subject:	A voice from the past!

Hi Laura!
Remember me??!! I was really pleased when I found your name on the Friends Reunited website – so (a) __6__ straight away.

(b) __1__ ? (c) __3__ . Last time we met you were still at university, but I guess you're working now. What are you doing? I remember you always wanted to work with children. Are you still with Simon or is that all in the past now? (d) __10__ ? What are your parents doing these days, and how about Joe and Katie? (e) __2__ ?

I now work for a big property company as a sales manager, and at the moment I'm living in Australia, working in the Sydney office. I absolutely love it over here, and even more exciting, I'm getting married next April to Matt – a gorgeous Australian guy I met here! We don't know yet if we're going to live in England or stay in Sydney.

As for my family, well unfortunately Gran died a couple of years ago, but (f) __4__ . Dad retired about three years ago, and they're travelling all over the world these days. They came to see me here a few months ago. And remember my big brother Anthony? He's married now (to Rosie, a girl he met at university) and they've got two-year-old twins, so his life's really changed!

Well, I think that's all the main news from me. (g) __7__ . Maybe we could meet up when I'm back in England?

(h) __5__
Love Charlotte
XXXX

(i) __9__

---

b Complete the e-mail with the following sentences. (There is one sentence too many.)

1 How are things with you?	7 Do write back – I'd love to hear your news.
2 Send them my love, won't you?	
3 I really hope you're well.	8 Keep in touch.
4 My parents are really well.	9 PS I've attached some photos of me now.
5 Take care of yourself.	
6 I decided to drop you a line.	10 How is all your family?

2 Here are some other ways of finishing an e-mail or letter. What do you think is the relationship between the people?

All my love   Regards   Lots of love   Best wishes

3 *Either* Write an e-mail to an old friend giving all your news.

Or Send an e-mail to either your teacher or another student telling them all about yourself.

14

PRACTISE...

1 Auxilliary verbs ☐

Choose the correct auxiliary verb.

a Where are / do your parents come from?

b Johnny is / has got sixteen cousins!

c I really enjoyed the concert, but the others weren't / didn't.

d A: Have you got any money with you?

B: No, I don't / haven't.

e Where were / did you born?

f My boyfriend likes my new hairstyle, but my mother isn't / doesn't.

g How is / does your course going?

▶ **Need to check? Language summary A, page 144.**

2 Present simple and continuous ☐

Which verbs are not correct in the Present continuous? Write the correct Present simple form.

a Tomas isn't usually speaking much in class.

b Paula says she'll call you back – she's making a cake.

c Shh! The children are having a little rest.

d Look, it's getting dark already!

e I'm not knowing your brother.

f Harry's having six older sisters.

g This city is becoming very expensive.

h I'm understanding the Present continuous perfectly.

▶ **Need to check? Language summary B, page 144.**

3 The correct form of the verb ☐

Which is the correct form after these expressions? Think of at least three other verbs or phrases followed by the same form.

a My sister's really into jog / jogging / to jog.

b I hate get / getting / to get up early in the winter.

c William's very good at swim / swimming / to swim.

▶ **Need to check? Vocabulary, page 8.**

4 People around you ☐

Write a word for each definition.

a your aunt's son or daughter _____

b your wife's brother _____

c a person who lives near you _____

d a person you work with _____

e someone you know, but not well _____

f someone you don't know _____

g your mother's new husband _____

h your sister's daughter _____

▶ **Need to check? Vocabulary, page 10.**

5 Words that go together ☐

Match A and B to make phrases.

A	B
a Doctors work long	1 after the children.
b I need to do	2 the Internet most days.
c Take	3 about grammar.
d We must keep	4 the housework.
e I can look	5 full-time.
f I use	6 hours.
g How do you spend	7 your homework, please.
h My mother works	8 your time?
i Do	9 in touch.
j She knows a lot	10 care of yourself.

▶ **Need to check? Reading and speaking, page 8.**

6 Quantities ☐

Match the phrases in A with the percentages in B.

A	B
a a fifth	1 ninety-five percent
b almost half	2 forty-eight percent
c the vast majority	3 fifty-three percent
d about two thirds	4 sixty-four percent
e over half	5 twenty percent

▶ **Need to check? Reading and speaking, page 9.**

Pronunciation spot

Stress and the /ə/ sound

You can use your mini-dictionary to find the stress (strong syllable) in new words.

acquaintance /əkweɪntəns/ n C someone you know, but do not know well

a Underline the stressed syllables in these words. Use your mini-dictionary, if necessary.

average   colleague   cousin
employee   father-in-law leisure
neighbour   parents   pensioner
percent   relative   stomachache

b T1.8 Many weak syllables have the sound /ə/. Listen and circle the /ə/ sounds in the words above. Which two words do not have an /ə/ sound?

ⓐcquaintⓐnce

c Practise saying the words, paying attention to the stress and /ə/ sounds.

REMEMBER!

Look back at the areas you have practised. Tick the ones you feel confident about. Now try the MINI-CHECK on page 156 to check what you know!

Memory

▶ Past simple and continuous; *used to*
▶ **Listening and speaking**: First meetings, A childhood memory
▶ **Pronunciation**: Past simple *-ed* endings, sounding polite
▶ **Song**: *Remember the days of the old schoolyard*
▶ **Reading**: *Ten ways to improve your memory*
▶ **Vocabulary**: Remembering and forgetting
▶ **Task**: Test your memory
▶ **Real life**: Showing interest

a Sung-Yarong
1 Cristian Vieri
b Andy
2 Richard Nixon US President 1969–1974
c Raul
3 Karen

Listening and speaking
First meetings

1 Discuss the following questions in small groups.

- What do you notice about people when you first meet: their voice, their face and hair, their clothes or something else?
- How accurate are your first impressions of people? Have you ever been completely wrong about someone?
- Have you ever met anyone famous? Where were you? What do you remember about him/her?

2 **T2.1** You will hear the people in photos a–c discussing how they met one of the people in photos 1–3. Listen and match the people.

3 Listen again and make a note of where and when each of the people met; and what they said to each other.

Language focus 1
Past simple and continuous

Look at Andy's tapescript on page 160. Find two examples of each of the following.

– regular Past simple verbs
– irregular Past simple verbs
– Past continuous verbs

How do we form the Past simple and Past continuous tenses?

Analysis

Look at the sentence and timeline below. Then choose the correct alternative in the rules a–d.

Andy met his girlfriend while he was working in a bar.

<··· he was working in a bar ···>

	X		⟶ future
past	he met his girlfriend	**now**	

a The Past simple / Past continuous shows complete actions in the story, usually the main events.

b The Past simple / Past continuous shows actions in progress at a time in the past. They start before and often continue after the main events.

c We often use *while* to link these two tenses. It goes before the Past simple / Past continuous.

d Look at Raul's tapescript. Another time word we use to link these tenses is ___when___. It goes before the Past simple / Past continuous.

▶ Read Language summaries A and B on page 145.

Practice

1 [T2.2] Complete Julia's story of how she met her husband, Mark. Put the verbs in brackets in the Past simple or continuous. Then listen and check.

I first (a) _____ (meet) Mark nine years ago, at a party at my friend Harry's house, and we (b) _____ (go) out on our first date three weeks later. Mark (c) _____ (stay) with Harry while he (d) _____ (visit) from Boston, and one Sunday Harry (e) _____ (invite) me to this barbecue in his garden. Mark (f) _____ (help) him to get it ready, supposedly, but when I (g) _____ (arrive) it was complete chaos! They (h) _____ (still tidy) the house, and there was no food ready at all, so I (i) _____ (offer) to help them.

Mark and I (j) _____ (start) chatting while we (k) _____ (prepare) the salads, but I remember thinking he (l) _____ (be) a bit strange because he (m) _____ (ask) me if I had a boyfriend. I think that Americans are much more direct than the British. Anyway, he (n) _____ (seem) a nice guy, and I (o) _____ (like) him a lot ... except for this awful Hawaiian shirt that he (p) _____ (wear) – it was just unbelievable!

Pronunciation

1 How many syllables are there in each of the following Past simple regular verbs?

arrived ☐	asked ☐	helped ☐	invited ☐
liked ☐	offered ☐	prepared ☐	seemed ☐
started ☐	stayed ☐	tidied ☐	visited ☐

2 [T2.3] Listen and check. In which verbs is the -ed form pronounced as a syllable /ɪd/? How is the form pronounced in the other verbs? Practise saying the verbs.

3 [T2.4] How are these -ed forms pronounced? Listen and check.

decided	expected	hoped	noticed
played	remembered	studied	talked
tried	wanted	watched	worked

2 a Match the beginnings of the sentences in A with the endings in B using *when*, *while* or *because*.

A

1 My dad (give) me a lift   *e; because*
2 My relatives (arrive)
3 The police (stop) him
4 It (snow)
5 You (fall) off your bike
6 I (wait) for the bus this morning
7 Anna (break) her leg
8 I (do) a summer job in a hotel

B

a we (have) dinner.
b she (ski) in Austria.
c I (meet) my husband.
d Marco (drive) past me.
e it (rain) so hard.
f I (open) my bedroom curtains this morning.
g he (drive) too fast.
h you (not pay) attention to the road.

b Write out the sentences with the verbs in the correct form, Past simple or continuous.

Example:
My dad gave me a lift because it was raining so hard.

3 Work in small groups. Tell each other about the first time you met someone who is now important in your life. Include details about some of these things.

your life at that time   where you were
the weather   what you noticed about this person
what you talked about   what he/she was wearing
your general impression of him/her

Language focus 2
used to

Remember the days of the old schoolyard

Remember the days of the old schoolyard
We used to laugh a lot
Don't you remember the days of the old schoolyard

When we (1)_____ imaginings
And we (2)_____ all kinds of things
And we (3)_____
And (4)_____ love
Yes, I do, oh and I (5)_____ you

Remember the days of the old schoolyard
We used to (6)_____ a lot
Don't you remember the days of the old schoolyard

When we (7)_____ simplicity
And we (8)_____ warm toast for tea
And we (9)_____ and (10)_____ love
Yes, I do, oh and I (11)_____ you

1 a You are going to listen to the song *Remember the days of the old schoolyard* by Cat Stevens. From the title what do you think the song is about?

b **T2.5** Can you complete the song with the following verbs? Compare with a partner. Then listen and check.

> cry had (x4) laughed (x2) needed (x2) remember (x2)

2 How does the writer of the song feel about his schooldays? Were they a completely happy time? What words/lines tell you this? Compare your opinions in groups.

Analysis

1 Which of the following sentences describes:
- a single action in the past?
- repeated actions/states in the past?
- repeated actions/states in the present?

a *We used to laugh a lot.*
b *We had warm toast for tea.*
c *We usually have toast for tea.*
d *I laughed when I saw him.*

2 a Which of the following sentences describes something that has changed from the past? Which describes something that hasn't changed? Underline the time phrases that show this.

His life isn't simple any more / any longer.
He still needs love.

b Rewrite the following sentence twice using each of the time phrases you underlined.

He thinks about his schooldays.

▶ Read Language summary C on page 145.

Practice

1 a Which of the following sentences are true about your schooldays? (If you are still at school, think about your primary schooldays.)

1 I used to love school.
2 I still remember the names of all my teachers.
3 I used to be frightened of some of the teachers.
4 I used to be frightened of some of the bigger children.
5 I still see my friends from those days.
6 I used to be very good at maths.
7 My work used to be very neat and tidy.
8 I still have my exercise books from school.
9 I always used to do my homework.
10 I never used to get into trouble.
11 I used to love sport and games.
12 I don't do sport any more.

b Use the sentences to talk about your childhood in groups. Did you learn anything surprising about your classmates?

> Actually, I used to hate school.

> Really? I liked it. I used to love art and history.

2 Think back to your life when you were ten years old. What are the differences and similarities between your life then and now? Think about:

– your home.
– your likes and dislikes (food, sports, animals, etc.).
– your skills and abilities.
– your personality (confident/studious, etc.)
– your fears and worries.
– the lives of your parents and family.

Write sentences using *used to*, *didn't use to*, *still* and *not ... any more / any longer.*

Examples:
We used to live in a small village, but we don't any more.
I still don't like eating vegetables!
I didn't use to like dogs, but I don't mind them now.

Listening and speaking
A childhood memory

1 a You will hear Justin and Helen talking about a childhood memory. Look at the pictures. What do you think happened?

Helen   Justin

b Check these words in your mini-dictionary. Which story do you think they belong to?

> to get the blame for something   slot machines
> to slide   the alarm went off   a fairground   a marble floor
> to bully someone   to win a prize   to cut your head open

2 **T2.6** Listen and check. Who do you think was happier at the end of the story, Justin or Helen? Why?

3 a Listen to Justin's story again and answer the following questions in pairs.

1 How old was Justin at the time of the story?
2 Who was Carl Foster and why didn't Justin like him?
3 What did Justin and his friends use to do after lunch?
4 How did he hurt himself?
5 Why does Justin say 'It serves him right' at the end?

b Now listen to Helen's story again and answer the questions.

6 Where did Helen and her family spend their holidays when she was a child?
7 Why did she get angry with the machine?
8 Why did the manager come out of his office?
9 What did Helen's brother tell her would happen?
10 Why was she frightened for the rest of the holiday?

4 a Think about an incident from your childhood. It could be:

– a funny or annoying incident at school.
– a holiday you particularly remember.
– a party or family celebration.
– a time when you did something naughty.

b Spend a few minutes thinking about how to describe what happened. Then work in groups and tell your story.

Reading

1 What methods do you use to remember things? Look at the pictures below. What methods is the man using to remember his shopping list? Have you ever tried any of these methods?

One day Charles the EGG woke up. For breakfast he had a bowl of MILK with SUGAR and the rest of last night's SPAGHETTI ...

Spaghetti, milk, sugar, eggs, spaghetti, milk, sugar, eggs ...

*MESS
M = milk,
E = eggs,
S = sugar,
S = spaghetti*

2 Which of the things below do you think improve your memory? Which don't help?

doing puzzles and crosswords	keeping fit
increasing your heart rate	listening to rock music
getting oxygen to your brain	chewing gum
eating fruit and vegetables	eating fish
listening to classical music	stress

3 a Read the text and check your answers to exercise 2.

b Which of the methods in the pictures in exercise 1 are mentioned in the text?

4 Mark the following statements *True*, *False* or *Don't know*. Then compare your answers with a partner.

a Schoolchildren often don't remember facts about history because they find it very boring.

b Repeating things is effective for long-term memory.

c Using a story to help you remember long lists is not very effective.

d Listening to all types of music helps to improve memory.

e 'Mental exercise' is more important for the memory than physical exercise.

f All fats and oils are bad for the brain.

g Chewing gum helps you to concentrate even better than coffee.

⑩ ways to improve your memory

A good memory is often seen as something that comes naturally, and a bad memory as something that cannot be changed, but actually there is a lot that you can do to improve your memory. However, it does mean taking responsibility and making an effort. Here are the experts' top tips.

① Take an interest – make an effort

We all remember the things we are interested in and forget the ones that bore us. This no doubt explains the reason why schoolboys remember football results effortlessly but struggle with dates from their history lessons! Take an active interest in what you want to remember, and focus on it consciously. One way to 'make' yourself more interested is to ask questions – the more the better!

② Repeat things

Repeating things is the best way to remember things for a short time, e.g. remembering a phone number for a few seconds. 'Chunking' or grouping numbers helps you to remember them, e.g. the following numbers would be impossible for most of us to remember: 1492178919318483. But look at them in 'chunks', and it becomes much easier: 1492 1789 1931 8483.

③ Form a mental picture

Another way to make something more memorable is to think about something visual associated with it. Form a mental picture, and the stranger the picture the better you will remember it! If an English person studying Spanish wanted to remember the Spanish word for duck, 'pato', he/she could associate it with the English verb 'to pat' and imagine a picture of someone patting a duck on the head.

④ Invent a story

To remember long lists, try inventing a story which includes all the items you want to remember. In experiments, people were asked to remember up to 120 words using this technique and when they were tested afterwards, on average they could remember ninety percent of them!

5 Organise your ideas

If we organise what we know in a logical way then when we learn more about that subject we understand that better, and so add to our knowledge more easily. Make well-organised notes. Be sure things are clear in your mind. If not, ask questions until you understand!

6 Listen to Mozart

Many experts believe that listening to classical music, especially Mozart, helps people to organise their ideas more clearly and so improves their memory. Sadly, rock music does not have the same effect!

7 Take mental exercise

If you do not want to lose your memory as you get older you need to keep your brain fit, just like your body: 'use it or lose it' is the experts' advice. Logic puzzles, crosswords and mental arithmetic are all good 'mental aerobics'.

8 Take physical exercise

Physical exercise is also important for your memory, because it increases your heart rate and sends more oxygen to your brain, and that makes your memory work better. Exercise also reduces stress, which is very bad for the memory.

9 Eat the right things

The old saying that 'eating fish makes you brainy' may be true after all. Scientists have discovered that the fats found in fish like tuna, sardines and salmon – as well as in olive oil – help to improve the memory. Vitamins C and E (found in fruits like oranges, strawberries and red grapes) and vitamin B (found in lean meat and green vegetables) are all good 'brain food', too.

10 Drink coffee

Caffeine may not be too good for you, but like exercise, it increases your heart rate and sends more oxygen to your brain. A cup of coffee really does help you concentrate when you sit down to study. And if you don't like coffee, don't worry – experts believe that chewing gum has the same effect!

5 Add the missing prepositions. Look back at the text, if necessary.

a   interested _____
b   struggle _____
c   focus _____
d   think _____
e   associated _____
f   add _____
g   listen _____
h   sit _____

6 Which of the tips in the text would be useful in helping you to learn English? Will you try any?

Vocabulary
Remembering and forgetting

1 The verbs on the left are related to memory. Cross out the phrases which cannot follow each verb.

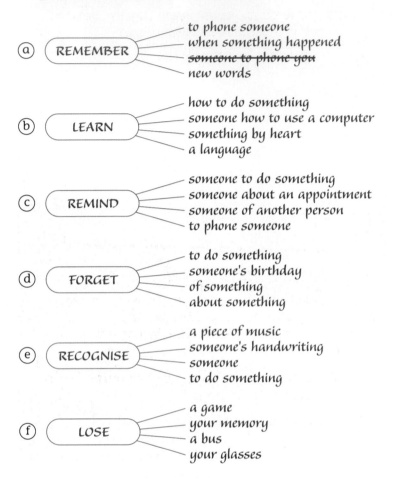

(a) REMEMBER
— to phone someone
— when something happened
— ~~someone to phone you~~
— new words

(b) LEARN
— how to do something
— someone how to use a computer
— something by heart
— a language

(c) REMIND
— someone to do something
— someone about an appointment
— someone of another person
— to phone someone

(d) FORGET
— to do something
— someone's birthday
— of something
— about something

(e) RECOGNISE
— a piece of music
— someone's handwriting
— someone
— to do something

(f) LOSE
— a game
— your memory
— a bus
— your glasses

2 a Complete the questions with one word, if necessary.

1 Have you learnt how _____ drive yet?
2 Did anyone important forget _____ your birthday this year?
3 Have you ever lost _____ a large amount of money?
4 Who usually reminds you _____ do things?
5 At school, what kind of things did you have to learn _____ heart?
6 Can you remember anything about _____ you were three? What can you remember?
7 Have you forgotten _____ do anything important this week?
8 Is there anyone in your class who reminds you _____ someone famous?
9 Do you usually recognise _____ pop songs quickly?
10 Is there anyone that you must remember _____ phone today?
11 Are you competitive? Do you get upset if you lose _____ games or competitions?
12 Have you ever seen anyone well-known in the street? How did you recognise _____ him /her?

b Work in pairs. Choose eight of the questions and ask your partner.

Task: Test your memory
Preparation: reading

1 Check the words in bold in the box in your mini-dictionary. Then discuss with other students which of the things you are good and bad at remembering.

appointments and **arrangements**
people's names/faces
the words of poems, songs, etc.
facts and **dates** you studied
details about people's lives
events from your childhood
things you need to do or buy
people's birthdays
the **plots** of films or books
new English vocabulary
phone numbers
things that happened last week

2 You are going to prepare for a memory quiz. Look at the memory tasks. You have ten minutes to remember as much as you can.

Task: speaking

1 Work in pairs. Student A: Test Student B using the memory quiz on page 136. Student B: Test Student A using the memory quiz on page 134. Take turns to ask questions. Keep a note of how well your partner answered.

▶ Useful language a and b

2 What kind of things is your partner good at remembering? What is he/she not very good at remembering? What are the differences between you? Tell the class.

▶ Useful language c

MEMORY TASKS

1 This is your new mobile phone number. Remember it.

☎ 05511 789312

2 These are the past tenses of six irregular verbs. Remember them.

bite – bit   eat – ate   hit – hit
hold – held   throw – threw   win – won

3 These are your new classmates. Remember their names.

Daniel

Saara

Chang

Nadine

Robin

4 You are going to sing the song from page 18 at a party! Memorise the first verse.

5 While you are out shopping after this lesson you need to buy the following things. Memorise your shopping list.

- a birthday card for gran
- some tomatoes for dinner
- some white sports socks
- a black pen
- a new English dictionary

6 You've just got married. Your new mother-in-law's birthday is on 27th June, and your new father-in-law's is on 22nd July. Your husband's/wife's is on 26th January. It's important that you don't forget them!

7 One of your classmates has given you her e-mail address. Remember it.

antonia.b@yahoo.net

Useful language

a Saying what you remember

I/We/He definitely …

I remember it perfectly …

I'm not a hundred percent sure but I think …

I find it easy to remember …

b Saying what you don't remember

Just let me think.

I'm afraid I can't remember …

I've got no idea!

c Comparing

He's/She's (not) very good at remembering …

He's/She's better than me at remembering …

He's/She's got a very good memory for …

Real life
Showing interest

1 **T2.7** Kirstin is the singer in a group called 'Steam Patrol'. She is telling her friend Tom about an experience she had when playing a concert in Germany. Listen and put the following events in the order she mentions them.

She saw the rest of the group. ☐
She couldn't find the bar. ☐
She decided to go for a walk. ☐1
She followed the man. ☐
She walked around for a bit. ☐
She saw someone in a 'Steam Patrol' T-shirt. ☐
She spoke to a woman. ☐
She decided to return to the bar. ☐
She left the bar. ☐

2 Look at the tapescript on page 160. Underline the phrases Tom uses to show he is interested.

▶ Read Language summary D on page 145.

Pronunciation

1 **T2.8** Listen to some phrases from Kirstin and Tom's conversation. Notice how Tom shows he is interested by his use of intonation.

Really? Uh-huh.

2 Look at the tapescript on page 161 and practise saying the phrases, copying the intonation from the recording.

---

3 Work in pairs. Think of a time when you got lost or something strange happened to you. Student A: Tell Student B your story. Student B: Show you are interested by using some of the phrases from the tapescript. When you have finished, swap roles.

STUDY...

Using the mini-dictionary

1 The mini-dictionary contains all the new words and phrases from the Students' Book. In Module 1 you saw how to use the mini-dictionary to help you with word stress. The mini-dictionary also tells you about the meaning, pronunciation and grammar of each word or phrase, and gives you an example sentence, like this:

arrangement /ə'reɪndʒmənt/ n **1** [C usually plural] plans and preparations that you must make so that something can happen in the future: *Lee is making the arrangements for the wedding.* | *We haven't finalized our travel arrangements yet.* **2** [C] something that has been organized or agreed on: *We made an arrangement to meet.*

2 The words in bold below all appear in Module 2. Use the mini-dictionary to answer the following questions.

a Is **pat** a noun, verb or adjective?
b Where is the stress in **arithmetic**?
c Is **toast** a countable or an uncountable noun?
d What preposition comes after the verb **to focus**?
e How do we form the opposite of the adjective **fit**?
f How do you pronounce the final letter in **asked**?
g What type of verb is **tell off**?
h What is the past simple of the verb **eat**?

For more information about the mini-dictionary, look at the welcome page of the mini-dictionary.

PRACTISE...

1 Past simple ☐

All the sentences below are in the Past simple. Which sentence refers to:

a an action which happened at a specific time?
b a state?
c a short, single action in the past?
d a repeated action in the past?
e a long action in the past?

1 He put the money on the table.
2 They got back from holiday last night.
3 I often walked to school as a child.
4 It rained for three days without stopping.
5 I felt very homesick at first.

▶ **Need to check? Language summary A, page 145.**

2 Past continuous ☐

Which verbs are not correct in the Past continuous? Write the correct Past simple form.

a At 7.30 I was having breakfast in the kitchen.
b It was raining hard when we were arriving at the station.
c I was sitting at home when the doorbell was ringing.
d We were having such a great time we weren't wanting to go home.
e I was driving home when I was hearing the news on the radio.
f At the age of eighteen, I was liking all kinds of sport.

▶ **Need to check? Language summary B, page 145.**

3 Contrasting past and present ☐

Complete the sentences with the words in the box.

any more still use used

a We _____ to have such a lot of fun when we went out together.
b I didn't _____ to like Thai food, but I do now.
c Mr Franks doesn't work here _____ longer.
d Once there was a huge factory here, but there isn't any _____ .
e There are _____ some beautiful old buildings in the town centre.

▶ **Need to check? Language summary C, page 145.**

4 Short questions to show interest ☐

Write the correct short question (Do you?, Is she?, etc.).

a A I'm really tired today.
  B _____ ?
b A I saw Paula last night.
  B _____ ?
c A He was wearing an awful shirt.
  B _____ ?
d A My parents were happy to meet you.
  B _____ ?
e A They didn't like the film.
  B _____ ?

▶ **Need to check? Language summary D, page 145.**

5 Remembering and forgetting ☐

Choose the correct alternative.

a Did you forget / learn / remember to phone your sister?
b Florence always recognises / reminds / remembers me of her father.
c I'm trying to learn / remember / remind the words of the song by heart.
d It seems that the young man forgot / lost / remembered his memory as a result of the crash.
e I almost didn't forget / recognise / learn her – she's really changed!

▶ **Need to check? Vocabulary, page 22.**

6 Words that go together ☐

Match the verbs in A with the prepositions in B.

A	B
a interested	1 about
b listen	2 on
c focus	3 down
d sit	4 in
e struggle	5 to
f think	6 with

▶ **Need to check? Reading, page 21.**

Pronunciation spot

The sound /w/

a **T2.9** Listen and count the number of /w/ sounds in these sentences.
1 While we were preparing the salad ...
2 He was wearing a Hawaiian shirt.
3 I was waiting for the bus.
4 When we were twelve years old ...
5 What was he wearing?

b Practise saying the sentences, paying attention to the /w/ sounds.

REMEMBER!

Look back at the areas you have practised. Tick the ones you feel confident about. Now try the MINI-CHECK on page 156 to check what you know!

Around the world

▶ Comparatives and superlatives
▶ Phrases for comparing
▶ Reading: *100 places to visit before you die*
▶ Pronunciation: Stress and /ə/ sounds
▶ Vocabulary and writing: Describing towns and cities
▶ Task: Design a tour
▶ Real life: Booking a flight

Language focus 1
Comparatives and superlatives

a Do the quiz below in groups or teams. Do not look at a map!

b [T3.1] Listen and check your answers. Note any answers you didn't get.

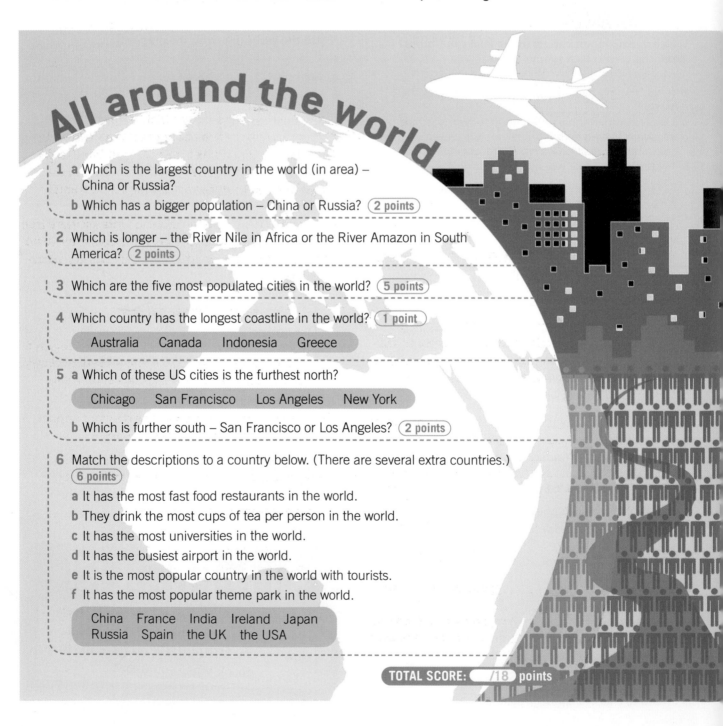

All around the world

1 a Which is the largest country in the world (in area) – China or Russia?

b Which has a bigger population – China or Russia? (2 points)

2 Which is longer – the River Nile in Africa or the River Amazon in South America? (2 points)

3 Which are the five most populated cities in the world? (5 points)

4 Which country has the longest coastline in the world? (1 point)

Australia   Canada   Indonesia   Greece

5 a Which of these US cities is the furthest north?

Chicago   San Francisco   Los Angeles   New York

b Which is further south – San Francisco or Los Angeles? (2 points)

6 Match the descriptions to a country below. (There are several extra countries.) (6 points)

a It has the most fast food restaurants in the world.

b They drink the most cups of tea per person in the world.

c It has the most universities in the world.

d It has the busiest airport in the world.

e It is the most popular country in the world with tourists.

f It has the most popular theme park in the world.

China   France   India   Ireland   Japan
Russia   Spain   the UK   the USA

TOTAL SCORE: /18 points

Analysis

1 Revision of basic forms

a What are the comparative and superlative forms of these adjectives?

> long big busy popular far

b What are the rules for one-, two- and three-syllable adjectives? Can you think of two more irregular adjectives like *far*?

2 Big and small differences

Match the sentences to the correct picture.

X is slightly higher than Y.
X is much higher than Y.
X is a little bit higher than Y.
X is a lot higher than Y.

3 Superlative phrases

Complete the missing words in the superlative phrases.

by *far* the biggest city _____ the world
second/third/fourth biggest city _____ the USA
one _____ the biggest cities

▶ Read Language summaries A, B and C on page 146.

Practice

1 Add two words to each sentence to complete the information from the quiz. Look at the tapescript on page 161, if necessary. Use the correct form of the adjectives in brackets.

a The Nile is only *slightly longer* (long) than the Amazon.
b Seoul is the _____ (populated) city in the world.
c Mumbai is a little _____ (big) than São Paulo.
d Moscow is the _____ (big) city in the world.
e The coast of Canada is _____ (long) than the coast of Indonesia.
f Los Angeles is a _____ (far) south than San Francisco.
g India has a _____ (big) university than any other country.
h France is much _____ (popular) with tourists than the USA.
i London has _____ (busy) airport in the world.
j Japan has the _____ (popular) theme park in the world.

2 a **T3.2** Listen to eight instructions and write your answers in random order below.

b Swap books with a partner. Ask questions to find out why your partner wrote down these places. Were any of your answers the same?

> Why did you write ...?

> Because it's the second biggest city in my country ... I think!

3 a **T3.3** Look at the table on page 138 that gives information about the UK and two of its neighbours, France and Ireland. Then listen to six statements and decide from the table if they are true or false. Then correct the false statements.

b Work in pairs. Use the table to write six more true or false statements about the three countries. Read your sentences to another pair. Can they say which are true?

4 a Choose one of these options.

- *If you are in your own country,* write down the name of a nearby country to compare with your country (preferably one that is very different from your country).

- *If you are in an English-speaking country,* compare that country with your own country.

Think of eight to ten differences, for example: size, population, cities, scenery, climate, cost of living.

b Compare your ideas in groups.

> ... is slightly more expensive than ...

> ... is much bigger than ...

Reading

1 What do you look for in a holiday destination? Discuss with a partner if these things are important or not.

– Natural wonders, such as waterfalls, mountains, etc.
– Ancient archeological sites and great monuments
– Romantic, historical cities
– Exciting modern cities
– Beautiful beaches and coastline

2 A TV travel programme asked its viewers to vote for 'The top 100 places to visit before you die'. They voted in the five categories in exercise 1. Scan the text and answer these questions.

a Which place won in each category? Which country is it in?
b Which ones have you heard of before? What do you already know about them?
c Check these words in your mini-dictionary. Which of the five places do you associate these things with?

canals and bridges	cliffs
layers of rock	neon lights
extravagant hotels	coconut trees
paintings and sculptures	temples
stretches for 443 kilometres	turquoise sea
white sand	gambling

3 Work in pairs or small groups. Find these pieces of information as quickly as you can.

a The names of two famous people married in Las Vegas.
b The age of the city of Petra.
c The name of the largest island in Thailand.
d Two 'ancient monuments' you can find in Las Vegas.
e The name of the second most popular natural wonder.
f Two things you will find in the Doge's Palace.
g The number of people who die falling into the Grand Canyon every year.
h The nationality of the traveller who found Petra about 200 years ago.
i Three things you can do on Koh Samui.
j The number of bridges in Venice.

4 Read the text again and think about the questions. Then compare your opinions in pairs or groups.

• Put the five places in order starting with the one you would most like to visit.
• Are there any other places in the world that you have always wanted to go?
• Have you been anywhere that you think 'everyone should see before they die'?

100 PLACES
TO VISIT BEFORE YOU DIE

We asked our viewers to vote – these were the top choices.

Natural wonder

 1st **The Grand Canyon, USA**

Known to native Americans as the 'Mountain lying down', the Grand Canyon stretches for 443 kilometres where the Colorado River cuts through northwest Arizona. The canyon is a baby by geological standards – only five or six million years old, although the rocks at the bottom are almost two billion years old. It is the incredible colours of these different layers of rock that delight visitors – over five million of them every year. Surprisingly though, after making the long journey there, the average visitor spends only fifteen minutes looking at the Canyon. Even so, visitors should still be careful: every year an average of five people fall over the edge.

A viewer's opinion: 'It's just incredible, you feel as if you have died and gone to heaven.'

2nd Iguazu Falls, Argentina/Brazil
3rd Great Barrier Reef, Australia
4th Rocky Mountains, Canada
5th Victoria Falls, Zimbabwe

Ancient wonder

1st Petra, Jordan

The location for a number of Hollywood films, including *Indiana Jones and the Last Crusade*, the city of Petra was built in rocky cliffs more than 2,000 years ago, and was once an important commercial city. Temples, palaces, and a huge amphitheatre were all cut out of the cliffs, whose amazing colours give the city its rose-red appearance. Historians believe that the citizens of Petra had to abandon it around 551 AD and this incredible archeological site was forgotten by the West, until a Swiss traveller 'rediscovered' it in 1812.

A viewer's opinion: 'It's very difficult to imagine how enormous and how splendid it is from photographs – you just have to see it in person. It'll blow your mind!'

2nd Machu Picchu, Peru **3rd** The Pyramids, Egypt
4th The Great Wall of China **5th** Angkor Wat, Cambodia

Romantic city

1st Venice, Italy

What could be more romantic than going down a Venetian canal in a gondola? No wonder Venice is the favourite of lovers all over the world.

This unique city is located on 118 flat islands, and has over 200 canals and 400 bridges. Visit the Piazza San Marco, one of the most beautiful squares in the world with its 500-year-old buildings, and marvel at the Basilica of St Mark, and the Doge's Palace, the home of many of Venice's most famous paintings and sculptures.

A viewer's opinion: 'Imagine going back in time to a life without cars, where magnificent art and architecture were all around you – this is what you experience when you go to Venice.'

2nd Prague, Czech Republic **3rd** Paris, France
4th Istanbul, Turkey **5th** St Petersburg, Russia

Modern city

1st Las Vegas, USA

A surprising choice as your favourite city, Las Vegas means the 'meadows' in Spanish, but meadows are probably the only thing you can't find here. Even for those who aren't interested in gambling, Las Vegas is one of the most exciting cities in the world. 'The strip', in the centre of town, is five kilometres of the most extravagant hotels you will ever see, including replicas of the Eiffel Tower, the Egyptian Pyramids and ancient Roman Palaces. It uses almost

24,000 kilometres of neon lights! Famous for its 'quickie' weddings (both Elvis Presley and Richard Gere were married here) you can even arrange a 'drive through wedding' and be back in the casinos in an hour!

A viewer's opinion: 'There can be no other place like this on earth – it's like entering a cartoon world.'

2nd Sydney, Australia **3rd** Hong Kong, China
4th New York, USA **5th** Rio de Janeiro, Brazil

Beach

1st Koh Samui, Thailand

A tropical paradise located in the warm blue waters to the southeast of Thailand. Although it is the kingdom's second largest island after Phuket, it was unknown to tourists until a few years ago. Easy to reach from Bangkok, it is covered with coconut trees and brightly-coloured flowers and is surrounded by

white sandy beaches and turquoise seas. Whether you want remote beaches, great shopping, first-class restaurants or an exciting night-life, you'll find it on Koh Samui.

A viewer's opinion: 'The most perfect paradise island in the Far East – such friendly people and good food! Everyone should go there before they die, but hopefully not at the same time!'

2nd Whithaven beach, Great Barrier Reef, Australia
3rd Cancún, Mexico **4th** Boulder's Beach, South Africa
5th Bora Bora, French Polynesia

Language focus 2
Phrases for comparing

Michael Tang is from Hong Kong. In 1997, the city changed from British to Chinese rule. He talks about the changes.

Irina Solokova is from Moscow. She talks about how 'Perestroika' (the changes after Communism) has changed her city.

1 Look at the photos of Michael and Irina. What do you know about Moscow and Hong Kong?

2 a **T3.4** Listen to Michael and Irina. Mark the things in the box they mention, *I* for Irina and *M* for Michael.

economic problems	street names
tourists	language(s) spoken
how clean/dirty the city is	pace of life
new shops and buildings	traffic and driving
standard of living, prices, etc.	

b Which changes do both Michael and Irina mention? Do they feel generally happy or unhappy about these changes?

3 Choose the correct alternative. Then listen again and check.

Hong Kong
a Daily life in Hong Kong feels very different from / more or less the same as how it was before.
b Michael thinks Hong Kong seems more / less Chinese now.
c The standard of living in Hong Kong is very similar / very different.
d The streets look slightly / completely different from before.

Moscow
e The streets of Moscow look slightly / completely different from the old days.
f Irina thinks Moscow feels more / less Russian.
g The traffic in Moscow is much worse than / more or less the same as before.
h Prices in Moscow are very similar to / very different from before.

Analysis

1 Match the adjectives on the left with the prepositions on the right.

different   than
the same   to
worse   as
similar   from

2 Put the phrases in the best place on the line.

very different from
very similar to
exactly the same as
slightly different from
about the same as
completely different from

same ↑
   a _____
   b the same as
   c _____
   d _____
   e similar to
   f _____
   g different from
   h _____
different ↓ i _____

► Read Language summary D on page 146.

Practice

1 a **T3.5** Look at the two pictures on page 135. Then listen and say whether the statements about the pictures are true or false.

b Work in pairs. Find six more similarities and differences between the pictures. Tell other students about them using the phrases in the analysis box.

2 Think about your town now and at some point in the past. Make sentences using comparative phrases. Then compare with other students.

Example:
The shops and restaurants are much better than before.

shops and restaurants	traffic
public transport	street names
cost of living	climate
how the place looks	daily life

Pronunciation

1 **T3.6** Listen and write down the eight sentences.

2 **T3.7** Notice the stress and /ə/ sounds in the comparative phrases. Practise saying the phrases.

/ə/ /ə/
better than ...

/ə/ /ə/ /ə/
a **lot bus**ier than ...

/ə/ /ə/
one of the **big**gest ...

/ə/ /ə/
different from ...

/ə/ /ə/
the **same** as ...

/ə/
similar to ...

3 Practise saying the sentences you wrote down in exercise 1 above. Pay attention to the /ə/ sounds.

Vocabulary and writing
Describing towns and cities

1 Check the words in bold below in your mini-dictionary. Then choose a place you know well and answer the questions.

- Is it a village, town or city? How big is it ? Describe its location, using some of the phrases below to help you.

  It's in the west / southeast / centre. It's near the **border** with ...
  It's on the river X.   It's famous for ...
  It's about 50 km from ...

- Which of the following things does the place have?

  an **industrial area**   a **carnival**, **festival** or other **events**
  beautiful **scenery nearby**   an **underground system** or **trams**
  sandy beaches   **docks** or **a harbour**
  spectacular views   **shopping malls** or street **markets**

  Does it have any other important things not on this list?

- Which of the following adjectives would you choose to describe the place?

  cosmopolitan crowded exciting **historical** industrial
  noisy ugly **old-fashioned** **peaceful** **polluted**
  popular with tourists romantic

- Which is your favourite area or place? Which place do you like least? What are the best and worst things about it?

2 Work in pairs.

- *If you have chosen the same place*, compare answers. Do you agree?
- *If you have chosen different places*, close your book and describe the place to your partner. Answer any questions your partner has.

3 Write a description of the place you have chosen, including answers to the questions in exercise 1.

Task: Design a tour
Preparation: listening

1 What do you know about Australia? Think about:
– the capital and main cities.
– the climate.
– the language and culture.
– the scenery and wildlife.

Compare ideas with other students.

2 **T3.8** Marco is going to Australia for two weeks on holiday. He is asking his Australian friend Elaine to recommend places to visit. Listen and number the four places on the map that Elaine suggests. How long do they decide he should spend in each place?

3 Work in pairs. In which place(s) does Elaine mention the following?

bars and cafés	climbing
beautiful beaches	jellyfish
cosmopolitan	snorkelling
the Opera House	the Outback
the Parliament building	the rainforest
Aboriginal culture	wine tasting

Listen again and check.

4 **T3.9** Listen and complete the phrases Elaine uses.

a   I think you'll really _____ Melbourne.
b   I don't think _____ to go to Perth.
c   Personally, _____ from Melbourne to Alice Springs.
d   I'd _____ about two days or so.
e   You've got to stay at least _____ .
f   _____ , I'd stay on an island.
g   You _____ at least four or five days in Sydney.
h   It would be _____ the Blue Mountains just outside Sydney, they're _____ .

5 Would you like to visit Australia? Which of the places described would you most like to see? Why?

Cairns;
Great Barrier Reef

Alice Springs;
Ayers Rock (Uluru)

Perth

Adelaide

Sydney;
Blue mountains

Canberra

1 Melbourne

Task: speaking

1 **a** Either in pairs or individually, you are going to design a tour similar to Elaine's. Choose one of the options below.

- Design a tour of your country or region for one of the following groups. (You will be the guide!)
  – other students in your class
  – a family with young children
  – a group of students on a budget holiday
  – a foreign film star, singer, sports personality, etc.
- Design a tour of either California or Scotland, using the information at the back of the book on page 137.
- Design a tour of an interesting country you have visited for other students in your class.
- Design a 'fantasy tour' of a region/country/continent that you would like to visit (for example, 'Great cities of Europe', 'Highlights of the USA', etc.).

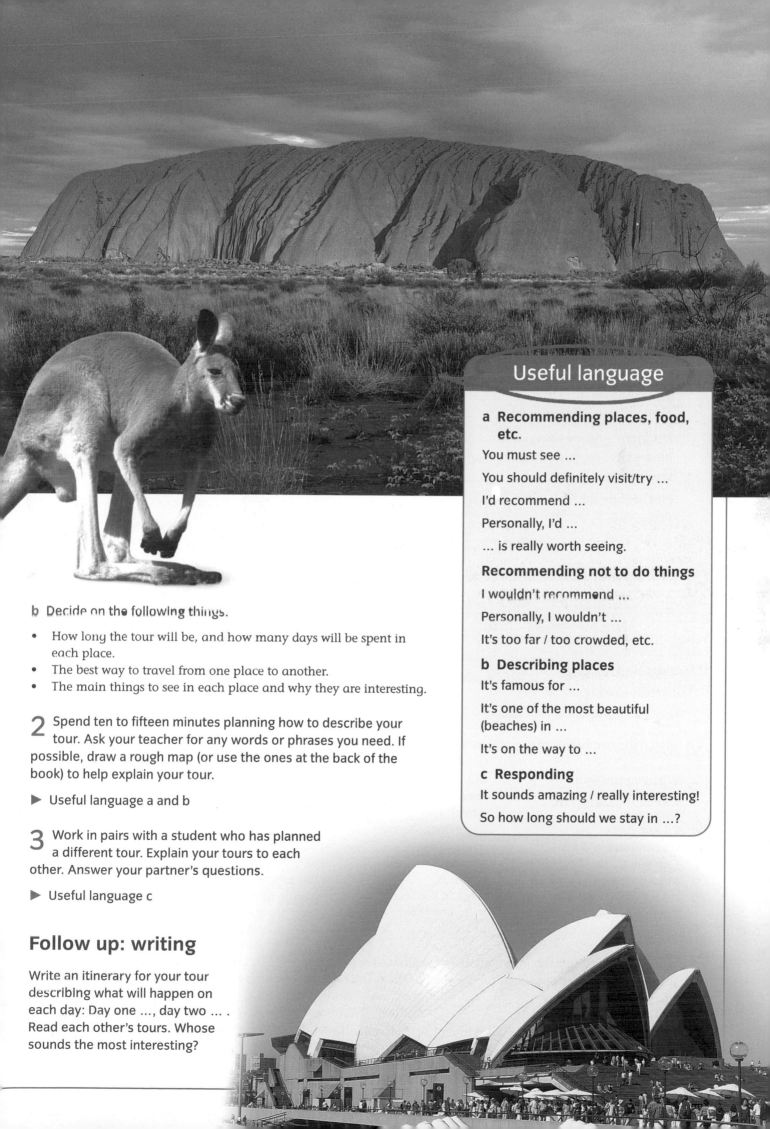

b Decide on the following things.

- How long the tour will be, and how many days will be spent in each place.
- The best way to travel from one place to another.
- The main things to see in each place and why they are interesting.

2 Spend ten to fifteen minutes planning how to describe your tour. Ask your teacher for any words or phrases you need. If possible, draw a rough map (or use the ones at the back of the book) to help explain your tour.

▶ Useful language a and b

3 Work in pairs with a student who has planned a different tour. Explain your tours to each other. Answer your partner's questions.

▶ Useful language c

Follow up: writing

Write an itinerary for your tour describing what will happen on each day: Day one ..., day two ... . Read each other's tours. Whose sounds the most interesting?

Useful language

a Recommending places, food, etc.

You must see ...

You should definitely visit/try ...

I'd recommend ...

Personally, I'd ...

... is really worth seeing.

Recommending not to do things

I wouldn't recommend ...

Personally, I wouldn't ...

It's too far / too crowded, etc.

b Describing places

It's famous for ...

It's one of the most beautiful (beaches) in ...

It's on the way to ...

c Responding

It sounds amazing / really interesting!

So how long should we stay in ...?

module 3 Around the world

Real life
Booking a flight

1 Rachael wants to book a flight to visit some friends in Buenos Aires. Think of four questions she will ask the travel agent.

2 **T3.10** Listen and complete the notes Rachael made. (The information in the recording is not in the same order as below.) Then check your answers in pairs.

> How much? (a) _____ return (Iberia)
>
> Depart London Heathrow on (b) _____ April at 19.15
> arrive Buenos Aires at (c) _____ on (d) _____
> April. (1 hour stopover in (e) _____)
>
> 17th April — depart Buenos Aires at (f) _____ arrive
> Madrid at 6.10 (18th). Depart Madrid at 7.00 arrive
> London Gatwick at (g) _____
>
> Can hold for (h) _____ days
> Phone Jude on 020 (i) _____

3 Listen again and complete the details that the travel agent took.

Mr ☐	Mrs ☐	Miss ☐	Ms ☐
Surname			
First name			
Contact number	07711		

4 Match the two halves of the sentences. Then practise saying them.

a When do you want   full, I'm afraid.
b And coming back   instead?
c How many   when?
d I'll just check   flight from Madrid.
e It's completely   availability.
f Can you try the 3rd of April   to travel?
g I can do it for €979 return   two days.
h It's a twelve hour   seats do you want?
i There's an hour stopover   including taxes.
j I can hold it for   in Madrid.

5 a Work in pairs. Use the information and sentences in exercises 2 to 4 to act out the conversation between Rachael and the travel agent.

b Act out two similar conversations. Student A: Go to page 134. Student B: Go to page 136.

Student A: Go to page 134.
Student B: Go to page 136.

STUDY...

Keeping notes

1 Whenever you learn a new word or phrase, make sure you write it down. Try to 'collect' at least six to eight new words in each lesson. You might also want to write:

- a definition or translation into your language.
- how the word is pronounced, the stressed syllable, etc.
- an example sentence. (You can use a dictionary for this.)

You could use underlining, highlighting and different colours to make your notes more attractive, for example:

> crowded (adjective) =
> full of people
> /ˈkraʊdɪd/
> The beach gets very
> crowded in summer.

2 The words below all appear in Module 3. Choose four and write similar notes using the advice above. This will make your notes easier to read later and it will help you to remember them and increase your vocabulary. Use your mini-dictionary to help you.

archaeological	cosmopolitan
crowded	extravagant
gambling	old-fashioned
polluted	recommend
scenery	spectacular

1 Comparative and superlative adjectives ☐

Write the opposite of the phrases below, using the adjective in brackets.

a the smallest (big) _____

b the quietest (busy) _____

c nearer than (far) _____

d the most polluted (clean) _____

e better than (bad) _____

f the easiest (difficult) _____

g more interesting than (boring) _____

▶ **Need to check? Language summary A, page 146.**

2 Large and small differences ☐

Complete the sentences with the words in the box.

> bit by lot much one slightly

a Louis is _____ far the most experienced player we've got.

b Michael is _____ of the best young musicians in the country.

c Surprisingly, the trip is only _____ more expensive if you travel first class.

d Since they moved house, Mark and Carla have been _____ happier.

e Tomorrow's weather will be just a little _____ cooler than today.

f Marianne is a _____ more relaxed since her holiday.

▶ **Need to check? Language summaries B and C, page 146.**

3 Making comparisons ☐

Replace the underlined word with the correct word.

a He's not as intelligent <u>like</u> his sister.

b This question isn't <u>quiet</u> as easy as the last one.

c Life here is <u>least</u> expensive than in the city.

d People seem to have <u>fewer</u> time than they used to.

e The new library looks very similar <u>than</u> the old one.

f The two designs are <u>complete</u> different – you can't compare them.

g The school is very different <u>as</u> the old one.

h This bag is <u>exact</u> the same as yours.

▶ **Need to check? Language summaries C and D, page 146.**

4 Prepositions ☐

Choose the correct preposition.

a It's on / in / at the southeast.

b It's about 150 kilometres away / from / of Mexico City.

c It's near the border at / in / with Turkey.

d The city of Liverpool stands at / in / on the River Mersey.

e The city of Petra is famous by / for / of its ancient ruins.

f It's a small town in / of / on the east coast of Australia.

▶ **Need to check? Vocabulary and Writing, page 31.**

5 Word building ☐

Write the adjectives from these nouns.

a industry _____

b history _____

c crowd _____

d romance _____

e pollution _____

▶ **Need to check? Vocabulary and Writing, page 31.**

Pronunciation spot

The sounds /ɪ/ and /iː/

a `T3.11` Listen to the pairs of words below. Can you hear the difference in the vowel sounds?
it / eat   fit / feet   sit / seat
The first words in each pair all have the short /ɪ/ sound. The second words all have a long /iː/ sound.

b `T3.12` Look at the underlined letters in these words from Module 3. Are the sounds /ɪ/ or /iː/? Listen and check.

b<u>ea</u>ch	b<u>i</u>g	b<u>ui</u>lt	b<u>u</u>sy
c<u>i</u>ty	cl<u>ea</u>n	<u>ea</u>sy	str<u>ee</u>t
t<u>ea</u>	thr<u>ee</u>	wh<u>i</u>ch	

c Practise saying the words, paying attention to the /ɪ/ and /iː/ sounds.

REMEMBER!

Look back at the areas you have practised. Tick the ones you feel confident about. Now try the MINI-CHECK on page 156 to check what you know!

Life stories

▶ Present perfect simple
▶ *for*, *since* and *ago* and Present perfect continuous
▶ Reading: *Parallel lives*
▶ Pronunciation: Strong and weak forms of *have*, Linking
▶ Vocabulary: Describing life events, Positive characteristics
▶ Task: Talk about someone you admire
▶ Wordspot: *take*
▶ Writing: A curriculum vitae

Reading

1 Work in pairs. Have you got any brothers or sisters? In what ways are you similar/different? Which of your parents/grandparents do you take after? Think about the following things.

facial expressions	opinions and attitudes
health	personality
looks	tastes and interests

> People say I look like my sister.

> I'm completely different from my mother – she's … but I'm …

> I think I take after my grandmother because I'm very …

2 Do you know any twins? If so, are they identical or not? What kind of relationship have they got?

3 Read the text quickly. Which twins do each of these statements refer to?

a They seemed almost telepathic.
b They got married on the same day without knowing.
c The similarities between their lives were truly remarkable.
d They had their own special language.

4 Check the words and phrases in the box in your mini-dictionary. Then read the text again and tick the statements that are true about Professor Bouchard's research.

to be adopted	a coincidence	genes/genetic
to influence someone		to be separated at birth
your upbringing / to be brought up		

a He contacted both identical and non-identical twins separated at birth.
b He collected as much information about them as he could.
c He found that the similarities between Terry and Margaret were very unusual.
d He found that twins who are brought up together always have more in common than twins who are brought up separately.
e He doesn't think upbringing has an important influence on personality.
f He has found that genes can influence:
  – the things we do in our free time.
  – how intelligent we are.
  – our political opinions.
  – the illnesses we have.
  – the things we like and dislike.

5 Discuss the following questions in small groups.

• Which of the similarities between the 'Jim Twins' do you find the most amazing?
• Which of the similarities do you think might be genetic, and which must be a coincidence?
• Which do you think is more important to our personality – our genes or our upbringing?

Parallel lives

Margaret Richardson and Terry Connelly have almost identical taste in clothes, both have four children of more or less the same age, and both were married on exactly the same day. Not surprising, perhaps, Margaret and Terry are identical twins. What is surprising is that they didn't even meet until they were in their mid-thirties – after their children were born.

It is well known that twins are closer than most brothers and sisters – after all, they spend more time in each other's company. Occasionally, this closeness becomes extreme: for example, Grace and Virginia Kennedy who as children invented their own language; or Greta and Freda Chapman who can speak the same words at the same time in the same voice, as if linked by telepathy.

But what happens if, like Terry and Margaret, identical twins are separated at birth and brought up in different families? Will their backgrounds make them completely different, or will their shared genes still mean that they have a lot in common? Professor Tom Bouchard from the University of Minnesota, set out to find the answer to this question. He traced more than a hundred pairs of twins who were adopted by different parents at birth, sixty-four of whom were identical twins. Each twin was then tested and interviewed about every detail of their life and personality.

It turned out that Margaret and Terry were not unusual. As well as looking very similar, many twins had the same IQ, the same health problems, the same hobbies and interests, the same attitudes and even the same tastes. Several pairs of twins arrived at their first meeting in the same clothes, and one pair of middle-aged women were wearing identical jewellery. Others had made the same career choices: Jerry and Mark Levy first met in their thirties to discover that they were both firefighters, who drank the same kind of beer and weighed exactly the same.

However, the most incredible story is that of Jim Springer and Jim Lewis from Ohio in the USA – in fact, the 'Jim Twins' made headline news across the USA when they finally met up at the age of thirty-nine. Born to a poor immigrant woman in 1939, they were adopted by different families when they were a few days old, and both were named Jim by their new families. This was just the first in an almost unbelievable number of similarities in their lives. (see below)

Of course, some of this must be coincidence. But Professor Bouchard has come to a remarkable conclusion. Identical twins brought up separately are more similar than non-identical twins brought up together. 'I am not saying that upbringing doesn't matter – it's very important of course – but this research shows that our genes influence almost every part of our lives: they influence our IQ, our hobbies; our personalities, our political attitudes, our health, even the clothes and food we like.'

The remarkable 'Jim Twins'

- Both grew up with an adopted brother called Larry.
- As children they both had dogs called Toy.
- Both men were divorced and remarried. Both first wives were called Linda, and both second wives were called Betty.
- Both had a first son called James Alan.
- Both were 184 cm tall and weighed 83 kg.
- Both loved motor racing and hated baseball.
- Both had the same handwriting and the same facial expressions.
- Both took their holidays at the same beach in Florida every year.
- Even their homes and gardens were very similar.
- In 2002, both men died of the same illness, on the same day.

Language focus 1
Present perfect simple

a Read the text below without doing the exercise. In what ways have the twins had an amazing life?

b [T4.1] Choose the correct verb form. Then listen and check your answers.

The world's most successful twins

Mary Kate and Ashley Olsen are the most successful twins in the world, and they are still teenagers. Read the fact file below.

■ The twins (1) **were / have been** born in Oakwood, California on 13th June 1986.

■ They (2) **were / have been** TV stars all their lives. They (3) **appeared / have appeared** in their first TV show, the popular American sitcom *Full House* at the age of just nine months!

■ At the age of six, they (4) **started / have started** their own production company, becoming the youngest Hollywood producers in history.

■ They (5) **appeared / have appeared** in *Full House* for eight years. The show (6) **finally ended / has finally ended** in 1995.

■ Since 1995, the twins (7) **become / have become** famous world-wide and have fan websites in dozens of languages.

■ They (8) **published / have published** their first book about twelve years ago: so far, their books (9) **sold / have sold** more than thirty million copies, and (10) **made / have made** more than $130 million.

■ The twins (11) **also produced / have also produced** their own clothing, jewellery, make-up and perfume ranges.

■ So far, the twins (12) **built up / have built up** a fortune of at least $150 million dollars each, and in 2003 they (13) **were / have been** the world's highest paid TV stars.

Analysis

1 How is the Present perfect simple formed? Which verbs in the text above are regular/irregular?

2 We use the Present perfect when a past action is related to the present in some way. Choose the correct alternative in the rules below.
  a If an action started in the past and continues to the present, we use the Past simple / Present perfect.
  b If we don't say when an action happened, but it is still important now, we use the Present perfect / Past simple.
  c If we say exactly when an action in the past happened (or this is clear from the context), we use the Present perfect / Past simple.

3 Which of the words and phrases below belong with the Past simple? Which belong with the Present perfect?
  all my life   ever?   since   ten minutes ago   when?   yesterday

▶ Read Language summaries A, B and C on pages 146–147.

Practice

1 Match the people in the photos to the texts and write the names in the spaces. Then put the verbs in the correct form.

a In 1965 _____ (1) _____ (write) the most popular song of all time, *Yesterday*. There (2) _____ (be) over 2,500 cover versions since then.

b Since he (3) _____ (die) in 1977, _____ (4) _____ (have) thirty-one hit singles! During his lifetime he (5) _____ (have) over sixty hits, including eighteen number ones.

c With a career lasting more than thirty years, _____ is still a major Hollywood actor. He (6) _____ (receive) twelve Oscar nominations – more than any other actor in the history of Hollywood – and he (7) _____ (win) three Oscars. He (8) _____ (win) the Best Actor Award in 1975 for *One Flew Over the Cuckoo's Nest,* and again in 1997 for *As Good as it Gets,* and in 1983 he (9) _____ (receive) the Best Supporting Actor Award for *Terms of Endearment.*

d _____ (10) _____ (star) in the most successful film of all time, *Titanic.* Since its release in 1997, the film (11) _____ (make) around $2 billion. However, it (12) _____ (cost) over $200 million to make – the most expensive film ever!

■ Jack Nicholson

■ Lennon and McCartney

■ Kate Winslet and
Leonardo DiCaprio

■ Elvis Presley

2 a `T4.2` Listen to five everyday conversations and match the dialogues to the descriptions.

A teacher talking to some students. ☐
A woman meeting her friend in the street. ☐
A couple at home. ☐ 1
Some business people meeting at a party. ☐
Some colleagues in an office. ☐

b Complete the gaps with the Present perfect of the verbs in the box.

> change   finish (x2)   go (x2)   lose (x2)   meet   see

1 _____ you _____ my glasses anywhere?
2 I _____ my glasses.
3 You _____ your hair – it's really nice!
4 You _____ weight, haven't you?
5 She was here – perhaps she _____ just _____ out for a minute.
6 She _____ home. She left about ten minutes ago.
7 We _____ . Can we go now?
8 Sorry, I _____ yet. Just a minute.
9 George, _____ you _____ Silvina?

c Look at the tapescript on page 163 and check your answers.

Pronunciation

1 `T4.3` Listen to the first dialogue from exercise 2 again. How many times do you hear *have*? How many times do you hear *'ve*?
  a When is *have* pronounced /hæv/ (= the strong form) ?
  b When is *have* pronounced /həv/ (= the weak form) ?
  c When is *have* pronounced /v/ (= the contracted form) ?

2 Practise the following phrases, starting with the strong words. Use the recording to help you.
  a seen → Have you seen → Have you seen my glasses?
  b lost → I've lost → I've lost my glasses.
  c have → I have ‣ I don't know if I have.

3 Look at the tapescript again for the other dialogues in exercise 2. Practise reading them with a partner. Pay attention to the stress and weak forms.

---

3 Work in pairs. You are going to find six things that you have done that your partner hasn't. First think about things you have done. Use the ideas on page 138 or your own ideas. Then ask and answer questions with your partner.

Example:
A Have you ever been in a newspaper?
B Yes, I was in a newspaper when my school won a prize.
A Really? So have I! I was in a swimming tournament. Have you ever won any money?
B No, I haven't.
A Okay, that's one for me – I won some money on the lottery last year …

Vocabulary 1
Describing life events

1 a Put the life events into the correct categories.

bring up your children	change job	fall in love
get a degree	get engaged	get a job
go to university	get promoted	get married
have children	leave home	leave school
rent or buy a house	pass your exams	move house
retire	start school	start work

love and relationships	
home and family	
education	*start school*
career	

b Discuss the following questions in pairs.

• What order do the things in each category happen?
  (There are different possibilities.)
• Which of these things have you done? Which haven't
  you done yet?

2 Here are some more life events. Which are positive
and which are negative? Which category in
exercise 1 do they go in?

become very successful	fail your exams	get divorced
get married again	lose your job	split up
make a lot of money		

3 Spend a few minutes studying the phrases, then do
the quiz on page 138 to check what you remember.

Language focus 2
for, *since* and *ago* and Present perfect continuous

1 **T4.4** Listen to a student
of English, Sara Rossi,
talking about her life.
Complete the 'lifeline'.

a Born in Alatri (near Rome)
in _____ .

b Started playing
volleyball when she
was _____ .

c Met Gianluigi.

d Worked for local
radio station.

e Started learning
English in 1998.

f Moved to Rome
in _____ .

g Began studying
medicine.

h Bought her car
in _____ .

i Bought her
_____
in 2003.

SCHOOL SCHOOL SCHOOL UNIVERSITY UNIVERSITY THIS YEAR

2 Use the lifeline and the tapescript on page 163 to
complete the following sentences. Where
necessary, complete the gaps with the correct form of
the verbs in brackets.

a Sara was born in Alatri _____ ago.
b She _____ (move) to Rome in _____ .
c She's been playing volleyball for _____ years.
d She worked as a radio announcer for _____ .
e She's lived in Rome since _____ .
f She _____ (met) her boyfriend when she was
   at school.
g She's lived in her present house since _____ .
h She _____ (know) Gianluigi for more than
   ten years.
i She's been learning English _____ 1998.
j She _____ (study) medicine since 1999.
k She _____ (had) her car since 2001.

Analysis

1 Which sentences in exercise 2 are in:
  - the Past simple?
  - the Present perfect simple?
  - the Present perfect continuous?

2 *for*, *since* and *ago*
  a Which tense is used with *ago?* Change these time phrases to use *ago.*
    last Tuesday 6.00 this morning last August 2001 1965
  b Look at sentences c and e in exercise 2. *For* and *since* are often used with the Present perfect simple and the Present perfect continuous. What is the difference between *for* and *since?* Decide which of these time phrases go with *for* and *since.*
    twenty years I was born 1999 six o'clock a long time
    five minutes
  c Notice we also use *for* with the Past simple if the time period is finished. Find an example of this in exercise 2.

3 **Present perfect continuous with *for* and *since***
  The Present perfect continuous is especially common with *for* and *since* because it emphasises that the action is long or repeated.
  a Find examples in exercise 2 that show this.
  b Why don't we use the Present perfect continuous in sentence h?

▶ Read Language summary D on page 147.

Practice

1 Read more about Sara and her family. Complete the gaps with the correct form of the verbs and circle the correct alternatives.

a Sara (1) _____ (drive) (2) for / since nearly six years. She first (3) _____ (take) her driving test in 1999, but unfortunately she (4) _____ (not pass) first time!

b Sara's brother (5) _____ (study) economics (6) for / since five years, and a few weeks ago he (7) _____ (start) working in an international bank.

c Sara's mother (8) _____ (be) a maths teacher (9) for / since over twenty years. Last Christmas she (10) _____ (be) promoted to head of department, and (11) for / since then she (12) _____ (work) really long hours.

d Sara's father (13) _____ (work) for a bank for over thirty years, but two years ago he (14) _____ (retire). However, he (15) _____ (be) very busy (16) for / since then. Not long ago he (17) _____ (buy) an old boat, and (18) for / since the last few months he (19) _____ (paint) it.

Pronunciation

1 **T4.5** In connected speech, if a word begins with a vowel sound, the previous consonant sound often 'links on'. Listen to these time phrases.

    for about six months
    a minute ago
    since April
    for a while
    a long time ago
    since eight o'clock

Practise saying the phrases, paying attention to the words that link together.

2 **T4.6** Listen and write down the six sentences. Then practise saying them.

2 a **T4.7** Listen and answer the ten questions using *for*, *since* or *ago*. Do not write full sentences.
Example: *for about three months*

b How many of the questions can you remember? Listen again and check. Choose five to ask a partner.

3 a Draw a lifeline like Sara's for yourself. Mark important dates and events in your life.

b You are going to explain your lifeline to other students. Spend a few minutes planning which verb forms, time words, etc. to use.

c Work in small groups. Explain your lifelines and answer any questions you are asked.

In 1998, my parents moved to …

How long have you known …?

d Write a short paragraph explaining your lifeline.

Vocabulary 2
Positive characteristics

1 a Work in pairs. Check these words in your mini-dictionary.

ambitious	clear-thinking
courageous	determined
fair	hardworking
imaginative	original
tolerant	talented

b Which of the things above should the people in the box be? Why?

an actor	a colleague
a manager	a teacher
a political leader	a scientist
a songwriter	
a top sportsperson	
a parent or grandparent	

c Think of someone you know (either personally or a famous person) who has these characteristics. Then tell your partner about this person.

2 Match the roles in exercise 1b with the following qualities.

– be a good leader
– be a good team player
– have strong principles
– have a good sense of humour
– stay calm in a crisis
– have a lot of self-confidence
– have a positive attitude

3 Discuss the following questions in small groups.

• Which of the characteristics above are important in almost any job/role?
• Which characteristics do you most admire in others? Which are unimportant to you?

Task: Talk about someone you admire
Preparation: listening

a Work in small groups. How many of the people in the photos do you recognise? Why do you think people admire them?

b **T4.8** Listen to two people talking about someone they particularly admire. Listen and note down details of each person's life.

c Listen again and note down why they admire each person.

Task: speaking

You are going to give a short talk, like the ones on the recording, about a person you particularly admire (either personally or a famous person).

a Decide quickly who you will talk about. You will need to know some basic facts about the person's life.

b Spend a few minutes making notes about what you want to say. Ask your teacher for any words or phrases you need.

▶ Useful language

c Practise your talks either individually, in pairs or with your teacher.

d Take turns to give your talks to the class. Be ready to answer any questions the class have.

Useful language

Explaining why you admire someone

She's the kind of person who always (does what she thinks is right).

He's someone who (has done a lot to help others).

She's achieved so much ...

He's got very strong principles ...

She's exceptionally talented/creative ...

I really admire the way he ...

Follow up: writing

Write a brief description of a person you really admire. Include information about the following.

brief biographical details
the person's achievements
the kind of person he/she is
why you particularly admire him/her

Wordspot
take

1 a The following phrases with *take* all feature in this module. Do you remember the meaning of each phrase?

1   Which of your parents/grandparents do you **take after**?

2   Both **took their holidays** at the same beach in Florida every year.

3   She first **took** her driving **test** in 1999, but unfortunately she didn't pass first time!

4   **Take turns to** give your talks to the class.

b Check the phrases in A in your mini-dictionary. Then tick if the phrases in A and B have the same meaning. Explain the difference if they are not the same.

	A	B
1	take after	look or behave like
2	take a holiday	have a holiday
3	take a test / an exam	pass an exam
4	take up a sport/hobby	begin a sport/hobby
5	take a picture	paint a picture
6	take someone out for a meal	invite someone out for a meal
7	take a train	catch a train
8	take care of	look after
9	take off (clothes)	put on (clothes)
10	take part in	participate in
11	take over	take control
12	take notes	write notes

2 Add the phrases from A in exercise 1 to the diagram below.

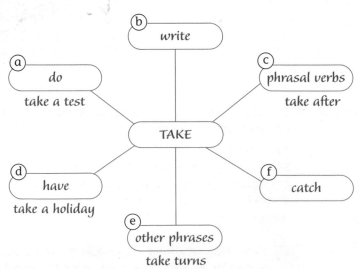

3 Work in pairs. You are going to interview each other.
Student A: Look at the questions on page 139.
Student B: Look at the questions on page 140.

Writing
A curriculum vitae

1 Birgitte is a fashion student looking for a part-time job. She sees this advertisement in the local newspaper. Read the advertisement and find out whether the job is suitable for her or not. Is it part-time? Which days would she have to work?

Retail Store Assistant
RIVA FASHIONS

Salary according to age/experience
Working Saturdays/Sundays,
16 hours per week.

We are seeking a dependable, friendly and capable person to work weekends in our busy town-centre fashion store. The successful candidate will have excellent personal and sales skills and experience in retail sales and/or the fashion industry.

Telephone Linda at Riva Fashions on 0278 547 3829 or e-mail your CV to linda@rivastores.co.uk

---

2 Birgitte decides to send her CV. Which topics do you think she should include? Can you think of any other topics?

> her contact details (address, telephone number, etc.)
> her work experience
> the name of her primary school
> the name of her secondary school
> her education and qualifications
> her date of birth
> her hobbies and interests
> whether or not she can drive
> a profile of her skills and achievements
> what kind of clothes she likes
> what languages she speaks
> what makes her suitable for the job

3 Read Birgitte's CV and tick the topics in exercise 2 which are included.

BIRGITTE JORGENSEN

Flat 7, 32 Sycamore Avenue
Marston MN42 7HD
Tel: (home) 0278 636 0237 (mob) 07971 226635
E-mail: birgittejorg@eserve.co.uk

Profile
Final year student in Fashion Design and Marketing at University of Marston.

Knowledge of all aspects of fashion industry (design, marketing, sales).

Proven ability to work under pressure as a member of a team, excellent personal skills.

Experience
Six-month work placement with independent fashion house (Ideas Inc, Marston) working on designs for two large retail stores.

Completed study comparing Danish and UK fashion industries as part of degree course.

Gained valuable retail experience during university vacations working in supermarkets in Denmark and UK.

Qualifications
High School graduate, Frederiksborg Gymnasium, Denmark.

BA Degree Fashion Design & Marketing, University of Marston (to be completed June 2005).

Languages
Danish (mother tongue), English (fluent in speech and writing), Swedish (fluent in speech), and German (fair in speech and writing).

Personal details
Danish nationality (EU citizen – work permit not required). Age 22. Single, non-smoker. Full clean driving licence (UK and Danish).

4 a Find words or phrases in Birgitte's CV that mean the following.

1 she has shown that she can do something
2 the ability to get on well with people
3 time spent getting work experience while you are a student
4 someone who has completed their course at school or university
5 it will be finished
6 first language
7 quite good
8 someone who doesn't smoke

b Notice how in a CV we miss out words which are unnecessary or obvious.

Examples:
~~I am a~~ final year student in Fashion Design and Marketing at ~~The~~ University of Marston.
~~I have~~ knowledge of all aspects of ~~the~~ fashion industry (design, marketing, sales).

5 *Either* Read the information about Pavel Cizek on page 139. Write a CV for him, using the headings in Birgitte's CV to help you.

Or Write a CV for yourself using the headings in Birgitte's CV to help you. You can invent experience and qualifications if you prefer.

A Questions and auxiliaries

1 The following answers were given by people talking at a party. What questions do you think they were asked? Write one possible question for each answer.

a

> Yes ... French.

b

> Only about a week.

c

> I'm working in an advertising agency.

d

> Oh, yeah,
> it was great – the scenery,
> the food, the weather
> ... fantastic!

e

> In Caracas. It's the capital of Venezuela.

f

> Oh, about once
> a week. I'd like to swim more
> often, though.

g

> I'm staying in
> St Paul's Square – right in the centre of town.

h

> Yes. I've got
> an older brother and two younger sisters.

2 **C1** Now listen to the questions they were asked. How many did you guess correctly?

B Present and past verb forms

Read the text and choose the correct alternative.

In 1911 the small, peaceful village of Hollywood (1) has voted / voted to become part of Los Angeles, because it (2) had / was having problems with its water supply. Today, nearly a hundred years (3) ago / later, this same village (4) grows / has grown into the home of one of the most glamorous industries in the world – the American film industry.

With this growth (5) came / were coming many other well-known symbols. There is the famous Hollywood sign which (6) is standing / stands above the hills of the town. The original sign was built in 1923, but the present one (7) has only been / is only there (8) in / since 1978. Then there is the Grauman's Chinese Theater, where great actors and actresses (9) are leaving / leave their hand and footprints. Norma Talmadge (10) has been / was the first actress to do this in 1927. But most famous of all are the Academy Awards, better known as the 'Oscars'. In March every year, actors and actresses still (11) are waiting / wait nervously to find out if they have won – although director Woody Allen (12) has once missed / once missed the ceremony because he (13) played / was playing the clarinet in his favourite jazz club!

Nowadays it (14) becomes / is becoming more and more common for films to be made away from Hollywood, but it remains the home of film, and thousands of hopeful young actors (15) still come / have still come to 'The Dream Factory' every year. But not all Hollywood dreams (16) have been / were happy ones – as one actress who later (17) died / has died tragically, said: 'Hollywood is a place where they'll pay $500 for a kiss, and fifty cents for your soul.'

C Listening and speaking: Comparing the past with the present

1 [C2] You are going to hear someone comparing her life now with her life ten years ago. Listen and tick the topics she talks about in the box.

> her home   her friends   her family
> her hairstyle   her studies   her clothes
> her personality   a typical Friday night

2 Listen again and make notes about the topics she says have changed in the last ten years.

3 How is your life different now from ten years ago? Work with a partner and compare your lives, using some of the topics in the box.

D Speaking: Getting to know you

1 Work in pairs. Imagine that you are two passengers sitting next to each other on a long flight. Spend a few minutes reading the cards below and thinking about what you will say.

> **STUDENT A**
> You are flying home to your own country. Invent some details about yourself (your name, age, job, family, interests, etc.). Student B is a tourist who has never visited your country before. Talk to him/her about yourself, and recommend places to visit and things to do during his/her visit.

> **STUDENT B**
> You are a tourist visiting Student A's country for the first time. Invent some details about yourself (your name, age, job, family, interests, reason for visiting, etc.). Talk to Student A about yourself, and ask him/her questions about himself/herself. Also ask about his/her country (places to visit, things to do, etc.).

2 You are ready to have your conversation. It is ten minutes until lunch is served, so try to keep the coversation going. Remember to use the ways of showing interest in Module 2.

E Vocabulary: Alphabet quiz

Work in pairs. Read the definitions and think of a word from Modules 1–4 which begins with the letter shown. (The number in brackets refers to the number of letters in the word.)

A = someone you know, but who is not a close friend *(noun)* (12)

B = frontier *(noun)* (6)

C = someone you work with *(noun)* (9)

D = you are this if you really want to do something and won't let anyone stop you *(adjective)* (10)

E = people who have agreed to get married are *(adjective)* (7)

F = the opposite of *pass*, e.g. an exam *(verb)* (4)

G = risking money on a game or race – Las Vegas is famous for this! *(verb)* (8)

H = the opposite of lazy *(adjective)* (11)

I = an _____ area is where there are many factories *(adjective)* (10)

J = a kind of sea animal that can sting you – common in Australia *(noun)* (9)

K = '_____ in touch' means 'to stay in contact' *(verb)* (4)

L = a _____ radio station can only be heard in a limited area *(adjective)* (5)

M = your husband's/wife's mother *(noun)* (6-2-3)

N = your brother's/sister's daughter *(noun)* (5)

O = not modern or new *(adjective)* (3-9)

P = if you enter a competition you may win a _____ *(noun)* (5)

R = to know what something is because you have seen it before (also for people) *(verb)* (9)

S = a woman who is married to your father, but is not your mother *(noun)* (10)

T = two children who are born at the same time to the same mother *(noun)* (5)

W = movements of water in the sea *(noun)* (5)

Success

▶ Future forms
▶ Future clauses with *if*, *when*, etc.
▶ Reading and vocabulary: *Have you got what it takes?*
▶ Pronunciation: Stressed syllables, Sounding polite
▶ Vocabulary: Work
▶ Listening and speaking: Doing something different
▶ Task: Choose the best candidate
▶ Writing: A covering letter
▶ Real life: A formal telephone call
▶ Song: *Manic Monday*

Have you

Reading and vocabulary

1 Work in small groups. What does success mean to you? Which of these are the most/least important?

– a good love life   – a nice home
– friends and fun   – a successful career
– a happy family life   – something else
– plenty of money

2 a Look at the 'psychometric test' (a test designed to assess your personality) and read the questions quickly. Which of the areas in exercise 1 is the questionnaire mainly about?

b Check these words and phrases in your mini-dictionary.

to concentrate on something	to distract someone
to be jealous	to run a training course
a steady job	variety
to be wise	a workaholic

c Work in pairs and do the test. Ask and answer the questions, and keep a note of your partner's answers. If you haven't got a job yet, imagine how you would react. Give reasons for your answer to each question.

3 Look at page 140 and work out your partner's score. Then read the assessment together. Discuss the following questions.

• Do you think your assessment is fair?
• Do you think this is a good test to assess personality?
• Which are the most/least useful questions? Why?

1 Do you find it easy to concentrate on one subject?
  a Not at all, I like to think about a variety of things.
  b I try hard but sometimes it's difficult.
  c Yes, I have no problem doing this.

2 Do your leisure interests ever distract you from your work?
  a No, never.   **b** Sometimes.   **c** Yes, often.

3 You are planning a weekend with your family and friends. On Friday afternoon something urgent comes up. What is your reaction?
  a You try to find someone else to do it for you.
  b You forget your weekend and get on with what you have to do.
  c You decide it will have to wait as you already have plans for the weekend.

4 You get a new job and discover that the local college is running a training course that will be very useful in your work. How do you react?
  a You're not very interested in doing it.
  b You decide to do the course even if you have to pay for it yourself.
  c You will go, but only if your new company pays for it.

5 Where do you see yourself in five years' time?
  a You'll probably be in the same position as now.
  b You hope you'll be in a better position.
  c You intend to advance your career considerably in the next five years.

got what it takes?

6 Do you talk about your job/studies outside work/college?
  a Sometimes.
  b Very frequently.
  c No, I 'switch off' from work as soon as I can at the end of the day.

7 Do you think intelligence leads to success?
  a Intelligence alone does not lead to success.
  b Yes, you have to be intelligent to be successful in life.
  c It's a big part of success.

8 One of your colleagues gets promoted. How do you feel?
  a You're a bit jealous.
  b You're pleased for your colleague.
  c You're upset. You want to find out why it wasn't you and what went wrong.

9 Do you believe in the saying 'practice makes perfect'?
  a No, nobody's perfect.
  b Yes, the harder you work at things, the better you become.
  c People don't have enough time to practise things these days.

10 Is it useful to look back at the past?
  a No, you can't change what has happened.
  b Yes, it's very important to look back and analyse our mistakes so that we don't repeat them.
  c Maybe sometimes, but everyone can be wise about the past.

11 What do you think about hard work?
  a It's the way to get what you want.
  b It's okay if you are paid well for it.
  c It's very tiring.

12 Where does your motivation come from?
  a From your family.
  b From your boss.
  c From inside yourself.

4 Complete the table with words from the test and the assessment on page 140.

Noun	Adjective
success	*successful*
jealousy	a
b	intelligent
importance	c
d	happy
e	ambitious
f	determined
g	imaginative
confidence	h
i	possible

Pronunciation

1 Mark the stressed syllable on the words in exercise 4.

  ●   ●
  success   successful

2 **T5.1** Listen and check. Which words change their stress pattern?

3 Practise saying the words, paying attention to the stressed syllables.

Language focus 1
Future forms

1 Is it easy for graduates and school leavers to find a job in your country? Do most people start a career immediately? What else might they do?

2 **a** A radio programme is interviewing students who are about to graduate, to find out what they intend to do. Check these phrases in your mini-dictionary.

to be a trainee manager	to be accepted for a job/course
to apply for a job/course	to do a degree (in law, etc.)
to do a master's degree	to do a temporary job
to join the army	

b **T5.2** Listen to six students and make a note of what they have been studying and their plans/ideas about their future career.

3 **a** **T5.3** Listen and complete these sentences.

Nora

1 _____ end up teaching drama in a secondary school.
2 _____ for anything this year ...
3 I've got family in Trinidad, so _____ there for a few months.

Oliver

4 _____ the army.
5 _____ my training in September.

Dino

6 First _____ a holiday with my family.
7 _____ in five days!
8 After that, _____ a master's degree.

Caroline

9 _____ work at the beginning of September.
10 _____ a couple of months break over the summer.
11 _____ a beach somewhere nice and hot.

Zak

12 _____ for a course in journalism.

Alice

13 _____ a lawyer.
14 I suppose _____ of temporary job for the next few months.

b Work in small groups. Which of the six students have already made arrangements to start a job / course? Who already knows what they want to do? Who doesn't really know what they want to do?

Nora   Oliver

Dino   Caroline

Zak   Alice

Analysis

There are many ways of expressing the future in English. The form used depends on how the speaker sees the future action.

1 Look at sentences 1, 7 and 11 in exercise 3. Then complete rules a–c below with *will* + verb, Present continuous or *going to* + verb.
 a We use _____ when there is no special plan, this is something you predict or see as a future fact.
 b We use _____ to describe a present intention about the future.
 c We use _____ to describe something we have already arranged to do.

Find another example of each use in exercise 3.

2 Sometimes other verbs and phrases can express plans and intentions.
I'm planning to do a master's degree.
I'm about to join the army.

Find three more phrases like this in exercise 3.

▶ Read Language summary A on pages 147–148.

Practice

1 Use the prompts to make future sentences.

a I / plan / study engineering.
b My sister / think / join the army.
c I / due / take my driving test next week.
d Alex says he / not going / apply for university.
e I know I / will not get the job.
f My boss / about / retire.
g My son / start / a new job on Monday.
h I / probably / not / see you before you go.

2 Write five sentences about yourself (or someone you know) using the prompts below.

a (apply for) a job as a … / course in …
b (take) … exams / driving test …
c (get) married …
d (train) to be a …
e (go into) the army …
f (travel) abroad …
g (change) job/school …
h (start/leave) university/school …

Examples:
My brother's due to go into the army soon.

I'm not planning to take my driving test until I'm twenty-one.

My cousin's going to start school next month.

3 Work in pairs. Take turns to choose three numbers from 1–12. Your partner reads out the instructions on page 141.

Both of you should write about the answer to each instruction, using an appropriate future form. Compare answers.

Vocabulary
Work

1 On a piece of paper write down three jobs you'd love to do, three you wouldn't mind doing and three you'd hate to do. Keep the paper, but do not show it to anyone yet.

2 **a** Check the words and phrases in bold in your mini-dictionary. Then divide the phrases into the three categories below.

* I would like a job like this.
* I wouldn't mind doing a job like this.
* I wouldn't want a job like this.

You have to be **physically fit**.
You have to be **good with money/numbers**.
You need good **people skills**.
You have to be very **well-organised**.
You have to be very **creative**.
You need **special training** and **qualifications**.
You have to **work long hours**.
It's very **secure**.
It's **well-paid**.
It's **badly-paid**.
It's **stressful**.
It's very **competitive**.
It's **challenging**.
There's a lot of **responsibility**.
There are lots of **opportunities to travel**.

---

b Explain your opinions to a partner. Tell your partner about anything else you would look for in a job.

3 Suggest some 'ideal jobs' to your partner, based on what he/she has told you. Compare your suggestions with the list your partner made in exercise 1.

Listening and speaking
Doing something different

1 Read about the people in the photos and answer the following questions for each person.

a What jobs did they use to do?
b What are they doing now?

2 **T5.4** Listen to the three people describing how it happened and answer the questions. (You may need to listen more than once.)

a Why did they leave their old job?
b What are the good things about the new job?
c What are the disadvantages?

3 Mark the following statements True or False. Then listen again or read the tapescript on page 165 and check.

a Clare was joking when she first said she wanted to be a plumber.
b She has problems with her male colleagues on the course.
c She sometimes finds that older people have less confidence in her work.
d Kevin became a house-husband because he wanted to spend more time with his children.
e He finds his life now harder work than his old job.
f He's made lots of new friends since he changed roles.
g Lorna and Ian weren't very successful in their old jobs.
h They worked much longer hours in London.
i She thinks it will be a good place to bring up children.

4 Discuss the following questions in groups.

- Would you like to do what any of these people are doing? Why / Why not?
- Do you think they have made the right decisions or do you think they will regret it?
- Are there any jobs that men/women are naturally better suited to, do you think?
- In your country, is it common for people to leave stressful jobs in the city and start a new life in the country? What do you think of this idea?

Clare
Last year Clare Davis, 26, resigned from her job as a geography teacher in a secondary school and started retraining as a plumber.

Kevin
When Kevin Dunstable, 31, lost his job as a supervisor in an electronics factory nine months ago, his wife Sally returned to her job as a legal secretary, leaving Kevin at home to look after their three young children: Jodie, 6, Daniel, 4 and Chloe, 18 months.

Lorna and Ian
Eighteen months ago, Lorna Whitwort, 29, and husband Ian gave up their well-paid jobs in the city of London (Lorna was a solicitor, and Ian an accountant) and moved to the country to run a small hotel. Lorna is now pregnant with their first child.

Language focus 2
Future clauses with *if*, *when*, etc.

Work in pairs. Read about the people in the photos again. Who do you think said these things?

a "If I don't enjoy it, I'll try something else. I'm never going to go back to teaching, though."

b "When she has the baby, we'll have to get more staff to help us."

c "I'll be fully-qualified in about three years, unless I fail my exams, of course!"

d "We can't both work full-time until our youngest child starts school in about three years' time."

e "As soon as he finds a job again, I'm going to change to working part-time."

f "I'm hoping to redecorate a lot of the hotel before I have the baby."

Analysis

1 These conjunctions join two clauses (parts) of a sentence.
as soon as   before   if   unless   until   when
Underline them in the sentences in exercise 1. Then underline the verb that follows the conjunction.

2 The sentences in exercise 1 are about the future, but what tense is used after the conjunctions?

3 What verb forms are used in the other clause?

▶ Read Language summary B on page 148.

Practice

1 Read what Clare, Kevin and Lorna's friends say about them. Choose the most appropriate conjunction and complete with the correct verb form, affirmative or negative.

a 'When / Before Clare _____ (qualify) as a plumber, she _____ (earn) a lot of money.'

b 'Lorna _____ (make) herself ill unless / as soon as she _____ (get) more rest.'

c 'I'm sure Kevin _____ (go) mad if / when he _____ (not find) work soon.'

d 'Lorna and Ian _____ (have) to sort out their financial problems before / until they _____ (have) the baby.'

e 'I'm sure Kevin _____ (go) back to work as soon as / until it _____ (be) right for the children.'

f 'Things _____ (not get) easier for Kevin and Sally unless / until the children _____ (be) a bit older.'

g 'It _____ (be) difficult for Kevin to find a job if / when he _____ (wait) too long.'

h 'I think Clare _____ (get) bored with plumbing, when / unless she _____ (have) to do it all day every day.'

2 Work in small groups. Complete the sentences to make them true for yourself. Then tell your group.

a I'm going to buy a ... as soon as ...
b I'll continue learning English until ...
c I'll be able to relax once ...
d I'll be home by ... o'clock tonight if/unless ...
e I'm (not) going out tonight if/unless ...
f I'm going to ... next weekend if/unless ...
g I will/won't be late home today if/unless ...
h My English will/won't improve if/unless ...

3 Work in small groups. Take turns to talk about the plans and ambitions of someone you know. The others think of a consequence if their plans come true.

My friend Mina wants to become a ballet dancer.

If she wants to go to ballet school, she'll have to work very hard.

She won't earn much money unless she gets into a really big ballet company.

She'll probably have to do something else if she has children.

Task: Choose the best candidate
Preparation: reading

1 Read the advertisement for Horizons Unlimited. What kind of jobs do they recruit for?

> ### Fed up with your daily routine? Looking for something different? Always wanted to travel?
>
> **Horizons Unlimited** is an international employment agency, recruiting for positions all over the world.
>
> Vacancies include:
> - management and office staff
> - hotel and restaurant staff
> - nannies, private teachers and nurses
>
> All applicants must be appropriately qualified. Write for an application form to: Horizons Unlimited, PO Box 444, Richmond, Surrey, SJ5 4TS Interviews will be arranged for suitable applicants.

2 a Look at the photos of Jean-Luc and Marion, and read the captions.

Jean-Luc Bertrand is the forty-five year old owner of a small hotel in a ski resort in the French Alps. He has used Horizons Unlimited before to find staff for him.

Marion O'Neill is the recruitment manager at Horizons Unlimited.

b Jean-Luc has sent an e-mail to Marion. Read the first two paragraphs of the e-mail on page 55 and answer these questions.

1 What has happened to Jean-Luc recently?
2 Why is his request to Marion difficult?

3 Work in pairs. Complete the table about the job.

Size/Location of the hotel	
Hotel duties	
Childcare duties	
Information about the children	
Essential qualifications	
Other useful qualifications	

Task: speaking

1 Marion has chosen the five best candidates in the photos on page 55. Work in small groups. Choose one candidate each and read Marion's notes about him/her on the page indicated. Mark the positive (+) and negative points (–) in the notes.

2 You are going to present the pros and cons of your candidate to your group. Spend a few minutes thinking about what you will say. Ask your teacher for any words or phrases you need.

▶ Useful language a and b

3 In your groups, listen to the pros and cons of each candidate. Discuss who would be first and second choice for the job.

▶ Useful language c

4 One person from each group presents their decisions to the class. Did you agree or not? Why / Why not?

Useful language

a Good points

He's got plenty of experience with ...

The good thing about ... is ...

What I like about ... is ...

b Bad points

I'm worried that he'll ...

I think ... is too young / isn't experienced enough.

c Other

I get the impression she's ...

He seems very energetic.

What'll happen if ...?

I prefer ... because ...

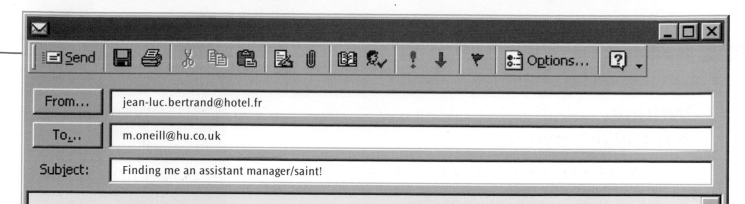

From... jean-luc.bertrand@hotel.fr

To... m.oneill@hu.co.uk

Subject: Finding me an assistant manager/saint!

Hi Marion,

I'm afraid I've got a difficult request for you this time! As you know, my wife Martine sadly died eighteen months ago. Since then I've been so busy looking after the children, I've been neglecting the hotel. Basically I need someone to do what Martine did! The job I'm offering is assistant hotel manager/part-time childminder – I know this is unusual but it's what I need.

To remind you about the hotel, we are a twenty-five-bedroom family hotel in rather a remote ski resort, so it's important that the person is prepared for this. We're very busy in winter and we also have quite a lot of guests in summer, but it's much quieter in spring and autumn.

The 'assistant hotel manager' duties would include:

– running reception/office during mornings and evenings.

– organising part-time staff (barman, cleaners, waiters) on my days off and when I'm absent on business. The chef will organise the kitchen so this is not a problem.

– helping out in the restaurant, bar, etc. when we are very busy.

For these duties the candidate needs fluent French and English (German also useful), good computer skills and previous experience of hotel work. Many of our guests are skiers of course, so knowledge of skiing is also useful.

In spring and autumn when things are very quiet, I have to go on some business trips and this is when I would need help with childcare. I've got two children – David (13) and Karine (8) both very well-behaved. I go away perhaps seven or eight times a year, usually for about four to seven days. During these trips, the person would have to take and pick up Karine from the local primary school, about two km away (David goes to school by bus), cook their dinner, get them to bed and look after them at the weekend, if I have a long trip.

Obviously the children have had a difficult two years so it's really important that it's someone kind and sympathetic. This is really the most important qualification of all for me. For the same reason I'd prefer someone who will stay for a minimum of two years, though if you cannot find this, I will have to take someone for just one year.

In return I can offer an excellent salary, free food/accommodation, six to eight weeks' paid holiday, a free ski pass and full-time use of a car. (I forgot to mention – it would be very useful if the candidate has a driving licence, both to take Karine to school, and also because he or she may feel a little lonely up here without a car.)

Well, Marion, I know that what I'm asking is very difficult, but you've always found me fantastic staff in the past, so I'm putting my trust in you! Please contact me if you need more information.

Very best wishes,

Jean-Luc

Peter Krajeck, page 134

Brenda MacDonald, page 136

Brigitte Schumann, page 139

John Bailey, page 141

Anne-Sophie Martin, page 143

Writing
A covering letter

1 Louisa Barry wants to apply for a job through Horizons Unlimited, so she is sending her CV and a covering letter. Match the addresses and date below with the correct position on the letter.

☐ 30th April 2005

☐ Horizons Unlimited
PO Box 444
Richmond
Surrey
SJ5 4TS

☐ 15 Thayers Farm Road
Abingdon
Northampton
NT12 4PF

2 Work in pairs. Put Louisa's letter in the correct order.

ⓐ ------------------

ⓑ ------------------

ⓒ ------------------

----

a ☐ I am interested in any secretarial positions you have, especially in France or Switzerland.

b ☐ I will be available to start work from the middle of June.

c ☐ I look forward to hearing from you soon.

d ☐ Yours faithfully,

e ☐ I enclose my CV as requested.

f ☐ I am a qualified and experienced PA, and am bilingual in Spanish and English. I also speak French fluently.

g ☐ I am writing in reply to your advertisement for temporary summer positions, which appeared in the *Western Mail* on 27th April.

h ☐ Dear Sir or Madam,

i ☐ However, I am willing to consider any kind of work.

j ☐ Louisa Barry

3 Is the layout of a formal letter the same or different in your language? Underline any phrases in exercise 2 that would be useful in a formal letter in English.

4 Write a similar letter to Horizons Unlimited in response to their advertisement on page 54. Mention where you would like to work and what kind of work you would be interested in. You can invent qualifications and experience!

Real life
A formal telephone call

1 a `T5.5` Louisa Barry is phoning Horizons Unlimited. Listen to the conversation. Why is she phoning? What is the secretary going to do?

b Complete the missing phrases in the conversation. Then listen again and check.

TELEPHONIST   Good morning, Horizons Unlimited.
LOUISE   Hello, (1) _____ to Marion O'Neill, please.
TELEPHONIST   Marion O'Neill ... just a moment, I'll (2) _____ .
SECRETARY   Hello, how can I help?
LOUISE   Err ... (3) _____ to Marion O'Neill, please?
SECRETARY   I'll just see if she's available, can I ask (4) _____ ?
LOUISE   Louisa Barry.
SECRETARY   One moment, please. (pause) Hello?
LOUISE   Yes, hello?
SECRETARY   Yes, I'm afraid Marion's in a meeting at the moment ... can I take (5) _____ or shall I ask (6) _____ back?
LOUISE   Well, I'm (7) _____ she interviewed me for a job about two weeks ago and I haven't heard anything yet.
SECRETARY   Okay, well, (8) _____ the message and ask her to call you back. Have you got a number (9) _____ ?
LOUISE   Well, I'll be here till about four o'clock ... the number's 01604 472472.
SECRETARY   Right, and (10) _____ ?
LOUISE   No, but she can (11) _____ on the answering machine.
SECRETARY   Okay, then, thanks (12) _____ .
LOUISE   Thank you, bye.
SECRETARY   Bye.

Pronunciation

1 `T5.6` Listen to how the speaker uses intonation to make the questions below polite.

a   How can I help?

b   Could I speak to Marion O'Neill, please?

c   Can I ask who's calling?

2 `T5.7` Listen to some more telephone phrases. Then look at the tapescript on page 165 and practise saying all the phrases, paying attention to the intonation.

---

2 Work in pairs. Act out the conversation below.

Student A: You are phoning Travel Direct to find out about some airline tickets you ordered. You want to speak to Sandi Elliott to find out what is happening.
Student B: You work at Travel Direct. Sandi Elliott is on the other line at the moment.

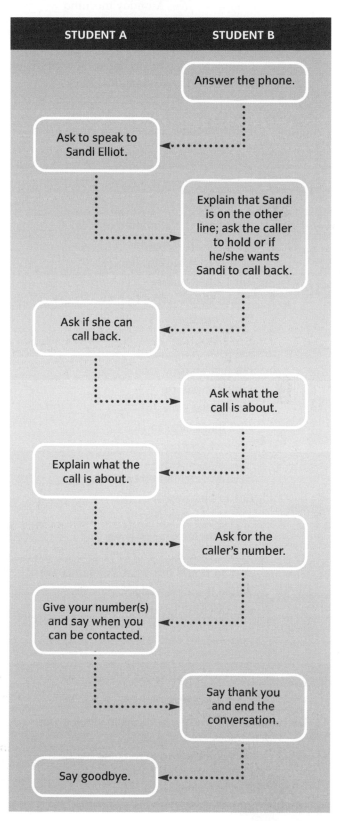

STUDENT A	STUDENT B
	Answer the phone.
Ask to speak to Sandi Elliot.	
	Explain that Sandi is on the other line; ask the caller to hold or if he/she wants Sandi to call back.
Ask if she can call back.	
	Ask what the call is about.
Explain what the call is about.	
	Ask for the caller's number.
Give your number(s) and say when you can be contacted.	
	Say thank you and end the conversation.
Say goodbye.	

Song
Manic Monday

1 Work in pairs. How do you typically feel at the following times?

- Friday afternoon
- Saturday evening
- Sunday morning
- Monday morning

Which is your favourite/least favourite day of the week? Why?

2 **T5.8** Complete the gaps in the song with the words and phrases in the box. Then listen and check.

> aeroplane dream fun day made Monday (x2) nine paid
> run day stream Sunday there time train wear

Six o'clock already
I was just in the middle of a (a) _____
I was kissin' Valentino
By a crystal blue Italian (b) _____
But I can't be late
'Cause then I guess I just won't get (c) _____
These are the days
When you wish your bed was already (d) _____

It's just another manic (e) _____
I wish it was (f) _____
'Cause that's my (g) _____
My I don't have to (h) _____
It's just another manic (i) _____

Have to catch an early (j) _____
Got to be at work by (k) _____
And if I had an (l) _____
I still couldn't make it on (m) _____
'Cause it takes me so long
Just to figure out what I'm gonna (n) _____
Blame it on the train
But the boss is already (o) _____

CHORUS

3 Discuss the following questions in small groups.

- What excuses is she going to make to her boss?
- Why is it important that she isn't late?
- Why is the song called 'Manic Monday'? Are your Mondays usually manic? Why?

STUDY...

Improving your spoken fluency

1 Here are some tips for improving your spoken fluency when doing the tasks in each module.

- Before the task, spend a few minutes thinking about what you are going to say and how you're going to say it. Try whispering to yourself to build fluency.

- Don't write every word of what you're going to say. Just make some short notes to help you.

- Check phrases with your teacher that you're not sure about, or if there is a better way to say something.

- When you're speaking, don't stop if you think you've made a mistake. Carry on speaking!

- After the speaking task, ask your teacher about the good points and the mistakes in what you said. He/She will give you feedback on the important mistakes you made.

2 Tick the things you do already and underline the things you would like to try.

BEFORE...

WHAT...I...ER...UM... LIKE...ABOUT...THIS... PERSON...

AFTER...

WHAT I LIKE ABOUT THIS PERSON IS...

PRACTISE...

1 Future plans and intentions ☐

Look at the sentences below. Which of them describes:

a an intention for the near future?
b an intention for the distant future?
c something arranged for the future?
d a future fact?
e an offer?

1 Shall I carry that suitcase for you?
2 My birthday will be on a Friday next year.
3 We're going to look for a new flat in a few years.
4 I'm having lunch with Simon on Friday.
5 I'm going to phone and tell him exactly what I think.

▶ **Need to check? Language summary A, pages 147–148.**

2 Talking about the future ☐

Cross out the word or phrase which cannot complete each sentence correctly.

a The course is due / going / planning to start on the 7th September.
b I'll tell him as soon as he gets back / he'll get back / I can.
c Are you due / going to / planning to take your holidays soon?
d We're hoping / planning / thinking of to go to Greece for our holiday this year.
e Can you phone me back before six o'clock / you leave / you will leave?

▶ **Need to check? Language summaries A4 and B, page 148.**

3 Future clauses ☐

Complete the sentences with the words in the box.

> as soon as   before   if   unless   until

a The bus won't arrive _____ after midnight.
b She'll be delighted _____ she gets the job.
c I want to finish my homework _____ I go out.
d _____ he gets home, I'll tell him the good news.
e We're going cycling, _____ it rains of course!

▶ **Need to check? Language summary B, page 148.**

4 Work ☐

Match A and B to make phrases connected with work. Can you remember any other phrases connected with work?

A		B	
a	well	1	a job
b	work	2	to travel
c	opportunities	3	time
d	apply for	4	training
e	good people	5	long hours
f	physically	6	skills
g	full	7	fit
h	special	8	-paid

▶ **Need to check? Vocabulary, page 51.**

5 Adjectives ☐

In each list, one word is not an adjective. Underline it, and make the necessary changes to make it an adjective.

a fit / important / success / intelligent
b ambitious / creative / happiness / stressful
c available / challenging / imagination / secure
d confident / determination / experienced / possible
e jealousy / kind / sympathetic / temporary

▶ **Need to check? Reading and vocabulary, page 49.**

6 Prepositions ☐

Choose the correct preposition.

a Goodbye. Thanks about / for / to calling.
b Sheila is interested about / in / of working with young people.
c Just a moment. I'll put you off / through / up to the right department.
d I look forward at / in / to meeting you tomorrow.
e I've already left several messages at / in / on the answering machine.
f I am fluent about / at / in French and Spanish.

▶ **Need to check? Writing and Real life, pages 56–57.**

Pronunciation spot

The sounds /ɒ/, /ɔː/ and /əʊ/

a **T5.9** Listen to the three sounds.

/ɒ/	want	box	hot
/ɔː/	warn	four	more
/əʊ/	don't	won't	coat

b **T5.10** Look at the lists of words below. Circle the word where the underlined vowel sound is different. Then listen and check.

1 got / long / old
2 course / important / qualification
3 bored / concentrate / job
4 alone / gone / most
5 boss / lost / told
6 confidence / score / walk

c Practise saying the words, paying attention to the vowel sounds.

REMEMBER!

Look back at the areas you have practised. Tick the ones you feel confident about. Now try the MINI-CHECK on page 157 to check what you know!

In the media

- ▶ -ed/-ing adjectives
- ▶ The passive
- ▶ Listening and vocabulary: TV and radio
- ▶ Reading and vocabulary: News stories
- ▶ Vocabulary: Extreme adjectives
- ▶ Pronunciation: Word stress
- ▶ Task: Review a book/CD/concert
- ▶ Writing: A consumer review

Listening and vocabulary
TV and radio

1 Discuss the following questions in pairs.

- How often do you listen to the radio? watch 'terrestrial' TV? watch satellite TV?
- When do you usually do these things?
- Which are your favourite / least favourite TV channels / radio stations? Why?

2 a Look at the types of programmes below. Do you usually find these on TV, on radio or on both?

documentaries	'reality' shows	phone-ins	sit coms
sports coverage	cartoons	local news	adverts
crime mysteries	national news	soap operas	
travel news	game shows and quizzes		

b What other kinds of programme are popular in your country?

3 Put the programmes in exercise 2 into these categories. Compare your opinions in pairs.

There are too many of these on the TV/radio in my country.	There aren't enough of these.
There are about the right number.	We haven't got this kind of programme in my country.

4 **T6.1** Listen to five short extracts from different types of radio or TV programme. What type of programme is each from? Is it more likely to be on TV, on radio, or could it be on either?

5 Listen again and answer these questions. Then compare answers in pairs.

a There are two questions in the quiz. Which categories do the questions belong to: art, geography, history, music, science?
b Where are the World Athletics Championships being held this year?
c Is Joe Rawlings a reporter, a runner or injured at the moment?
d What is the subject of the phone-in?
e What do we learn about Kerry's opinions?
f In the travel news, what is the cause of the delays on the M4?
g Is the situation on the M6 better or worse than before?
h What is the young man in the soap trying to tell the young woman?
i Does the young woman respond positively?

Language focus 1
-ed/-ing adjectives

1 Which of the following statements do you agree with? Compare your opinions in groups.

a You can't believe most of what you read and see in the media – half the time the journalists invent 'news' to fill their newspapers and programmes.

b They only ever show bad news on TV, never the good news.

c TV is better nowadays than it used to be.

d There's too much sex and violence on TV early in the evening when young children are still watching.

2 **T6.2** Listen to four people giving their opinion. Match the opinions to the statements in exercise 1. Do they agree, partly agree, or completely disagree?

3 Listen again. Which of these words did each person use? Did they use the -ed or -ing form?

excited/exciting	upset/upsetting
worried/worrying	annoyed/annoying
bored/boring	confused/confusing
depressed/depressing	interested/interesting

Analysis

1 Look at the picture. Who/What is:
– excited?
– exciting?

2 When do we use an -ed adjective and when do we use an -ing adjective?

▶ Read Language summary A on page 148.

Practice

1 Choose the correct alternative.

a Did you see that documentary about political corruption last night? It was a really interested / interesting programme – I was quite shocked / shocking.

b The Prime Minister said he was very pleased / pleasing with the country's economic progress, although there are some worried / worrying signs that there may be difficult times ahead.

c There was a very excited / exciting basketball game on TV last night, but I was a bit surprised / surprising that my team lost.

d I know that people are always fascinated / fascinating by celebrities' private lives, but I do think some of the personal questions they ask on chat shows can be a bit embarrassed / embarrassing.

e The instructions for this DVD player are so confused / confusing, it's so frustrated / frustrating trying to follow them.

f I was a bit annoyed / annoying that I forgot to record that Julia Roberts film last night, although the review in the paper said it was very disappointed / disappointing.

g I was really frightened / frightening by that ghost story you told us last weekend.

2 Work in groups. Discuss how you would feel in the following situations.

Example:
You switch on the TV to watch your favourite soap and discover that it's the football instead!

I'd be really pleased – I love football!

I'd be really annoyed – I find football really boring!

a You find out there's a chat show on TV with your favourite actor or rock star.

b You suddenly see your best friend on TV.

c You finish watching a scary film on your own at home and have to go to bed in an empty house.

d You watch a news item about civil war in a developing country.

e One of your friends phones for a chat in the middle of the news.

Reading and vocabulary
News stories

1 a Work in pairs. Which newspapers and magazines do you read? Do you usually read the serious news stories first, or do you turn to more light-hearted articles?

b Here are some common topics for news stories. Think of at least two more.

- accidents
- celebrities
- court cases
- crime
- rescues

2 a Cover the articles and read the headlines below. Choose two headlines below and try to guess what the article is about.

1 **Bono's hat goes first class**

2 **False alarm at airport**

3 Firefighter rescues old flame

4 **Home is a dangerous place**

5 **Lottery winner takes a day off**

6 **Mum is always there**

7 The case of the disappearing bridegroom

8 **Trainers make life worth living**

b Can you guess which headlines these words relate to?

air traffic controllers	wallpaper
baseball bat	giant cheque
hijack	ink
marriage register	pay off debts
slippers	soft toys

3 Read the articles quickly and match them to the headlines.

a A Cambodian immigrant who arrived in New York as a teenager has won $128m in the city's lottery. Phin Suy, a gardener in Central Park, says he will use the money to pay off his debts, but has got no plans to give up his job. He was presented with a giant cheque in a ceremony at Madison Square Garden, where his boss shouted: 'Phin, is this a vacation day or a sick day?' to which Suy modestly replied 'Vacation day'.

c A teenager who tried to rob a bus in Chile was horrified to discover that his mother was one of the passengers. Emilio Sanchez, together with two of his friends, was threatening the driver with knives and a baseball bat, when he heard a familiar voice telling him to stop it at once and ordering him off the bus.

e A youth who threatened to jump off a London bridge after breaking up with his girlfriend was persuaded down after an hour when the police offered him a new pair of trainers. Billy Camlin remained on Chelsea Bridge while he tried the Reeboks on for size, then decided that life wasn't so bad after all.

b Raul Hortena, 24, from Barcelona thought he had the perfect plan to escape his marriage any time he wanted. He signed the marriage register in disappearing ink. However, in court last week the judge refused to annul the marriage and Hortena was fined €130.

d There was panic at Chicago airport when Pete Twigger, a passenger boarding a plane greeted the pilot, whom he knew, with the words 'Hi Jack'. Air traffic controllers listening in the control tower ordered armed security teams to board the plane before realising their mistake.

f The most ordinary items in your home can cause an accident, according to government figures. Every year, more than 2,000 people are injured by soft toys, 700 by envelopes and 1,500 by tissue paper. Another 37,000 people blame slippers for their injuries, nearly 2,000 blame wallpaper, and almost 18,000 accidents are caused by armchairs. But by far the greatest danger in the home comes from carpets. Last year around 165,000 accidents involving carpets were reported.

g

U2 star Bono reportedly paid out €1,300 to fly his trilby hat first class to Italy. The singer had forgotten to pack his favourite hat for a charity concert with Italian tenor Luciano Pavarotti, so complicated arrangements were made to get the hat safely from England. A taxi took it from West London to Gatwick Airport where it was put in a first-class seat on a British Airways flight to Bologna. A hired driver then picked up the hat and sped to Modena – Pavarotti's home and the venue for the concert. A spokesman for the star said, 'including tips and insurance it cost about €1,300 to fly the hat here, but that is nothing compared to the money that will be raised for charity tonight.'

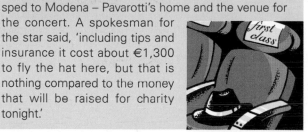

h

When Brisbane firefighter Shaun Kenna rescued a woman from a burning house, her face was so black that he did not at first recognise his ex-wife. 'Then when I recognised her voice I was amazed,' said Shaun, 'I had forgotten how beautiful she is.' The couple are now planning to remarry.

4 Work in pairs. Cover the articles again and check the words in bold in your mini-dictionary. Can you remember who or what ...

a   tried to **rob** a bus?
b   **threatened** to **commit suicide**?
c   **caused panic** at Chicago airport?
d   was **raising money for charity**?
e   was **fined** €130 **by a judge**?
f   **rescued** his ex-wife **from** a burning house?
g   was **presented with** a giant cheque?
h   has a **spokesman**?
i   thought there was a **hijacker** on board a plane?
j   **caused** 165,000 **accidents** last year?
k   cause 700 **injuries** every year?

Read the articles again and check.

5 Discuss the following questions in groups.

• Which of the stories have happy endings for the people concerned? Which have unhappy endings?
• Which story do you think is the most romantic, the funniest and the most unbelievable?

Language focus 2
The passive

1 Read the following sentences about the news stories and underline the main verb in each.

a   Shaun Kenna, a Brisbane firefighter, <u>rescued</u> his ex-wife from a burning house.
b   A Melbourne woman was rescued from a burning house by her ex-husband.
c   A Chilean teenager tried to rob a bus with his mother on board.
d   Bono's hat was put on a first-class seat for the flight to Italy.
e   Every year thousands of accidents are caused by ordinary items.
f   A lot of money will be raised for charity at the concert tonight.
g   Raul Hortena has been fined €130.

2 Who/What did each action? Do the sentences always tell us?

Analysis

1   Active and passive
Look at sentences a and b in exercise 1.
a   Which verb is active and which is passive?
b   Who is the subject of the active sentence? Who is the subject of the passive sentence?

2   Forming the passive
The passive is formed with *be* + the past participle. Find an example in exercise 1 of the following.
– Present simple passive   – Past simple passive
– Present perfect passive   – Future passive

3   The 'doer' (agent) in passive sentences
In passive sentences, the main focus is on the action or the person it happened to, <u>not</u> the person who does the action.
a   Often the person who does the action is not mentioned because:
  – this is obvious. Find an example.
  – the doer is unimportant or unknown. Find an example.
b   Sometimes the doer of the action is mentioned after the verb using *by*. Find two examples.

▶ Read Language summary B on pages 148–149.

Practice

1 Read the articles below and choose the correct verb form.

A woman from Port Headland in Australia (a) attacked / was attacked by a burglar while she was on the phone to her brother in Leeds, England. Her brother (b) heard / was heard strange noises and (c) phoned / was phoned his local police station in Leeds. The Port Headland police (d) contacted / were contacted immediately, and an officer (e) sent / was sent to the woman's house. She (f) rescued / was rescued just eighteen minutes after the attack (g) happened / was happened.

Yorkshire Electricity Company (h) has apologised / has been apologised after they (i) sent / were sent a customer a bill for €2 billion. Tanya Holland, from Huddersfield, (j) told / was told that she (k) owed / was owed €2,131,474,163, but the company (l) said / was said that she could pay in instalments. They later (m) admitted / was admitted that they had made a mistake and a new bill for €21.31 (n) sent / was sent.

It (o) has estimated / has been estimated that a towel (p) steals / is stolen from a Holiday Inn hotel every twelve seconds – that makes a total of 2.7 million towels a year!

2 a Work in pairs. Do the quiz and if you don't know the answers, guess!

b `T6.3` Listen and check your answers. Then underline the passive verb forms in the quiz.

MEDIA & FILM QUIZ

1 Where were the world's first newspapers produced?
  a In Ancient China   b In Ancient Rome
  c In seventeenth-century Germany

2 Which TV series is most widely watched around the world?
  a *Friends*   b *Baywatch*   c *The X Files*
3 China Central TV (CCTV) is regularly watched by
  a 100 million viewers   b 300 million viewers
  c 750 million viewers
4 The radio was first used for communication by
  a an Italian   b a Scot   c a Frenchman
5 Who was *The Simpsons* created by?
  a Walt Disney   b Steven Spielberg
  c Matt Groening
6 Since the first film, *Dr No* in 1962, how many James Bond films have been made?
  a Around twenty   b Around thirty
  c Around forty
7 Which writer's work has most often been made into films?
  a Agatha Christie   b Jane Austen
  c William Shakespeare

8 How many TVs are manufactured in the world every year?
  a Around seven million
  b Around seventy million
  c Around 700 million

3 Complete the sentences from the recording with the correct form of the verbs in brackets.

a The very first newspapers _____ (write) by hand.
b *Baywatch* _____ (translate) into 142 different languages.
c CNN _____ (watch) in 212 countries around the world.
d The radio _____ (first use) for communication by Marconi.
e Marconi _____ (award) the Nobel prize for his work in 1909.
f *The Simpsons* _____ (create) in 1986.
g Matt Groening _____ (name) the characters after his own family.
h Around four hundred films _____ (base) on plays by Shakespeare.
i The Bond movies _____ (make) over €13 billion since 1962.
j Around 70 million TVs _____ (manufacture) every year.

4 a Work in small groups. Write your own quiz of at least five questions using passive phrases.

was/were written by	was/were built by/in
was/were painted by	is/are made in
was/were composed by	is/are based on
was/were directed by	

Examples:

Who were 'The Matrix' films directed by?
a Larry and Andy Wachowski
b James Cameron
c Ridley Scott

Was 'Guernica' painted by
a Matisse?   b Miro?   c Picasso?

b Do your quizzes in teams, taking turns to read out the questions. Which team got the highest score?

Vocabulary
Extreme adjectives

1 Work in pairs. Read the extracts below from reviews for different films. Is each review good, bad or mixed? What kind of film does each review describe?

a
'Terrific … has more thrills than all of this summer's blockbusters put together … the special effects are superb and the action non-stop.'

b
'Basically a one-joke comedy. Even Steve Bristow's biggest fans will have to admit that doing this film was a terrible mistake …'

c
'Sam Harris is hilarious as the commanding officer of a group of soldiers whose main aim in life is to stay as far away as possible from the action …'

d
'If you forget about the ridiculous plot, and the dreadful dialogue – the movie is actually quite good fun, and Hollywood's latest stars Lucy Martinez and Jason Stone bring youthful glamour to this love story …'

2 Find words in the extracts in exercise 1 that mean the following.

a   very good (x2)   c   very funny
b   very bad (x2)   d   very silly

3 a Match the extreme adjectives in A with an adjective in B.

A	B
1 astonished	very frightened
2 boiling	very happy
3 brilliant	very angry
4 delighted	very sad
5 freezing	very surprised
6 furious	very hot
7 terrified	very good
8 tragic	very cold

b Which of these adverbs cannot be used with the extreme adjectives in A: *absolutely, really, very*?

▶ Read Language summary C on page 149.

4 Extreme adjectives are often used to make newspaper headlines and articles more interesting. Rewrite the headlines below, using an extreme adjective to replace the adjective(s) underlined.

a   United manager <u>very happy</u> with <u>very good</u> performance
b   <u>Very sad</u> death of teenager
c   Prime Minister <u>very angry</u> at opposition's criticism
d   We made some <u>very bad</u> mistakes admits United captain
e   <u>Very cold</u> temperatures in north of country
f   <u>Very hot</u> weather to continue
g   Film star <u>very surprised</u> at Oscar nomination

Pronunciation

1 **T6.4** Listen and write the words in the correct column according to the word stress.

●●	●●●	●●●●	●●●
			astonished

2 Practise saying the words, paying attention to the word stress.

Task: Review a book/CD/concert
Preparation: listening

1 Mark the following activities 1–4 (1 = I never do it; 4 = I do it all the time). Then compare your answers in groups.

go to a musical	watch TV
go to the cinema	read novels
watch films on video/DVD	go to the ballet
go to a classical concert	go to a rock concert
listen to music at home	go to see a play
play computer games	

2 Which of the activities in exercise 1 do you associate with these words? You can use your mini-dictionary to help you.

acting characters costumes graphics language lyrics music photography set singing special effects story

3 a **T6.5** Listen to three people talking about something they have seen, read or listened to recently. Make notes about the following.

1   What are they talking about?
2   Did they like it or not?
3   What were its strong points?
4   What were its weak points?

b Have you seen / read / listened to any of these things? Do you agree with the speaker or not? Would you like to see / read / listen to them?

Task: speaking

1 **a** Work individually. Choose one of the things in Preparation exercise 1 that you have seen / read / listened to recently and which you think your classmates will be interested in.

b You are going to review this for the class. Spend about fifteen minutes deciding what you will say. Use these questions to help you prepare your review. Ask your teacher for any words or phrases you need.

What is it?
Where/When did you see it?
Who is it by, who does it star, etc.?
Did you like it or not?
What were its strong points?
What were the weak points?
What words would you use to describe it?
Do you think your classmates would enjoy it?

▶ Useful language a and b

2 Work in pairs. Practise your reviews and answer any questions your partner has. Can your partner suggest any improvements to your review?

3 *Either* Present your review to the class. Other students should listen and note down which programmes, films, etc. they would like to see and any questions they would like to ask.

Or Make a class radio/TV programme called *Arts Round-up* and record it on cassette/video. Practise your reviews first, until you feel confident to record them. Then decide together the best order to put the programmes in, who will be the presenter and what he/she will say.

Useful language

a Describing what it is

It's called …

It's by …

It was (written/directed/produced/ published/ designed) by/in …

It's by the same (writer/director) as …

It's his/her third (album/book).

It stars …

It's set in …

It's based on …

It lasts/lasted (one and a half hours).

The story is very simple/complicated.

It's about …

b Giving your opinion

The (acting/story/graphics) is/are brilliant/terrible.

The best/worst thing about it is …

… is really boring/annoying/exciting.

Another thing I really liked/hated was …

One weak point was …

I'd recommend it to anyone who likes …

I wouldn't recommend it to anyone!

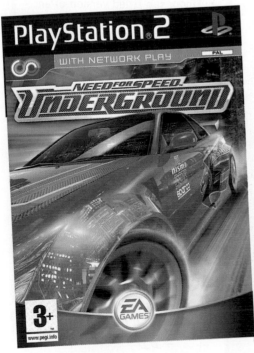

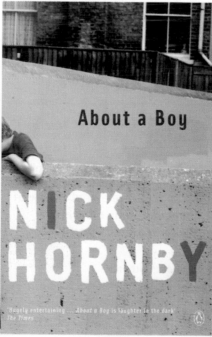

Writing
A consumer review

1 reviewbase.com is an online database of short reviews for books, CDs, films and computer games written by Internet users. The reviewer gives brief comments and a star rating (***** = Fantastic, *** = OK, 0 = awful). People use these reviews when deciding what to buy online.

Read the reviews below and answer the questions.

a   Is the review for a book, a CD, a film or a computer game?

b   What star rating (out of 5) do you think the reviewer gave?

Title: Love and hate   Review 1365 by Kate   23rd January   **Star Rating:**

This is not a movie I'd recommend. The special effects are OK, and some of the acting is quite good, but the plot is really hard to follow and by the end I'd lost interest.

Title: Desert island   Review 8397 by moo moo   13th April   **Star rating:**

The first time I played this, I'm afraid I was bored. The graphics are quite nice, the sound is OK (though the characters' voices are really annoying!) and the game got repetitive really quickly. Overall this game is a waste of money. Don't buy it.

Title: Attack!   Review 8674 by Danni   14th May   **Star rating:**

To my mind, this is easily the best thing on the market right now: there's fighting, shooting, a great storyline, great game play and the overall look is really cool. What more could you ask? Highly recommended!

Title: The real me   Review 16369 by Izzie   17th June   **Star rating:**

A terrific, funny read! As a rule I hardly ever read autobiographies, but I made an exception in this case and I'm glad I did. It's well written, very truthful and it had me laughing out loud on the bus … very embarrassing!! Buy it now – you won't regret it!

Title: Manic Days   Review 1611 by Paul   8th September   **Star rating:**

There are a few good tracks on here, but to be honest the rest of the album isn't up to much: everything sounds the same after a while and his voice isn't really any different from hundreds of other singers.

---

2 Complete the table with words and phrases from the reviews.

positive words and phrases	negative words and phrases
terrific funny	… not a movie I'd recommend

3 Make a list of five books, CDs, etc. you know. Write a brief review of each one and give each one a star rating. Use some or all of the phrases below, and the words and phrases from exercise 2 to help you.

Examples:

To my mind, … is the best book on the market right now …

A CD/book I'd/wouldn't recommend is …

I'd definitely recommend …

One computer game you should definitely buy is …

STUDY...

English outside the classroom (1): Using the media

1 Here are some things you can do to improve your English outside the classroom. Tick any of these things you've done. Did you find them useful?

- Use a good monolingual dictionary – *The Longman Active Study Dictionary* or *The Longman Dictionary of Contemporary English* are ideal.

- Find an English-language song you like and write down any words or phrases you understand.

- Watch an English-language TV channel (e.g. BBC World Service or CNN) for a few minutes every day.

- The BBC World Service offers a wide variety of radio programmes in English.

- Is there an English-language newspaper in your city (e.g. *Moscow Times* in Russia)? Choose an article to read.

- Choose a reader from the Penguin Reader series.

- Choose an article to read in an English-language magazine (e.g. *Time*).

- Find out about your nearest British Council library.

- Find a sub-titled version of an English-language movie. Watch without reading the sub-titles.

2 Discuss with other students which activities you think would be most useful. Underline the activities you would like to try.

PRACTISE...

1 -ed/-ing adjectives ☐

Choose the correct adjective.

a That's a very interested / interesting suggestion.

b It's not surprised / surprising.

c There's no need to feel embarrassed / embarrassing.

d Why are you always late? Have you any idea how annoyed / annoying it is!

e I'm afraid it was rather a bored / boring evening.

f It was very upset / upsetting to hear the news in that way.

g The news report was extremely worrying / worried.

h I don't understand. I'm really confused / confusing!

▶ **Need to check? Language summary A, page 148.**

2 The passive ☐

Put these active sentences into the passive, omitting the underlined word(s).

a The police arrested over thirty demonstrators.

_____

b The recent storms have damaged a number of buildings.

_____

c People destroy thousands of trees every year.

_____

d The judge will sentence the man tomorrow.

_____

e Someone had stolen my computer.

_____

f Is anybody looking after you?

_____

g They presented Sarah with a gold watch.

_____

h Davison built the museum in 1874.

_____

▶ **Need to check? Language summary B, page 148.**

3 Extreme adjectives ☐

Write extreme adjectives which are similar in meaning to the words below. Can you remember any others?

a very good _____

b very bad _____

c very sad _____

d very angry _____

e very silly _____

f very funny _____

▶ **Need to check? Vocabulary, page 65.**

4 Words that go together ☐

Match A and B to make a suitable verb + noun combination.

A	B
a commit	1 accident
b raise	2 day off
c cause an	3 money (for charity)
d hear a	4 voice
e to give up	5 suicide
f take a	6 your job

▶ **Need to check? Reading and vocabulary, page 63.**

5 Prepositions ☐

Choose the correct preposition.

a The film is based at / on / with a novel by Charles Dickens.

b Who would you recommend this film at / to / with?

c The film is set at / in / on New York.

d What was the best thing about / for / of the book in your opinion?

e The book has been translated in / into / on over thirty different languages.

f This film is by / from / of my favourite director.

▶ **Need to check? Task, page 67.**

Pronunciation spot

The sounds /æ/ and /ʌ/

a **T6.6** Listen to the pairs of words below. Can you hear the difference in the vowel sounds?

1 sang / sung		4	began / begun
2 rang / rung		5	drank / drunk
3 ran / run		6	swam / swum

b **T6.7** Listen and circle the phrase you hear.

c Practise saying the phrases, paying attention to the vowel sounds.

1 The match began / has begun.

2 I rang / 've rung lots of times.

3 They ran / 've run away.

4 We drank / 've drunk the whole bottle!

5 He swam / has swum every day this summer.

6 I sang / 've sung in public many times.

REMEMBER!

Look back at the areas you have practised. Tick the ones you feel confident about. Now try the MINI-CHECK on page 157 to check what you know!

Socialising

▶ Polite requests
▶ *will* for offers and instant decisions
▶ Making generalisations
▶ Reading and vocabulary: *The great international night out*
▶ Pronunciation: Sounding polite, *'ll*
▶ Vocabulary and speaking: Social behaviour
▶ Listening: Social customs in Thailand
▶ Task: Give tips on how to behave
▶ Real life: Making a social arrangement
▶ Wordspot: *go*

Reading and vocabulary

1 Which of these do you do if you go out with your friends? Which do you never do? Why not?

go to the cinema	watch live music
go out for a coffee	go for a pizza
go dancing	go to a bar
have dinner in a restaurant	go for a walk
go to a karaoke bar	

2 a Read the first paragraph of the article. Which three of the activities in exercise 1 are mentioned? Which country/countries do you associate with these things?

b Which of the three activities do you associate these phrases with?

to applaud   to bake   a chain of restaurants
a live band   an oven   a dance craze   a DJ
an ingredient   an international dish   laser lights

3 Work in pairs. Read the rest of the article and complete the sentences.

a _____ were banned in Paris nightclubs during the war.
b The first tomatoes were brought to Europe in _____ .
c Karaoke started in a bar in the city of _____ in _____ .
d The first Margarita pizza was created by _____ .
e The biggest pizza ever was baked in _____ .
f 'The Twist' became popular in _____ .
g Pizzas were brought to America by _____ .
h Karaoke started about _____ years ago.

The great

Go out any Saturday night in cities as far apart as Beijing and Berlin, and the chances are you'll find people eating pizzas, dancing in clubs and discos or enjoying a little karaoke. But have you ever wondered how these things started?

PIZZA

Pizza has a long history. The ancient Greeks first had the idea of putting vegetables on large flat pieces of bread, and 'pizza ovens' have been found in the ruins of Roman cities. But for
5 centuries one vital ingredient was missing – the first tomatoes were not brought to Europe until the sixteenth century, from South America. It was the nineteenth century before Rafaele Esposito, a baker from Naples, began to sell the first modern
10 pizzas. He was asked to bake a special pizza for a visit by the Italian King and Queen in 1889, and so the first pizza Margarita was created, named after the Queen.

Pizza became a favourite dish in Italy, but it
15 was after the Second World War, when thousands of American soldiers went home from Europe, that pizza really became an international dish. Soon there were pizzerias all over the USA, and American chains like Pizza Hut spread the idea
20 around the world. Today the average American eats over ten kilogrammes of pizza a year, and the world's largest pizza (measuring thirty metres across) was baked not in Italy, but in Havana, Cuba!

international night out

DISCOS

25 Have you ever wondered where the modern disco started? Before the Second World War, men and women going to nightclubs danced in couples to live bands. But in Paris during the war, jazz bands were banned in clubs. People still wanted to dance, so they took along
30 their gramophone players instead, and the very first 'discotheques' were created. The idea remained popular after the war, partly because it was cheaper to pay a DJ than a whole band, and soon Parisian discotheques were copied in the USA and other countries.

35 It was the arrival of a dance craze called 'The Twist' in 1961 that really made discos though, as for the first time couples danced without touching each other. Even Jacqueline Kennedy, the wife of the US President, was photographed doing the dance. Fashion, music and
40 technology have moved on quite a bit since then, but the basic idea has never lost its popularity.

KARAOKE

If dancing isn't your thing, perhaps you prefer singing? Everyone knows that karaoke comes from Japan, but it is not the Japanese for 'drunk and tone-deaf' as you might
45 think! It actually means 'empty orchestra'. It all started in a small music bar in the city of Kobe. One night when the usual guitarist
50 didn't turn up, the desperate bar owner recorded some music and invited his customers
55 to sing instead. The craze soon spread, and special karaoke machines were invented. The idea
60 was that however badly you sang everyone applauded at the end, and it proved the perfect way for stressed Japanese businessmen to unwind.

Today, just twenty years after it started in Kobe, you can find karaoke bars all over the world. It is so popular
65 in China that restaurants normally have several karaoke machines going at the same time. These days, you can hire karaoke machines that not only play music and videos, but also have smoke machines, laser lights, and even dancers and a DJ to accompany you, while you
70 make-believe for a few minutes that you are a star. As one karaoke fan put it, 'It's something everyone should try at least once in their life.'

4 Can you guess the meaning of these words and phrases from the context? Check in your mini-dictionary, if necessary.

a   flat (line 2)
b   to spread (line 19)
c   banned (line 28)
d   moved on (line 40)
e   not your thing (line 42)
f   tone-deaf (line 44)
g   to unwind (line 62)
h   to make-believe (line 70)

5 Discuss these questions in small groups.

• How popular are the activities mentioned in your country? Are there any other forms of entertainment from abroad that are currently popular?
• Do people around the world enjoy food, music, etc. from your country?
• Is American/international influence increasing where you live? In what ways? If so, do you think this is a good or a bad thing?

Language focus 1
Polite requests

1 In your culture, which of the following things are most important if you need to be polite?

- Use particular grammatical forms (e.g. different words for you)
- Body language (e.g. smiling, bowing)
- Use polite intonation
- Use polite phrases (e.g. please, Would you mind …?)

2 The two pictures show people having a night out. Which people are making requests? Try to guess what they are saying.

3 **a** **T7.1** Listen and find the person who is making the request each time.

b Listen again and make a note of the exact words used. Your teacher will pause the recording after each sentence.

4 **T7.2** Listen to the actual conversations. Does the other person say yes or no to the request? What reason do they give for refusing?

a

b

Analysis

Look at the recording script on page 167. Underline the phrases used to:
- ask if you can do something.
- ask another person to do something.
- say yes.
- say no.

▶ Read Language summary A on page 149.

Pronunciation

1 **T7.3** Listen to the first four requests again. Notice the polite intonation pattern.
Could I have the bill, please?
Is it okay if I take this chair?
Excuse me, can I get past, please?
Could you pass me the water, please?

2 Practise saying the requests, paying attention to the polite intonation.

Practice

1 Work in pairs. Rewrite the dialogues to make them sound polite. Then act out the dialogues.

     Can I
A: ~~I want to~~ speak to Maria. *please?*
I'm sorry *Could you*
  B: ⌄ She's out. ⌄ Call back later?

a A: I want to use your pen.
    B: Yes.
b A: Pass me my coat.
    B: Here you are.
c A: Lend me €10 till tomorrow.
    B: I haven't got any money.
d A: Bring me another coffee.
    B: Yes.
e A: Lend me your phone.
    B: It needs charging.
f A: If you're going into town give me a lift.
    B: Yes.
g A: Tell me the way to the bus station.
    B: I don't know this area.
h A: Pick up my suit from the dry cleaner's.
    B: I won't be able to. I'll have too much to carry.

2 **a** Think of six requests to ask politely, using these verbs.

1 help (me) to do something
2 open or close
3 move something
4 lend or borrow
5 pass (me)
6 turn on/off

b Take it in turns to make requests for your partner to answer. Make sure your requests and answers sound polite.

> Would you mind opening the window?

> I'm sorry, it doesn't open.

> Yes, of course. It's a bit hot in here.

Language focus 2
will for offers and instant decisions

1 **a** Look at the pictures. What is the relationship between the people? In each case there is a small problem. Guess what it is.

b **T7.4** Listen and check. How is the problem resolved?

2 Complete the following sentences from the recording. Then listen again and check.

a _____ and see what he wants.
b Look, tell Tony _____ in early tomorrow.
c Don't worry, _____ you a lift home.
d No, really, _____ for a taxi.

Analysis

1 In each of the situations, the speakers decide what to do about a small problem. When do they decide what to do? What verb form do they use?

2 We use *going to* when we have already decided/planned to do something.
We're going to see that new film at the Ritzy.

▶ Read Language summary B on page 149.

Practice

a Look at the situation below. Which do you think is the best answer?

> You are about to be served in a burger bar and your friend tells you he's left his wallet at home. What do you say?

  a Don't worry, I'll buy you a burger.
  b I'll lend you some money, if you like.
  c Never mind, I'll give you a bite of mine.

b Work in pairs. Look at page 142 and do the rest of the quiz.

Pronunciation

1 **T7.5** Listen to six answers to the situations in exercise b. In which sentences is *I'll* pronounced correctly?

2 Look at the recording script on page 167. Practise saying the sentences, paying attention to the correct pronunciation.

3 Use some of the situations from exercise b to write dialogues like those in recording 4 on page 167. Act them out with a partner.

Vocabulary and speaking
Social behaviour

1 Work individually. Check the words and phrases in bold in your mini-dictionary. Then answer the questions. (You can choose more than one answer.)

1 You go out to a restaurant for dinner. Do you:
a **dress up**?
b wear **smart casual** clothes?
c wear the traditional dress of your country?
d wear whatever you feel like?

2 Which of these things should you normally do in a restaurant in your country?
a **book in advance**
b **order** your starter and main course at the same time
c **tip** the waiter about 10%
d go somewhere else for coffee

3 If a man and woman **go out on a date**, which of these things should happen?
a The man should **pick** her **up** from her house.
b He should **pay for** her dinner.
c They should **split the bill**.
d He should **give** her a **lift** home.

4 You've been **invited to dinner** at a friend or colleague's house. Which of these should/shouldn't you do?
a take something, e.g. flowers, a dessert
b **refuse** food that you are offered
c **offer to wash up** after dinner
d **send a card or e-mail** afterwards to say thank you

5 While you are out, you meet some friends in the street. Do you:
a **shake** hands?
b **kiss each other on both cheeks**?
c **bow** to each other?
d just say hello?

2 Compare your answers in groups. Do any of these things depend on the circumstances? Explain why.

> I think it depends on the restaurant. If it's a really smart one, you should …

> But if it's just an ordinary restaurant, you can …

Listening
Social customs in Thailand

1 What do you know about Thailand? Do you know anything about the food or the social customs?

2 Read the extract from a travel guide to Thailand giving tips on social customs. Can you guess which alternative is correct for any of the tips?

3 a (T7.6) Nikam Nipotam is half Thai. One of his colleagues is going to visit Thailand, and has asked him about social customs there. Listen to their conversation and choose the correct alternatives in the guide.

b What things are the same and different for your culture?

Nikam Nipotam

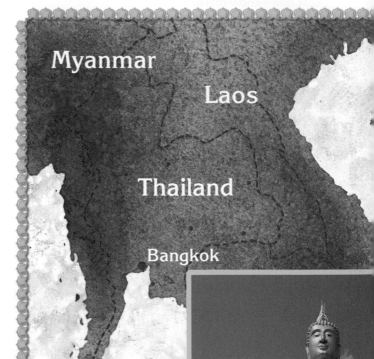

74

Tips for visitors to Thailand

Thailand is famous for its hospitality, and the average visitor will have no difficulty in adapting to local customs. The following tips are mostly common sense, but to avoid giving offence foreign visitors may find them useful.

a When addressing a Thai person it is polite to use just their first name / surname.

b In more formal situations you should use the word 'Khun'. This is like 'Mr' and is used for addressing men / both men and women.

c It is not usual to shake hands when you meet a Thai person – instead you do a wai – you put your hands together as if you are saying a prayer, and bow your head slightly. You should always do this when you meet older people / your friends.

d Couples should be careful how they behave. Thai couples tend not to hold hands in public and it is acceptable / not acceptable for couples to kiss in public.

e The head is very important in Thai culture. It is not respectful / acceptable to touch another person's head.

f Remember, if you are invited to someone's home it is important to take your shoes off / keep your shoes on.

g In Thailand, people tend to serve food in large bowls in the centre of the table. Everyone helps themselves, using chopsticks / a spoon and fork.

Finally remember that it is very important to show respect to the Thai royal family. Thai people always do this, and expect visitors to do the same.

Language focus 3
Making generalisations

Analysis

1 The following generalisations about Thai culture come from the travel guide. Notice how we use *It* to introduce generalisations.
   It is important to take your shoes off.
   It is not usual to shake hands.
   It is not acceptable for couples to kiss in public.
   Underline three more generalisations introduced by *It* in the travel guide. Think of some more adjectives you can use in this way.

2 *Tend to* + verb is also used to make generalisations.
   People **tend to** serve food in large bowls in the middle of the table.
   Thai couples **tend not to** hold hands.

▶ Read Language summary C on pages 149–150.

Practice

1 Choose adjectives from the box to make true sentences about your country, starting with *It's*.

(not) acceptable (not) important (perfectly) normal
(not) okay (not) respectful rude/polite (not) usual

a keep your shoes on in people's houses
b treat old people with respect
c friends shake hands when they meet
d strangers call you by your first name
e use 'Mr' and 'Mrs' when you address people
f say rude things about royalty or politicians
g men bow to women
h serve food in large bowls in the middle of the table
i touch people on the head
j couples hold hands in public

2 Tick the sentences that are true about your country. If they are not true, change them.

a People in offices tend to wear casual clothes to work.
b People don't tend to dress up when they go out.
c Women tend to wear a lot of make-up and jewellery.
d Young women don't tend to go out in groups.
e Parents tend to be strict with their daughters about going out.

3 Compare your answers to exercises 1 and 2 in groups. Do you disagree about anything?

Task: Give tips on how to behave
Preparation: listening

1 a [T7.7] Listen to eight people talk about a social custom in their country. Make a note of which of the topics in the box each one mentioned.

Amy, 25 from Canada
Pawel, 39 from Russia
Rosa, 33 from Peru
Ian, 30 from England
Dong-Min, 18 from Korea
Lee Kuan, 20 from Singapore
Ramon, 24 from Spain
Khalid, 22 from Bahrain

---
behaviour between the sexes
being late
how you greet and address people
smoking
the way people dress
typical times for going out / eating
what people do when they go out

---

b Listen again. What do they say about these things in their country?

2 [T7.8] Listen and complete the missing phrases.

a _____ pay fifty-fifty for everything.
b And you _____ to pay.
c Men _____ hands when they greet each other.
d It's _____ to shake hands with all the other men in the room.
e _____ arrive an hour late.
f _____, it's _____ to smoke in people's houses.
g _____ to dress smartly.
h _____ to be fashionable.
i _____ go out late in Spain.

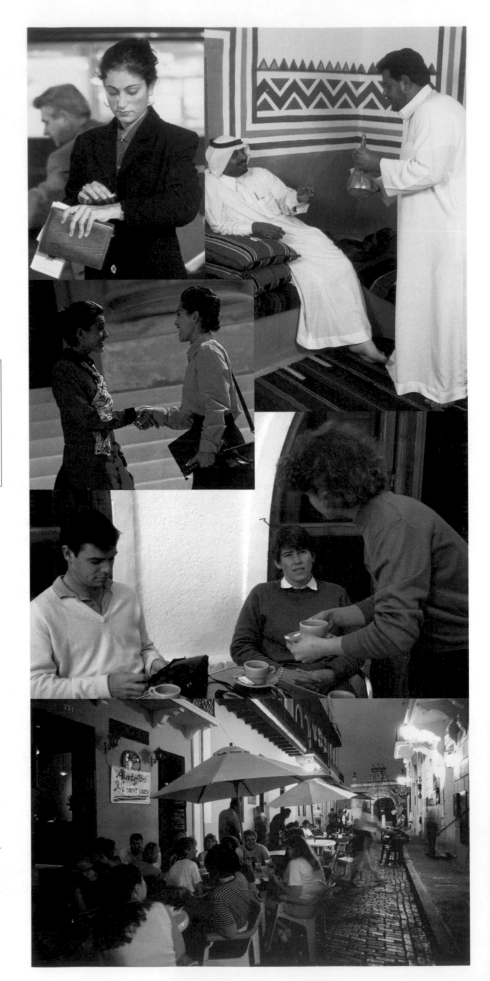

Task: speaking

1 Work in groups. You are going to make a list of tips about how to behave when you go out. Choose one of the options below.

Either Write some tips for a foreign visitor to your country. Write notes about the topics in the preparation section. Which things would a visitor find different in your country?

Or Imagine you have been asked to appear on a radio programme aimed at people over fifty. This week they are giving a 'guide' to the way young people behave when they go out. Think about the topics in the preparation section and prepare what you are going to say.

▶ Useful language a and b

2 *Either* Compare your list of tips with another group. Which ideas were the same/different?

Or Work in pairs. Give your short radio talk about social behaviour in your country.

Useful language

a What to do

Generally people ...

Most Spanish/young people ...

Always remember to ...

It's polite / usual / important / perfectly OK / common to ...

Don't be surprised if ...

People expect you to ...

b What not to do

You should never ...

These days, nobody ...

Nobody cares about ...

It might seem strange if you ...

It's not acceptable to ...

Real life
Making a social arrangement

1 **T7.9** Laurence is phoning Roger. Listen and answer the following questions.

a What do you think is the relationship between Roger, Laurence and Millie?
b Why is Roger busy at the moment?
c Where and when does Laurence invite Roger for a meal?
d What plans have Roger and Millie for that day?
e What suggestion does Laurence make to solve the problem?
f When should Roger give Laurence another ring?

2 Look at the tapescript on page 168 and underline useful phrases for the telephone, and for inviting and arranging.

3 a Mark the phrases below *A* if they are for accepting invitations and *R* if they are for refusing.

1 I think that should be fine, I'll call you back if there's any problem.
2 Sorry, but we're busy.
3 Thank you very much, that would be lovely.
4 We can't, I'm afraid.
5 What a shame!

b Listen again and tick the phrases that Roger uses. Then practise saying the phrases.

4 Work in pairs. Choose a situation below and have a conversation like Roger and Laurence's. Invite your partner:

* to a concert/football match/club/film/exhibition.
* to your house for a drink/meal/party.
* out for a drink/meal/coffee or to play sport.

Suggest a day and time. Your partner will accept or refuse, giving a reason. When you have finished, swap roles.

Wordspot
go

1 a The diagram below shows some common phrases with *go*.
   Study the diagram.

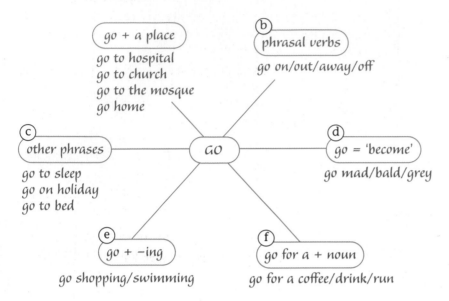

go + a place
go to hospital
go to church
go to the mosque
go home

b
phrasal verbs
go on/out/away/off

c
other phrases
go to sleep
go on holiday
go to bed

GO

d
go = 'become'
go mad/bald/grey

e
go + –ing
go shopping/swimming

f
go for a + noun
go for a coffee/drink/run

b Find a phrase with *go* that means the following.

1 to continue 2 to explode 3 to lose your hair

c Think of a situation where you might say the following.

1 Go away! 2 Go to sleep! 3 Oh, no! I'm going grey!

4 He went mad at me! 5 Let's go for a drink!

2 Walk around the classroom and find someone who ...

a went to bed late last night.
b goes to church / the mosque regularly.
c would like to go for a coffee/drink after class.
d is going on holiday soon.
e is going out tomorrow night.
f usually goes home immediately after class.
g goes for a run regularly.
h hates going shopping.
i likes going swimming at the weekend.
j sometimes has difficulty going to sleep.
k usually goes for a walk at the weekend.
l has never been to hospital.

Decide what questions you will ask before you begin, and speak to as
many students in the class as you can.

Using revision techniques

1 Here are some techniques for revising. Which of these have you tried? Discuss with other students which activities you think would be most useful.

- Read through the Language summary for a particular module. Highlight the sections that you haven't read before or have forgotten. Reread the highlighted sections again a day or two later. How much do you remember?

- Work in pairs. Choose a page in the mini-dictionary and read out the definitions to your partner. Can he/she guess the word?

- Choose one of the reading texts you have used in class. Write down any phrases/information you remember from the text. Then read the text again to check.

- Choose one of the recordings at the back of the book. Read it to yourself (or listen to the recording). Then close your book and write down as many words and phrases as you can remember.

- Look through one of the exercises you have done in the Workbook. Then close the book and try to write out the exercise yourself.

2 Try some of the techniques. How effective did you find them? Can you think of any others?

LIST of THINGS to REMEMBER

PRACTISE...

1 Offers and requests ☐

Match the sentences in A to an explanation in B.

A
a Do you mind if I open the window?
b No, not at all.
c Could you open the window, please?
d Sure, go ahead.
e Sorry, but I can't.

B
1 the speaker is making a request
2 the speaker is asking for permission
3 the speaker is refusing a request
4 the speaker is giving permission
5 the speaker is agreeing to a request

▶ **Need to check? Language summary A, page 149.**

2 *will* for instant decisions and responses ☐

Match the beginnings of sentences in A to the endings in B. Which sentences are:
• offers?
• decisions made at the moment of speaking?
• decisions made before the moment of speaking?

A
a I'll carry your books
b I'll try again later
c I'm going to get fit this summer
d I'll do the washing up
e I'll take the red pair of shoes
f I'm going to cook this evening

B
1 I've signed up for a course at the gym.
2 I don't like the black ones so much.
3 they look very heavy.
4 I bought all the ingredients this morning.
5 his phone's off at the moment.
6 you cooked so it's only fair.

▶ **Need to check? Language summary B, page 149.**

3 Words that go together ☐

Underline the word or phrase in B which makes a correct combination with A.

A	B
a order	1 some food / a tip / the waiter
b book	2 your food / in advance / the bill
c split	3 the bill / a lift / a tip
d give someone	4 a date / a lift home / a waiter
e send someone	5 a card / a lift / a date

▶ **Need to check? Vocabulary and speaking, page 74.**

4 Word building ☐

Write the adjectives from these words.

a accept   b respect   c importance

▶ **Need to check? Language focus 3, page 75.**

5 Making generalisations ☐

Choose the correct alternative. (— means 'no word'.)

a It's normal go / going / to go out in a large group.
b It's quite difficult for / that / — young people to find a good job.
c A lot of / the / — young people enjoy dancing.
d Very few of / the / — people stay out late.
e People tend never / not / not to blow their nose in public – it's considered impolite.

▶ **Need to check? Language summary C, pages 149–150.**

6 Phrases with *go* ☐

What phrases with *go* mean:

a to lose your hair?   _____

b to continue?   _____

c to leave?   _____ and _____

d to return home?   _____

Can you remember any other phrases with *go*?

▶ **Need to check? Wordspot, page 78.**

Pronunciation spot

The sounds /θ/ and /ð/

a **T7.10** Listen to the different ways of pronouncing the letters 'th'.
th = /θ/   thing   thief   three
th = /ð/   the   these   that

b **T7.11** Listen to these phrases from the text on pages 70 and 71. Is 'th' pronounced /θ/ or /ð/?
1 thousands of American soldiers
2 other countries
3 without touching each other
4 dancing isn't your thing
5 at the same time
6 it's something everyone should try

c Practise saying the phrases.

d Make a list of other words containing the sounds /θ/ and /ð/. Use your mini-dictionary to help you.

REMEMBER!

Look back at the areas you have practised. Tick the ones you feel confident about. Now try the MINI-CHECK on page 157 to check what you know!

Things you can't live without

▶ Defining relative clauses
▶ Quantifiers
▶ **Pronunciation:** Stress in compound nouns
▶ **Reading:** *Machines behaving badly*
▶ **Vocabulary:** How machines work, Describing everyday objects
▶ **Task:** Make a list of things you'd hate to be without
▶ **Real life:** Buying things
▶ **Writing:** Saying thank you

Reading

1 Look at the photos taken from unusual angles. Can you identify the objects?

2 Which of these do you have experience of? Do you feel positively about them? Why / Why not?

call centres	mobile phones
the Internet	e-mail
computer help desks	texting
laptops / palm tops	digital TV

3 Which thing(s) in exercise 2 do you associate the following words and phrases with?

a better quality picture	the customer care department
hardware	instruction manuals
being out of date	saving time
a spare part	software
using your thumbs	

4 a Read the article written by someone who is a 'technophobe' (someone who doesn't like modern machines). Then match the headings below with the seven paragraphs.

1 It does things you don't need
2 It doesn't save you time
3 It was out of date before you bought it
4 It's anti-social
5 It's destroying the English language
6 More choice does not mean better
7 No one takes responsibility when things go wrong

b Compare your answers in groups.

5 Work in pairs. Answer the following questions according to the author.

a Why doesn't a PC save you time?
b Why do people have to replace their computers so often?
c Why is it easy for help desks and call centres to not 'take responsibility'?
d What is the problem with digital TV?
e What three effects is text messaging having on young people?

MACHINES BEHAVING BADLY

Everyone, it seems, has a mobile these days, even children in kindergarten. Billions of text messages fly round the world every day, and computers and call centres run every aspect of our lives. But is all (5) **this really making life better? Here are seven good reasons to hate modern technology.**

A *It doesn't save you time*

Many people make the mistake of thinking that technology is there to save you time. Wrong. It is there to give people new ways of filling their time. Take (10) personal computers. Learning how to use all the features of a new PC uses up all the time that having a computer saves. And what about all the hours you spend staring at incomprehensible instruction manuals for your new phone / TV / digital doorbell?

B

(15) Of course it's wonderful to have a CD player, a mobile, a home computer, or an electric toaster, for that matter. But do you really want to play computer games on the 4 cm screen of your mobile phone? Do you need your computer to answer the phone, or your (20) TV to make toast?

C

Digital TV is a perfect example. When it arrived, we were promised a better quality picture and more choice. But at eleven o'clock at night as you flick through the 97 channels you can now get, it is not (25) the quality of the picture that you worry about. More the fact that not one single programme is worth watching.

D

After several frustrating weeks of finding all the right software for your new PC, then phoning 'help' desks (30) when it doesn't work, you will proudly show off your new machine to friends only to hear 'Oh, are you still using that one? I'm thinking of buying the new PYX 5000, myself.' A few months later, when you try to buy some minor spare part, you find it is no longer (35) manufactured, and that it would be much cheaper to replace the whole computer with the new PYX 7500.

E

This is easy, because very few people really understand how the machines they have bought work. So you phone the software company and they will tell (40) you it's a hardware problem. You then phone the hardware company and they tell you it's a software problem. Call centres are the worst. Phone the so-called 'customer care' number, and after waiting on hold for fifteen minutes you will be told you need the (45) sales department. The sales department assure you that it's the technical department you need, but surprise, surprise, the technical department put you back through to customer care. People can spend weeks of their lives like this.

F

(50) Apparently, teenagers now do so much texting and e-mailing that their thumbs are getting bigger. Unfortunately, they are also forgetting how to spell. One American schoolgirl recently wrote her entire essay on 'My summer holidays' in text speak. It began

(55) 'B4 we used 2go2 NY 2C my bro, his GF & thr 3 kids. ILNY it's a GR8 plc.'

Or for you and me: 'Before we used to go to New York to see my brother, his girlfriend and their three kids. I love New York it's a great place.'

G

(60) A recent survey showed that more than eight out of ten young people would rather text their friends or family than actually speak to them in person. And according to the same survey, twentyfive percent of people would answer their mobile phone even during (65) a moment of passion. I ask you, is this really a better world?

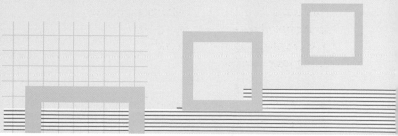

6 Can you guess the meaning of these words and phrases from the context? Check in your mini-dictionary.

a   anti-social (heading 4 in exercise 4a)
b   filling your time (line 10)
c   staring at (line 14)
d   flick through (line 25)
e   show off (line 32)
f   waiting on hold (line 47)
g   text speak (line 58)

7 **a** Discuss the following questions in small groups.

• Do you think the author is male or female, young or middle-aged? What makes you think this?
• Do you agree with him/her or do you think he/she is living in the past?

b *Either* Think of some more ways in which technology drives you mad.

Or Make your own list of 'seven reasons to love technology'.

Language focus 1
Defining relative clauses

Do the quiz below to find out how computer friendly you are.

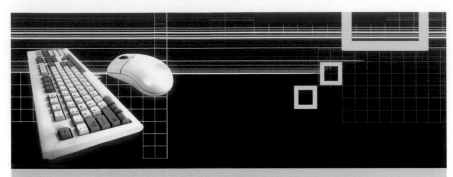

Are you a 'techie' or a technophobe?

Match each word in the box with a definition.

an anti-virus

broadband

cyberspace

the Internet

a mouse

a techie

a technophobe

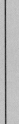

a A person who doesn't like machines, especially computers.

b A computer system which allows millions of computer users around the world to exchange information.

c A system that is able to send different types of communication signals down a telephone line at the same time.

d A piece of software you install on your computer to protect it from viruses.

e A small object which you move with your hands to give instructions to the computer.

f The imaginary place where electronic messages, information, pictures, etc. exist when they are sent from one computer to another.

g Someone whose life is dominated by technology – especially computers.

Analysis

1 Look at the quiz and underline the relative pronouns.
A person <u>who</u> doesn't like machines, especially computers.

2 Complete the following rules.
a _____ and *that* are used to refer to people.
b _____ and _____ are used to refer to things.
c _____ is used to refer to possessions.
d _____ is used to refer to places or locations.

3 Why is there no relative pronoun in definition d? In which other sentence can we leave out the relative pronoun?

▶ Read Language summary A on page 150.

Practice

1 a Which words in the box do the definitions below describe? Complete them with the correct relative pronoun.

boiler bodyguard cleaner cook
cooker decorator dry cleaner's
freezer launderette photocopier
plumber stationer's typewriter
vacuum cleaner

1 A _____ is a machine .... makes copies of documents.

2 A _____ is a person .... protects important people from being attacked.

3 A _____ is a place with washing machines .... you can wash your clothes.

4 A _____ is a person .... job is to mend central heating, taps, etc.

5 A _____ is a machine .... you use to clean floors and carpets.

b Match the other words in the box to the prompts below. Then write definitions. Use *which, that, who, whose* or *where*, if necessary.

Example:
machine / keep / food very cold
A freezer is a machine which keeps food very cold.

1 machine / cook / food
2 person / you pay / cook for you
3 person / you pay / clean your house or office
4 old-fashioned machine / you use for typing
5 machine / heat water for baths, etc.
6 shop / they clean jackets, suits, etc. for you
7 person / job is to paint houses
8 shop / you buy office supplies

2 Work in pairs. Student A: Close your book. Student B: Read five definitions from exercise 1 to see if Student A can remember the correct words. Then swap roles.

> What do you call a machine which keeps food very cold?

3 Work in teams to make a vocabulary revision quiz for other students. Team A: Look at page 140. Team B: Look at page 142.

Vocabulary 1
How machines work

1 a **T8.1** Listen to four short conversations. Which of the machines below are the people talking about? Which words and phrases tell you this?

| an answering machine   a cassette player |
| a digital camera   a laptop computer   a mobile phone |
| a photocopier   a radio   a vacuum cleaner   a watch |

b Listen again and look at the tapescript on page 168. Underline all the verbs that refer to machines.

Example:
Well, it just keeps <u>crashing</u> every time I try ...

2 **T8.2** Match a word or phrase from A with a phrase from B. Then listen and check.

A		B
a	switch on/off	the button
b	plug in	your mobile phone
c	press	the tape
d	rewind/fast forward	the vacuum cleaner
e	restart	the volume
f	turn up/down	your messages
g	replay	your computer
h	shut down	the tape
i	hold down	your computer
j	pause	the button
k	My computer	needs recharging
l	My mobile phone	's crashed
m	The batteries	need replacing

3 Work in pairs. Write three sentences about five of the items below, using some of the phrases from exercise 2. Then swap sentences with another pair and see if they can guess what you're describing.

a digital camera	a DVD player	an electric cooker
a fax machine	a games console	an MP3 player
a Walkman	a washing machine	

Example: (a dishwasher)
You can switch it on and off.
It doesn't need batteries.
It has to be plugged in before it'll work.

Pronunciation

1 Notice the stress patterns in compound nouns.

NOUN + NOUN	ADJECTIVE + NOUN
•	• •
phone message	central heating

2 How do you think the following compound nouns are pronounced?

call centre	fan heater
spare part	instruction manual
swimming pool	dark glasses
mobile phone	video recorder
dining room	personal computer
washing machine	car radio

3 **T8.3** Listen and check. Practise saying the words, paying attention to the stress.

Language focus 2
Quantifiers

1 Discuss the following questions in small groups.

- Have you ever driven or been for a walk in the desert? Would you like to? Why / Why not?
- What do you think are the possible dangers?
- Make a list of ten things you would need to take on a trip into the desert.

2 **T8.4** Jeff Wilkinson works for a centre for tourism in Queensland, Australia. He specialises in providing safety advice for visitors to the Queensland desert.

Listen to his advice. Which of the items in your list in exercise 1 does he mention?

3 **T8.5** Listen and complete the gaps.

a Every year we have _____ cases where people have to be rescued.

b If people just use _____ common sense …

c … and follow _____ basic rules for survival, this could so easily be avoided.

d Let _____ people know where and when you're going.

e There's not really _____ chance of finding you if we don't know where to look.

f You must be sure to take _____ water.

g In the desert there really is no such thing as _____ water.

h Definitely _____ alcohol – not even a cold beer.

i Check you've got _____ spare fuel for your vehicle.

j Be sure to take a small first-aid kit with a pair of scissors, _____ bandages …

k Take _____ matches so you can start a fire if need be.

l You'll need to have _____ sun screen if you don't want a bad case of sunburn.

m Very often people don't take _____ warm clothes to put on at night.

Analysis

1 Which of the words below are countable? Which are uncountable?
chance fuel rule water

2 Look at the words in the gaps in exercise 3 above. All these words are known as quantifiers. Make three lists.
   a Quantifiers which are used with countable nouns, e.g. *several*
   b Quantifiers which are used with uncountable nouns, e.g. *a bit of*
   c Quantifiers which are used with both, e.g. *plenty of*

▶ Read Language summary B on page 150.

Practice

1 Work in pairs. Discuss which quantifiers best complete the following sentences about your classroom or place of work.

a There's _____ space for everyone to work.
b There are _____ comfortable chairs.
c There's _____ natural light.
d There's _____ fresh air.
e There are _____ notices on the wall.
f There are _____ plants.
g There's _____ valuable equipment.
h There are _____ stairs.
i There's _____ noise from outside.
j There are _____ of people to talk to.

2 Work in small groups. Discuss the place where you live using appropriate quantifiers. Think about the following things.

cinemas	places to eat
sports facilities	green space
pollution	traffic
Internet cafés	theatres
shops	

I think there's too much traffic.

There are loads of shops.

There definitely isn't enough green space.

Vocabulary 2
Describing everyday objects

1 How many objects in the photo below can you name? Check the others in your mini-dictionary.

2 a Spend a few minutes memorising the new words, then close your book.

b Write down as many objects as you can remember in three minutes. Who remembered the most?

3 a Match each phrase below to an object in the photo.

1 It's made of glass / leather / silver / plastic / …
2 It's sharp / valuable / tiny / easy to break / soft / …
3 It's round / long and thin / …
4 It's got a lid / a handle(s) / buttons / batteries.
5 It's used for cutting / sticking things together / carrying things.

b Think of at least two more words to go in 1, 2 and 3 above.

4 Work in pairs. Choose an object in the photo and write three clues to describe it. Can your partner guess what it is?

It's round, it's made of metal — gold or silver very often — and it can be very valuable.

Is it a ring?

5 Choose an everyday object that is not in the photo. Other students can ask you a maximum of ten yes/no questions to find out what it is.

Has it got a lid?

Is it made of metal?

Is it used for carrying something?

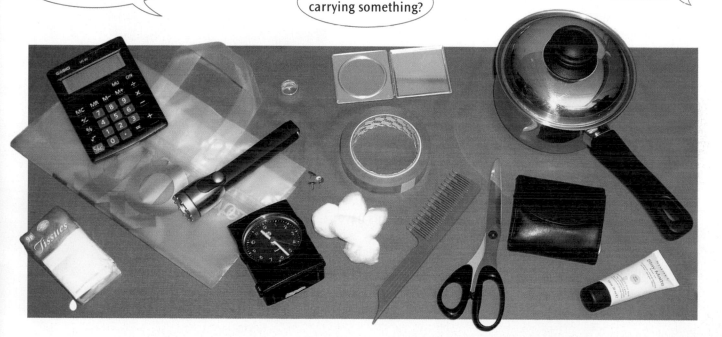

Task: Make a list of things you'd hate to be without

Preparation: listening

T8.6 You will hear six people talking about something they would hate to be without. Listen and complete the table.

	object	how he/she describes it	why it is important to him/her
1			
2			
3			
4			
5			
6			

Task: speaking

1 You are going to present your own list of five things you'd hate to be without. You could include some of the following.

furniture and ornaments	CDs or books
machines and technology	photos
things of sentimental value	clothes
useful everyday objects	jewellery

2 Spend a few minutes thinking about how to describe these things and why they are important to you. Mention some or all of the following.

– what the object is
– where/how/when you got it
– description of the object (colour, size, etc.)
– why it's important to you
– what you use it for
– why you couldn't live without it
– any stories/memories associated with it

Ask your teacher for any words or phrases you need.

► Useful language a, b and c

3 Work in small groups. Tell the other students about the objects on your list, and if you have the object with you, show it to the group. Answer any questions the other students have.

4 Which were the most common objects chosen? Which was the most unusual object chosen by your group? Tell the class about it.

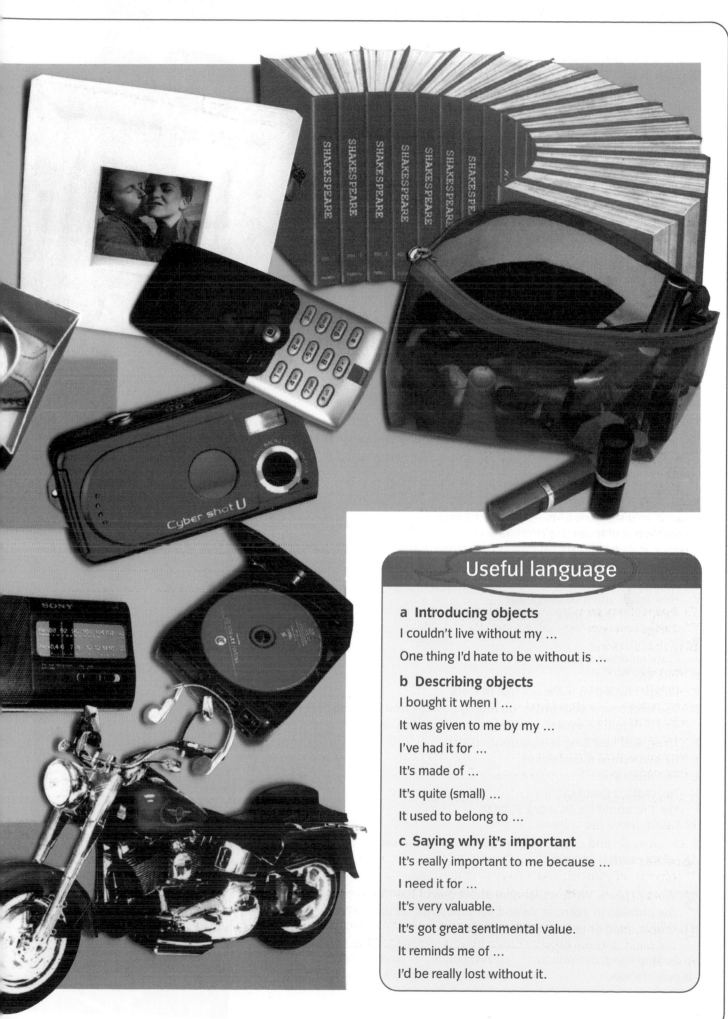

Useful language

a Introducing objects

I couldn't live without my …

One thing I'd hate to be without is …

b Describing objects

I bought it when I …

It was given to me by my …

I've had it for …

It's made of …

It's quite (small) …

It used to belong to …

c Saying why it's important

It's really important to me because …

I need it for …

It's very valuable.

It's got great sentimental value.

It reminds me of …

I'd be really lost without it.

Real life
Buying things

1 a **Look at the photos. Where/How are the people shopping? What other types of shopping can you think of? Which do/don't you enjoy?**

b **T8.7** **Listen to two conversations. Which photos do they relate to?**

c **Listen again and complete the table.**

	Conversation 1	Conversation 2
Item	TV	
Reference number		
Cost of item		
Cost of delivery		
Pay by credit card?		
Other useful information		

2 a **Check the words and phrases in bold in your mini-dictionary, if necessary. Match the sentences in A with the responses in B.**

A
1 I'd like to buy a Toshiba 50 cm screen television.
2 Do I have to pay for **delivery**?
3 How would you like to pay, sir?
4 Could you give me your **postcode**, please?
5 Keep your **receipt** sir, because it's your **guarantee**.
6 Do you want to **make an enquiry** or **place an order**?
7 Anything else?
8 How much will it be altogether?
9 Can I send them back if they **don't fit**?

B
A Place an order, please.
B BR5 8KS.
C I'll just check that we've got one **in stock**.
D The total cost of your **order**, **including postage and packing**, is €42.49, and it should be with you in three to five **working days**.
E Okay, and how long is it guaranteed for?
F By Mastercard if that's okay.
G Yes, that's fine.
H No, that's it thanks.
I Yes. I'm afraid it's an extra €20.00.

b **Listen again and check. Then practise saying the sentences and responses with a partner.**

3 **Work in pairs. Write a dialogue about one of the things below. Use the phrases in exercise 2a and the tapescript on page 170 to help you. If possible, read or act out your dialogue.**

a desktop computer/printer	a DVD player	some shirts
a pair of shoes	a new skirt	a washing machine

Writing
Saying thank you

1 Discuss the following questions in pairs.

- If you receive a present or are invited to someone's house, how do you usually say thank you?
- Are you offended if other people forget to thank you for these things?

2 a Read the note, card, e-mail and letter below. What is each person saying thank you for?

b Complete the gaps with the sentences below.

1   I've worn it lots of times already.
2   We haven't eaten so much for ages.
3   We thoroughly enjoyed ourselves.
4   Just what I needed for the party.

c How old do you think the writer is in each case? What do you think is their relationship with the person they are thanking?

3 a Underline the phrases used to say thank you in each text.

b Which text is the least formal? Which is the most formal? Find three differences in the way that they are written that show you this.

c In what other ways do the writers express friendly feelings to the person they are thanking?

4 Think of a present or social invitation that you have received recently, or a favour someone has done for you. Write a note or e-mail thanking them.

①

Laura,
Thanks a million for lending me your gorgeous leather jacket. (a) _____ You saved my life! Anyway here it is, safely returned. Am giving it to your mum as probably won't see you till Monday. Have a great weekend, and hope I can do the same for you some time!
Love and kisses,
Anna
XXXXX

②

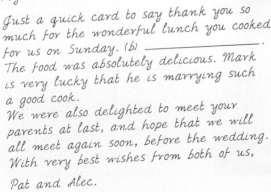

My dear Emma,
Just a quick card to say thank you so much for the wonderful lunch you cooked for us on Sunday. (b) _____.
The food was absolutely delicious. Mark is very lucky that he is marrying such a good cook.
We were also delighted to meet your parents at last, and hope that we will all meet again soon, before the wedding.
With very best wishes from both of us,
Pat and Alec.

③

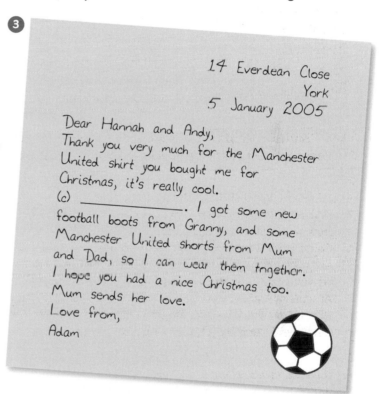

14 Everdean Close
York
5 January 2005

Dear Hannah and Andy,
Thank you very much for the Manchester United shirt you bought me for Christmas, it's really cool.
(c) _____. I got some new football boots from Granny, and some Manchester United shorts from Mum and Dad, so I can wear them together. I hope you had a nice Christmas too. Mum sends her love.
Love from,
Adam

④

Subject: Thank you

Hi Julie and Max,
Just a quick line to say thank you so much for having us to stay at the weekend, we had such fun! Your new flat is lovely, and it was lovely to have a relaxing walk by the river –
(d) _____ ! You must come and stay with us too – it's lovely here in the summer with the beach so near. You know you're always welcome.
Anyway, must hurry, but thanks again.
Lots of love from both of us,
Rosa and Martin
XXXXXX

A Future forms / Future time clauses

Read the article and choose the correct alternatives.

... HOT GOSSIP ... HOT GOSSIP ... HOT GOSSIP ...

For the hottest gossip on the good, the bad and the famous, read Immelda!!

Actress Glynnis Parsley and tennis star Andy Martinez have finally decided (1) get / getting / to get married – (2) once / unless / until Andy's first wife Alana agrees to a divorce!! However, I have heard that Alana (3) doesn't give / hasn't given / won't give Andy a divorce (4) because / once / until he hands over the couple's twenty-five million dollar mansion in Palm Beach. 'We hope (5) get married / getting married / to get married later this year,' a smiling Glynnis told me. 'Or maybe next ...'

CSN TV have announced that Britain's Duchess of Cumberland (6) about to / due to / is to present her own chat show on cable television later this year. Filming (7) is about to start / started / will start when the Duchess (8) is returning / returns / will return from her latest skiing holiday in Austria – and she says that the programme is (9) featuring / going to feature / will feature Hollywood celebrities as well as many of the Duchess's own friends. 'I want (10) do / doing / to do the best job I can as a TV presenter,' the Duchess told me last week. 'I would like people (11) recognise / recognising / to recognise me as a talented TV presenter, and not just as one of the best-dressed and most glamorous women in the world.'

Rock star, actress and mother Myra Bellina is about (12) buy / buying / to buy a very special home for herself and her baby daughter, Dolores – the Mediterranean island of Santo Domingo! She is also (13) planning / thinking / wants to build a copy of the cathedral in Florence at her home in Florida and is apparently thinking (14) of converting / on converting / to convert her ranch in Colorado into a private zoo for Dolores and herself. But she will not allow Dolores to have a boyfriend (15) unless / once / until she is twenty-one. 'Like any mother, I just want Dolores (16) has / have / to have a normal life,' Myra told me.

Show business legend Valerie Reinhard, who (17) going to hold / holds / is holding her seventieth birthday celebration at the Astoria Hotel, Las Vegas on Friday next week, says she plans (18) invite / inviting / to invite all seven of her ex-husbands to the party. 'What if they all (19) are arriving / arrive / will arrive at the same time?' I asked Valerie last week. 'I'm sure (20) they all have / they'll all have / they're all having a lot to talk about,' she replied.

... HOT GOSSIP ... HOT GOSSIP ... HOT GOSSIP ...

B Vocabulary: Megamemory

1 Work in pairs. The box below contains twenty-four words/phrases you have studied in Modules 5–8. As quickly as possible, find three of each of the following.

a names of jobs
b adjectives that describe a job
c phrases you might use on the telephone
d adjectives to describe negative feelings
e types of TV programme
f things you might do in the evening
g machines you might have in your home
h things you might do with a machine

annoyed	go for a run
an answering machine	go to sleep
arrange a night out	a freezer
Hello, it's Lawrence	furious
badly-paid	switch off
I'll call you back	a cook
a cartoon	jealous
challenging	plug in
Thanks for calling	a plumber
a dishwasher	a soap opera
a documentary	stressful
a firefighter	switch on

2 You have five minutes to memorise the words/phrases. Then close your books. Write down as many of the phrases as you can remember with a partner. Which pair remembered the most?

3 Look at the categories of words in exercise 1 again. Can you add any other words or phrases to each group?

C Listening: Famous firsts

C1 You are going to hear about some famous firsts. Complete the sentences, using the appropriate active or passive form of the verbs in brackets. Then listen and check.

a On 17th July, 1938, American aviator, Douglas Corrigan (1)_____ (give) permission to take off from an airfield near New York.

He (2)_____ (become) the first pilot to cross the Atlantic in a solo plane, by accident.

Corrigan (3)_____ (give) a hero's welcome on his return to New York.

Since then he (4)_____ (know) as 'Wrong Way' Corrigan.

b Sirimavo Bandaranaike was the first woman to (1)_____ (elect) Prime Minister of her country.

Her husband had been Prime Minister of Sri Lanka in the 1950s, until he (2)_____ (murder) in 1959.

Bandaranaike (3)_____ (decide) to enter politics herself.

The following year she (4)_____ (elect) as Prime Minister – the first female prime minister in the world.

She (5)_____ (die) in 2000 at the age of eighty-four.

c Almost fifty years ago, Laika (1)_____ (became) the most famous dog in the world – she was the first animal in space.

Sputnik 2 (2)_____ (launch) in November 1957.

Laika could not (3)_____ (bring) back to Earth.

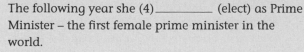

She (4)_____ (die) in space about a week after the launch.

The Laika Foundation in Moscow (5)_____ (name) after her.

D Speaking: Asking favours

1 Work in pairs. You are going to write and act out a dialogue in which A asks B a favour. Choose one thing from each of the boxes below. Spend about fifteen minutes writing and practising your dialogue.

Who are you?
- parent and child
- two friends/colleagues
- boss and employee
- husband and wife

Where are you?
- on the phone
- at home
- at work
- in a café/restaurant
- somewhere else

What favour does A want?
- help with filling in an important form or writing an important e-mail/letter (what?)
- to borrow something (money / an item of clothing, etc.)
- to have a lift somewhere (where?)
- someone to look after your baby / pet / plants, etc.
- someone to mend your radio / washing machine, etc.

Why?
- you're going on holiday
- you've got an appointment
- you haven't got any money
- you're very worried about it
- another reason

What problem does B have?
- you're tired / ill / busy yourself at the moment
- you have to be somewhere else at that time
- you're fed up with Student A always asking you to do things

How does A try to persuade B? What happens in the end?

2 Act out your dialogues for the rest of the class. Listen to the other students' dialogues and try to answer the questions in the boxes above.

3 **C2** You are going to hear two conversations with some native speakers in one of the situations above. Listen and answer the questions in the boxes above. Did they use any words/phrases which might have been useful in your dialogue? Listen again and check.

Future society

- ▶ Making predictions
- ▶ Hypothetical possibilities with *if*
- ▶ **Reading and vocabulary:** Getting it *wrong!* Getting it *right?*
- ▶ **Vocabulary:** Society and change
- ▶ **Prounciation:** Shifting stress, *'ll* or *'d*
- ▶ **Wordspot:** *make*
- ▶ **Task:** Decide how to spend lottery money
- ▶ **Real life:** Ways of saying numbers

Reading and vocabulary

1 Do you ever read horoscopes or experts' predictions about the future of society? Do you believe they are usually true?

2 a Read the first text about the world's worst predictions: *Getting it wrong!* and match the predictions to the topics below.

> Computers   Fashion   Film and TV   Music
> Science and technology

b Which prediction has actually come true? Which invention is the writer predicting?

3 Can you guess the meaning of these words and phrases from the context?

a   amount to anything (quote 1)
b   value (quote 4)
c   nonsense (quote 6)
d   launched (quote 6)
e   glued to (quote 7)
f   on their way out (quote 8)
g   turned down (quote 8)
h   devices (quote 10)

4 Which of the 'wrong' predictions do you find most amusing? Why? Can you think of any other predictions that didn't come true?

5 James Martin, the author who correctly predicted the invention and uses of the Internet in 1977, has recently written another book called *After the Internet: Alien intelligence*. Read some of his predictions for the next few years in *Getting it right?* checking the meaning of the words and phrases in bold.

Getting it **wrong**!

Ever since ancient times 'experts' have been predicting the future. If you were frightened that the end of the world was coming in the year 2000, you needn't have worried: the same prediction was made in the years AD 500, 1000 and 1500. But it's not just astrologers who get it wrong. Here is a selection of the world's worst predictions, made by people who should have known better.

1 'It doesn't matter what he does, he will never amount to anything.' *Albert Einstein's teacher talking to his father, 1895.*

2 'Who will want to hear an actor talk?' *H.M. Warner, Warner Bros, 1927 on the first talking films.*

3 'I think there is a world market for maybe five computers.' *Thomas Watson, Chairman of IBM, 1943.*

4 'Airplanes are interesting toys, but they will be of no military value.' *Marechal Ferdinand Foch, French professor of military strategy, 1910.*

5 'You'd better learn secretarial work or get married.' *Director of Blue Book Modelling Agency advising Marilyn Monroe, 1944.*

6 'The idea of space travel is nonsense.' *Sir Harold Spencer Jones, Astronomer Royal of Great Britain, 1957. Two weeks later the Russians launched Sputnik (the world's first space satellite).*

7 'The problem with television is that people must sit and keep their eyes glued to the screen, and the average American family just hasn't time for it.' *New York Times, 1939.*

8 'We don't like their sound, groups of guitars are on their way out.' *Decca Recording company when turning down The Beatles, 1962. The group were also turned down by Pye, Columbia and HMV.*

9 'It's a bad joke that won't last. Not with the winter coming.' *Fashion designer Coco Chanel, speaking about the mini-skirt, 1966.*

10 'By 2000, computers and other devices linked by telephones and radio waves will allow millions of people to exchange electronic mail, shop, work at home, take classes, pay taxes, plan holidays and entertain themselves.' *James Martin in The Wired Society, 1977.*

11 'By 2000, more than 1,000 people will live and work on the moon, according to NASA predictions.' *Omni Future Almanac, 1982.*

12 'Everything that can be invented has already been invented.' *Charles H Duell, Chief of the US Office of Patents, 1899.*

Getting it **right**?

■ 'All the things we need at present to **prove our identity** will disappear: credit cards, driving licences, keys, and so on. Computer programmes will be able to recognise our **unique appearance**. Doors will open, cars will start, pay phones and **parking meters** will automatically **bill** you.'

■ 'It will be a very comfortable world, there will be technology to keep your house tidy and the grass in your garden green. Televisions will be able to study and learn their owners' reactions and suggest programmes to watch. It will make sure that **commercials** that annoy you are not repeated.'

■ 'The world economy will change. The **wealth** of a country will depend on its workers' technical knowledge. India has already become a high-tech superpower. Any **developing country** could do the same in ten years.'

■ 'Computers themselves will design and **'breed'** new computers programmed in ways that no human being can understand.'

■ 'We will have machines that are a billion times more intelligent than we are, but only in **narrow**, specific ways. Computers won't ever be intelligent in the ways that we are; we cannot programme a computer to do what a mosquito does, certainly not what a human being does. Machines will do what they are good at and people will do what they are good at. Humans will do the creative tasks, leaving the boring work to computers.'

6 Are these sentences the same or different from what James Martin predicts? Write *S* for the same and *D* for different.

a We won't have to carry so many forms of identification because machines will be able to recognise us.
b We won't have to pay for telephones and parking.
c Technology will do a lot of the housework that humans do now.
d Our TVs will be able to analyse our tastes.
e Developing countries will become wealthy if they educate their workers correctly.
f Computers will be able to create newer computers without human help.
g One day, computers will be able to do everything human beings can do.
h Humans will no longer have to do boring tasks.

7 Discuss the following questions in pairs.

• Which of James Martin's predictions would you like to happen?
• Which do you find worrying?
• Which predictions do you think will come true?

Language focus 1
Making predictions

All the predictions in the *Getting it right?* text on page 93 use *will* or *won't.* Underline six examples.

Analysis

1 When you make predictions there are different ways of showing how sure you are.

 a **Adverbs with *will/won't*** (Notice the word order.)
 *The world economy **will probably** change.*
 *Computers **definitely won't** be as intelligent as human beings.*

 b **Modals**
 *India **may** become a rich country.*

 c ***is (not) likely to***
 *Life in the future **is likely to** be very comfortable.*

2 Put the words/phrases below in the best place on the line to show how sure we are that the prediction will happen.

will probably	probably won't
will almost certainly	almost certainly won't
is/are likely to	isn't/aren't likely to
may/might (not)	could / may well

```
100%  ↑   will definitely
          a _____
          b _____
          c _____
          d _____
          e _____
          f _____
          g _____
          h _____
0%    ↓   definitely won't
```

▶ Read Language summary A on page 151.

Practice

1 a Look at the predictions below. Add phrases from the Analysis that show what you think.

1 Children will study at home rather than at school.
 Children probably won't study at home rather than at school.

2 All housework will be done by robots.
3 There will be no more need for dentists.
4 There will be a cure for most diseases.
5 All teaching will be done by computers.
6 Chinese will be the world's number one language.
7 Small shops will disappear.
8 There will be no newspapers.
9 People will live to the age of 130.
10 Cars will report bad driving to the police.

b Compare your opinions with other students.

2 Write ten predictions of your own about:

– famous people   – the rest of this lesson
– sporting events   – your friends and classmates
– the weather   – yourself and your family

Examples:
My friend Sonia may well get married next year.
It will almost certainly be hot tomorrow.

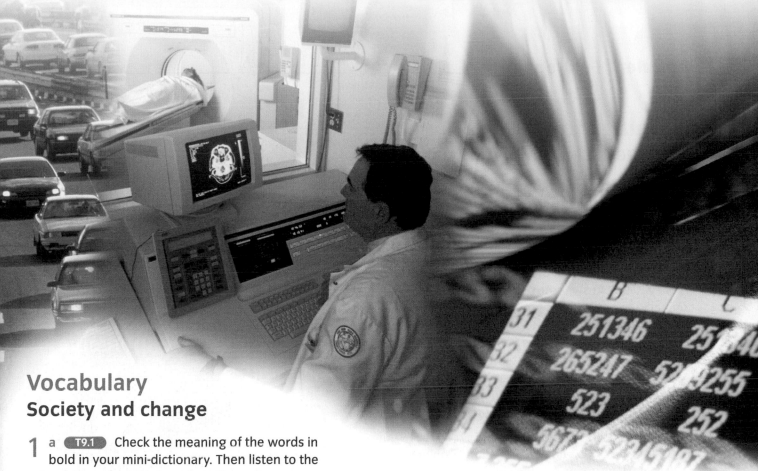

Vocabulary
Society and change

1 **a** (T9.1) Check the meaning of the words in bold in your mini-dictionary. Then listen to the extracts from news items where these items are discussed. Match A and B, according to the recording.

	A	B
1	Health care	is getting worse. is getting better.
2	The number of people learning English	is **decreasing**. is **increasing**.
3	Roads	are becoming more dangerous. are becoming less dangerous.
4	The cost of travel	is going up. is going down.
5	Unemployment	is falling. is **rising**.
6	The quality of TV programmes	is **deteriorating**. is improving.
7	The economic situation	is getting worse. is getting better.
8	The number of people going abroad for their holidays	is rising. is falling.
9	The education system	is deteriorating. is improving.
10	The number of people who take regular exercise	is decreasing. is increasing.

b Look at the tapescript on page 171. Underline the words and phrases that helped you find the answer.

Pronunciation

1 Complete the table. Use your mini-dictionary, if necessary.

	Noun	Verb	Adjective
a	_____	to decrease	_____
b	_____	—	economic
c	education	_____	_____
d	_____	to improve	_____
e	_____	to increase	_____
f	unemployment	—	_____

2 (T9.2) Listen and check. Then mark the stressed syllables. Is the same syllable stressed in each form of the word?

3 Practise saying the words, paying attention to the stressed syllable.

2 Discuss which of these things are happening in your country. Give reasons for your opinions.

> Do you think health care is getting better?

> Yes, I think it's improving. Technology and doctors' skills are getting better all the time.

Language focus 2
Hypothetical possibilities with *if*

1 Read the article on the right from a British magazine. Which results do you think would be different in your country?

2 Work individually. Look at the questionnaire under the article. Which of these and similar things would you do? Answer the questionnaire. Then compare your answers in groups.

3 a **T9.3** Listen to three people talking about the questionnaire. Which questions are they dicussing?

b Listen again and complete the gaps.

1 I _____ travel on a train without a ticket ... I _____ bad about it at all!

2 I _____ break the speed limit in an area with lots of people around ... If a child _____ in front of my car and I _____ , I _____ forgive myself.

3 I _____ a lot of the things here apart from one thing. I _____ drop litter. I _____ my rubbish in my bag and take it home if there _____ any litter bins around.

Analysis

1 Which sentence below describes
a a real future situation?
b an imaginary situation?
I'll definitely travel by train.
I'd definitely travel without a train ticket.

Which verb forms are used in each? Underline the other sentences with *would/wouldn't* in exercise 3.

2 We often talk about hypothetical situations using *if*. Find two examples in exercise 3. Which tense is used after *if*? Does this describe things that happened in the past?

3 Cross out the sentence below that is incorrect.
If the ticket office was closed, I would travel without a ticket.
I might travel without a ticket if the ticket office was closed.
If the ticket office would be closed, I would travel without a ticket.
I would travel without a ticket if the ticket office were closed.

▶ Read Language summary B on page 151.

According to a *Reader's Digest / Daily Mail* poll, 46% of Britons would hide income in order to pay less tax, compared to 16% of Europeans. 80% of Britons would return the money if they were given too much change in a shop or restaurant, and 76% would hand in a wallet they found in the street. However, 60% would steal office stationery, 66% would travel by train without a ticket, and 36% would park in a disabled parking space. Only 5% would drink-drive.

How socially responsible are you?

Would you ...

	yes	no	depends
a hand in a wallet you found in the street?	☐	☐	☐
b tell a shop assistant if she charged you too little?	☐	☐	☐
c steal office or school stationery?	☐	☐	☐
d travel by train without a ticket?	☐	☐	☐
e drive above the speed limit?	☐	☐	☐
f keep a book borrowed from a library?	☐	☐	☐
g pretend to be sick to take a day off work or school?	☐	☐	☐
h avoid paying income tax?	☐	☐	☐
i park in a disabled parking space?	☐	☐	☐
j drop litter?	☐	☐	☐

Practice

1 Complete these opinions with the correct forms of the verbs in brackets.

a　'I (1)_____ (definitely hand in) a wallet if I
(2)_____ (find) it in the street. It (3)_____ (be)
awful to lose all your credit cards. And I hope if I (4)_____
(ever lose) my wallet, someone (5)_____ (hand) it in.'

b　'I (6)_____ (probably steal) paper and things from my office if
I (7)_____ (know) other people (8)_____ (do)
it too … but I (9)_____ (be) terribly embarrassed if my boss
(10)_____ (catch) me!'

c　I (11)_____ (definitely tell) a shop assistant if he or she
(12)_____ (not charge) me enough, I'm extremely honest!'

d　'I (13)_____ (take) a day off work if I (14)_____
(be) really fed up or tired … everyone does it, don't they? But I
(15)_____ (feel) a bit guilty the next day.'

e　'I (16)_____ (park) in a disabled parking space if there
(17)_____ (be) a real emergency, I suppose, but I
(18)_____ (not do) it otherwise, I think it's totally
unacceptable.'

2 **a** Read the situations below and decide whether/when you would do these things.

Never say never

Under what circumstances, if any, would you …

1 lie to someone close to you?

2 walk out of your job, or drop out of college?

3 give a lift in your car to a complete stranger?

4 walk out of a restaurant without paying the bill?

5 lend a large sum of money to a friend?

6 hit someone?

7 steal something from a shop?

8 go to live in another country?

b Compare your answers in small groups.

> I might lie to a close friend about something very small, like why I was late.

> I would never lie to a close friend about anything.

3 **a** Do the following refer to real possibilities in the future or imaginary situations? Make questions using the pronoun *you*.

1 If / can / live / anywhere in the world / where / live?
If you could live anywhere in the world, where would you live?

2 What / do / if / have some free time this evening?
What will you do if you have some free time this evening?

3 If / can / become / a famous person for a day / who / be? Why / choose / that person?

4 If / go shopping / this week / what / buy?

5 Where / go / if / have a holiday next year? Who / go / with?

6 How / your life / be different / if you / be a millionaire? What be / the best and worst things about it?

b Work in groups. Ask and answer the questions above.

> I'd probably live in Paris.

> Perhaps I'll phone some friends.

Pronunciation

1 **T9.4** Listen to ten sentences about the topics in exercise 3. Write the form you hear: 'll (= will) or 'd (= would).

2 Look at the tapescript on page 171. Practise saying the sentences, paying attention to the form.

Wordspot
make

1 Match a question/statement in A with a response in B.

A

a I can't decide what to wear.
b Why's the car making that strange noise?
c Have you locked all the doors?
d What a lovely shirt … what material is it?
e Sorry, but I don't think that's a good idea.
f There's a hole in my T-shirt.
g So what can I do to help?

B

1 Can you make a better suggestion then?
2 Don't put your finger in it! You'll make it worse!
3 If I make the dinner, will you tidy up a bit?
4 I'm not sure. I think it's made of cotton.
5 It sounds okay to me.
6 Well, hurry up and make up your mind!
7 I think so … I'll just make sure.

2 **T9.5** Listen and check. Then practise the dialogues with a partner.

3 Underline the phrases with *make* in exercise 1 and add them to the correct section of the diagram.

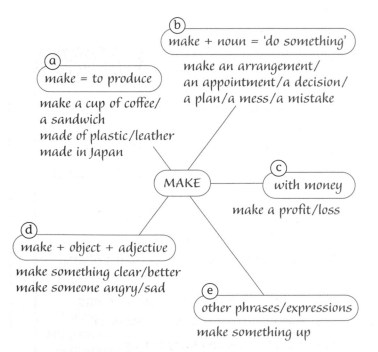

b *make + noun = 'do something'*
*make an arrangement/
an appointment/a decision/
a plan/a mess/a mistake*

a *make = to produce*
*make a cup of coffee/
a sandwich
made of plastic/leather
made in Japan*

MAKE

c *with money*
make a profit/loss

d *make + object + adjective*
*make something clear/better
make someone angry/sad*

e *other phrases/expressions*
make something up

4 Work in pairs. Look at the puzzle on page 143. Read the clues and complete the gaps. What is the hidden message?

Task: Decide how to spend lottery money
Preparation: listening

1 **a** Do you have a state lottery in your country? How does it work?

b Read about the state lottery in St Ambrosia. How much money has it made?

St Ambrosia

Port Thomas

Grand Bay

Area: 630km²
Population: 250,000
Unemployment: 15%
Capital: Port Thomas (population 55,000)
Climate: Warm, coastal 18–30%
Currency: St Ambrosian dollars (SA$)

Six months ago, St Ambrosia decided to organise a state lottery for the first time. It was agreed that profits from the lottery should go to 'help improve the lives of St Ambrosians'. It has been a great success; SA$10 million have been made in profit. Many applications have been received asking for money to help various projects. Now the Lottery Committee must decide how the money will be spent.

2 **T9.6** Listen to five representatives from organisations who would like to receive the money and complete the information on the photos.

3 **a** Check the words and phrases in bold in your mini-dictionary. Which organisation says the following things?

1 It will **provide** a social centre for the island.
2 There may be large **oil deposits** near the island.
3 Young people will no longer have to go abroad for their education.
4 It will bring in 50,000 tourists a year and create hundreds of jobs for local people.
5 It cannot get enough money from **foreign investors**.
6 It needs money for beds and **medical equipment** to help the poor.
7 It will help us to send a team to the Olympics.
8 It is **taking a risk** by **investing** in St Ambrosia.

b Look at the tapescript on page 172 and check.

1

St Ambrosian Hotel and Tourism Association

Needs SA$

What for?

2

St Ambrosian Sports Association

Needs SA$

What for?

3

University of St Ambrosia

Needs SA$

What for?

4

International Petroleum Incorporated

Needs SA$

What for?

5

St Ambrosian Children's Hospital

Needs SA$

What for?

Task: speaking

1 **a** Work individually. You are on the lottery commission. Decide how you think the money should be divided between different organisations.

b Plan how you will justify your suggestions. Ask your teacher for any words or phrases you need.

▶ Useful language a

2 Work in small groups. Discuss the best way to spend the money and agree together on a budget.

▶ Useful language b

3 Present your budget to the class, explaining your decisions. Which organisations were the most/least popular? What differences were there between the budgets?

Useful language

a Explaining advantages/disadvantages

If we give ... to ...

... will create a lot of / won't create any jobs.

... will/won't make the country wealthier / better educated.

... will/won't be good for everybody.

... will/could be a waste of money.

The most important thing for the future of the country is ...

b Discussing/Presenting your opinions

We should definitely give some money to ...

I don't think ... deserves any money.

I (don't) agree.

Yes, but what about ...?

We found it difficult to agree on ...

Real life
Ways of saying numbers

1 `T9.7` Look at the following figures. How do you say each one? Listen and practise saying them.

71%	€27,753	483,080 m^2
6.3 billion	55,680,000 km	300,000 km/sec
199,859	7%	126,000,000
–89° C		

2 a What do you think the figures represent? Can you match the figures with the following?

1 The proportion of the world's surface covered in water.
2 The lowest temperature ever recorded.
3 The average cost of a wedding in the UK.
4 The closest distance between Earth and the planet Mars.
5 The estimated world population in 2005.
6 The speed of light.
7 The population of Japan.
8 The area of the world's largest shopping mall.
9 The percentage of British people who are over sixty-five.
10 The largest crowd ever for a sporting event.

b `T9.8` Listen and check your answers.

3 a Work in pairs. Student A: Look at the information about China on page 141. Student B: Look at the information about the United Arab Emirates on page 142.

b Ask and answer questions to complete the information on your chart about the other country. Do not show each other the numbers – say them! Which statistics do you find most surprising?

STUDY...

English outside the classroom (2): Using the Internet

1 Here are four ways of improving your English using the Internet – there are many others!

- You can follow the latest world news, find out about BBC World Service radio programmes and download quizzes and song lyrics at www.bbc.co.uk/worldservice/learningenglish.

- You can use a variety of online dictionary resources at www.longman-elt.com/dictionaries.

- The British Council has a free website where you can find a variety of games, activities and a list of links suitable both for adults and younger learners at www.learnenglish.org.uk.

- And last but not least, *New Cutting Edge* has its own dedicated website with a wide variety of free resources.

2 Log on to the Cutting Edge website at www.longman.com/cuttingedge. Now practise your English (and have fun!) with the following activities:

- choose a book to read (Level 4 is Intermediate)
- enter the competition
- find three pieces of information about the authors
- improve your reading and vocabulary with the monthly article
- learn new slang
- make new friends in Student Talk
- test yourself with a short, interactive quiz

PRACTISE...

1 Making predictions ☐

Cross out the word or phrase which cannot complete each sentence.

a It will definitely / may / probably be sunny tomorrow.

b We could / may / might not be able to get tickets.

c They definitely won't / may definitely / will definitely be here by eight o'clock.

d The road is likely / may / won't re-open this week.

e There is definitely / is likely to / will probably be a big argument about this.

f The President may be / may not / may well resign this week.

▶ **Need to check? Language summary A, page 151.**

2 Hypothetical possibilities with *if* ☐

Match the halves of the conditional sentences.

A	B
a I'd help you	1 if I can.
b I wouldn't help you	2 I'd tell you.
c If I knew the answer,	3 if I could.
d If I find out the answer,	4 if you don't want me to.
e I'll help you,	5 even if you asked me.
f I won't do anything	6 I'll tell you.

▶ **Need to check? Language summary B1, page 151.**

3 Real and hypothetical possibilities ☐

Complete the sentences with the words in the box.

could	had	might	were	will	would

a If I _____ enough money, I'd go on holiday.

b He _____ call you after lunch, I promise!

c If I _____ you, I wouldn't trust him.

d It _____ be great if I could speak fluently.

e You _____ not enjoy that film; it's really scary in places.

f We _____ get a take-away pizza if you are too tired to cook.

▶ **Need to check? Language summary B2, page 151.**

4 Phrases with *make* ☐

Cross out the phrases not used with *make*. Can you remember any other phrases with *make*?

an appointment	a party	a mess	a risk
an arrangement	a profit	a mistake	

▶ **Need to check? Wordspot, page 98.**

5 Describing trends ☐

Match the words and phrases in A with their opposite meanings in B.

A	B
a get worse	1 decrease
b improve	2 deteriorate
c increase	3 fall
d less	4 get better
e rise	5 go down
f go up	6 more

▶ **Need to check? Vocabulary, page 95.**

6 Saying numbers ☐

Write these numbers out in full.

a 6,000 _____

b 6,000,000 _____

c 6,000,000,000 _____

d 6.6 _____

e 6% _____

f 66 km^2 _____

▶ **Need to check? Real life, page 100.**

Pronunciation spot

The sounds /b/ and /v/

a Look at the phrases below, which all come from the text on page 92. Is the missing letter b or v?

a no military _alue

b the pro_lem with tele_ision

c the a_erage American family

d may_e fi_e computers

e You'd _etter learn secretarial work

f has _een in_ented

b **T9.9** Listen and check. Notice the difference in pronunciation between b and v. Then practise saying the phrases, paying attention to the /b/ and /v/ sounds.

REMEMBER!

Look back at the areas you have practised. Tick the ones you feel confident about. Now try the MINI-CHECK on page 158 to check what you know!

An amazing story

THE FULL ORIGINAL VERSION
EVEN GREATER ON THE BIG SCREEN

FOR THOSE WHO HAVE NEVER SEEN IT... FOR THOSE WHO WILL WANT TO SEE IT AGAIN...

DAVID O. SELZNICK'S PRODUCTION OF MARGARET MITCHELL'S "GONE WITH THE WIND" IN TECHNICOLOR

- ▶ Past perfect
- ▶ Reported speech
- ▶ **Vocabulary and speaking**: Types of story, Adverbs for telling stories
- ▶ **Reading and vocabulary**: *The perfect crime ... well almost!*
- ▶ **Pronunciation**: Past simple or Past perfect, Sentence stress
- ▶ **Wordspot**: *say* and *tell*
- ▶ **Task**: Tell a ghost story
- ▶ **Writing**: A narrative

Vocabulary and speaking
Types of story

1 **a** The photos show well-known stories. Which ones do you know? Match each photo with some of the categories below.

1	adventure stories	5	comedies
2	detective and crime stories	6	fairy tales
3	myths and legends	7	romances
4	science fiction and fantasy	8	ghost stories

b Which of these types do you most enjoy generally? Which don't you like?

2 **a** Check the words in bold in your mini-dictionary. What type of story might people say these things about? Which descriptions are positive and which are negative? Which could be either?

1 The plot's very complicated.
2 It's completely **unrealistic**.
3 The story's very **slow**.
4 It has **a happy ending**.
5 It made me cry.
6 The plot's really clever.
7 It's very moving.
8 It's really scary.
9 It's very imaginative.
10 It's got a moral.

b Look at sentences 1–6 again. How do you say the opposite of these things?

3 Choose a favourite story from a book, film, etc. Explain to other students why you like it so much.

Language focus 1
Past perfect

1 Work in groups. Read the lateral thinking story below and discuss what you think happened.

In the middle of some grass lay a carrot, a scarf and some coal. No one had put them on the grass, but there was a perfectly good reason why they were there. Explain.

2 **T10.1** Listen to some people asking questions to find the solution. Is the solution the same as yours?

Analysis

1 a In the sentences below, which verb is in the Past simple? Which verb is in the Past perfect?

In the middle of some grass lay a carrot, a scarf and some coal. No one had put them on the grass.

b Which tense shows which events happened first? How is this tense formed?

2 Cross out the wrong explanation for the Past perfect.
- It describes actions that happened a long time ago.
- We use it when we are talking about an event in the past and we want to explain something that happened before that.

▶ Read Language summary A on page 151.

Practice

1 Match the beginnings of the sentences in A with the endings in B using *so* or *because*. Then write out the sentences with the correct form of the verbs in brackets.

Examples:
She spoke French well because she had lived in Paris as a child.
I had left my umbrella at home so I got really wet.

A
1 She (speak) French well
2 I (leave) my umbrella at home
3 My uncle (not want) to move
4 There (be) no food in the house
5 My grandparents (never fly) before
6 When I (get) home my father was angry
7 They (already sell) all the tickets
8 We (not have to) queue in the restaurant

B
a we (not get) into the concert.
b they (be) nervous when they got on the plane.
c I (not) phone him.
d I (forget) to go to the supermarket.
e my uncle (reserve) a table.
f she (live) in Paris as a child.
g he (live) in the same house for forty years.
h I (got) really wet.

Pronunciation

1 **T10.2** Listen to eight sentences and write the form you hear: *PS* for Past simple or *PP* for Past perfect.

2 Look at the tapescript on page 172. Practise saying the sentences, paying attention to the tense.

2 a Work in pairs. Student A: Look at puzzle A below and the solution to puzzle B on page 141. Student B: Look at puzzle B below and the solution to puzzle A on page 142. Check the words in bold in your mini-dictionary, if necessary.

A
There was a phone box close to the sea. Inside the phone box a man was lying dead on the floor. The **receiver** was **hanging** off the phone, and the windows were broken on either side of the phone box. What had happened?

B
A man went to a party and drank some **punch**. Then he left early. Everyone else who drank the punch later died of **poisoning**. Why didn't the man die?

b Ask and answer questions to find the solution to your puzzle. Who got the answer the quickest?

Reading and vocabulary

1 Discuss the following questions in small groups.

- Do you ever read crime stories in the newspapers or watch TV programmes about real life crimes?
- Which crimes have been in the news recently?
- Have there been any famous robberies in your country in the last few years? What happened?

2 **a** Check the words and phrases in bold in your mini-dictionary. When a crime takes place, in what order would these things normally happen?

The police **suspect** someone. ☐
He is **arrested.** ☐
He appears **in court.** ☐
He **pleads innocent** or **guilty.** ☐
He is **sentenced.** ☐
A serious crime is **attempted.** ☐ [1]
The suspect is **charged.** ☐
He is **questioned** by the police. ☐
He is **found guilty.** ☐
The suspect is **followed.** ☐

b What is the difference between fraud, mugging, robbery and theft? Use your mini-dictionary, if necessary.

3 Read the beginnings of crime stories 1–3. Which crime in exercise 2b is each story about? What exactly was each criminal trying to steal?

4 Which criminal(s) used these things to help commit the crime? How?

a cargo crate   a driving licence   a JCB digger
a pocket knife   smoke bombs   a speedboat
women's clothes

5 **a** Work in pairs. Guess what went wrong in each story.

b Match the endings A–D on page 105 to the correct story. (There is one extra ending.) Who guessed correctly?

The perfect crime

1 A daring criminal has finally been arrested in Málaga, Spain, two years after attempting to steal over three million euros. Spanish police yesterday told the story of how the forty-year-old man, Martin Dempsey from Manchester, was caught.

Two years ago, professional thief Dempsey discovered that the cash was going to be sent to Spain on a special flight, in the luggage hold. So Dempsey packed himself into a cargo crate, and got himself booked onto the same flight as the money. Once the plane took off, he cut his way out of the crate with a pocket knife, found the money successfully, and packed himself and money back into the crate. The plane landed safely, and everything seemed to be going perfectly to plan, when unfortunately …

2 Guildford Crown Court yesterday heard how mugger Toby Williams, twenty-four, unemployed, had snatched the handbag of Barbara Walsh a sixty-five-year-old retired teacher, in Crowndale Road last June. Inside Williams had found not only cash, but also a cheque for five thousand pounds, made out to Mrs Walsh.

Williams, who pleaded guilty to charges of theft and fraud, told the court how he discovered that he had all the correct identity documents to cash the cheque, the only problem being that he was not a sixty-five-year-old woman.

However, the ingenious Williams did not give up. Using the photograph on Mrs Walsh's driving licence as a guide, he dressed himself up as an elderly woman, and went to present the cheque at a local bank.

At first, all went according to plan: the bank clerk did not seem to suspect anything wrong. That was, not until she looked at the cheque …

3 If it had been successful it would have been the world's biggest robbery. Several years ago, a team of over 200 police officers foiled an attempt by a gang of professional thieves to steal diamonds worth around $350 million from the Millennium Dome in Greenwich, London. The plan was remarkably simple. The thieves crashed a JCB digger into the side of the Dome near where the 'Millennium Star' and twelve other priceless diamonds were displayed. They then threw smoke bombs and smashed holes in the security glass protecting the diamonds. They planned to escape with the diamonds in a speedboat waiting outside the Dome on the River Thames. But what they did not realise was that …

... well almost!

A ... for by an amazing coincidence, the bank clerk was Alexandra Walsh, Mrs Walsh's thirty-two-year-old daughter. She recognised her mother's cheque immediately and Williams was soon under arrest. Williams, who has been found guilty, will be sentenced later today.

B ... the police had been watching them for weeks. The gang had already attempted a couple of unsuccessful robberies, and all of the members were being followed. They had noticed how often they visited the diamonds at the Dome and had worked out what they were planning. On the morning of the attempted robbery, the Dome was actually full of police officers who were dressed as cleaners, with their guns hidden in bin liners.

However, as it happened, the whole gang were arrested without a shot being fired. But even if they hadn't been stopped, the gang would have been sadly disappointed – the diamonds had been replaced with replicas: the real ones were safe in the bank!

C ... the baggage handlers who were unloading the plane dropped Dempsey's crate and he fell out. Dempsey grabbed as much money as he could, yelled 'Don't worry about me, I'm fine' to the astonished baggage handlers and disappeared across the runway before anyone could catch him.

And he would have remained free, if he hadn't been arrested two years later for drink-driving in the Costa del Sol where he was now living. His DNA was found to match DNA from the airline crate, and Dempsey has at last been charged with the robbery.

D ... one member of the gang was in fact a police officer who had been keeping his colleagues in touch with developments via his mobile phone. The moment the gang entered the building and started loading the gold into sacks, a group of armed police officers leapt out from their hiding places and began arresting the horrified robbers. Desperate to escape, some the gang abandoned the gold and ran into the street outside – only to find they were completely surrounded.

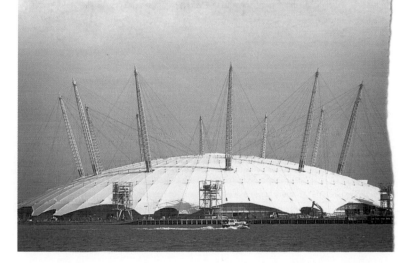

6 **a** Find words in the stories that mean the following.

1 took something quickly and perhaps violently. (two words: text 2 and text C)
2 clever; good at thinking of new ideas (text 2)
3 stopped something bad that someone is planning (text 3)
4 extremely valuable (text 3)
5 broke violently (text 3)
6 shouted (text C)
7 very surprised (text C)
8 jumped (text D)
9 shocked and upset (text D)
10 needing or wanting something very much (text D)

b Why did the writers choose these words, and not a more ordinary word?

Pronunciation

1 **T10.3** Listen and notice how the important words are stressed and how many smaller words are weak in the sentence.

/ə/   /ə/   /iː/
A **da**ring **crim**inal has **fi**nally been

arrested in **Ma**laga, **Spain**, **two years**
                         /ə/
after at**temp**ting to **steal** over **three**

million **pounds**.

2 **T10.4** Listen to the next sentence and mark the stressed syllables. Which words have weak forms?

Spanish police yesterday told the

story of how the forty-year-old man,

Martin Dempsey from Manchester,

was caught.

3 Practise saying the two sentences paying attention to the stress and weak forms.

7 Discuss the following questions in pairs.

- Which criminal(s) were most unlucky?
- Which crime was the cleverest?
- Do you know any other stories of crimes that went wrong? What happened?

Language focus 2
Reported speech

1 You are going to read a true story. Read Part one and answer the following questions.

a What had happened to Michael and Harry Findlater when they were young?

b What could Michael remember about his brother?

c Why did Michael look in his secretary's diary on that day? What did he find there?

2 **a** Read Part two of the story. Put the sentences in the correct order to find out how Michael and Harry were reunited.

b Below is the beginning of the actual conversation that Michael had. Read Part two of the story again and complete the rest of the conversation.

MICHAEL:	Can I speak to Mr Bell?
WOMAN:	I'm sorry, but I've only just started working here, and I don't know who Mr Bell is. Can you ...?
MICHAEL:	_____

c **T10.5** Listen and check.

Analysis

1 Tenses in reported speech
The dialogue in Part two is in reported speech. The one in exercise 2b is in direct speech.
a Underline the verbs in each one. What differences are there in the tenses used?
b Complete the table with examples from exercise 2.

Direct speech	Reported speech
Present simple *I don't know who Mr Bell is.*	Past simple *She said she didn't know who Mr Bell was.*
Present perfect	
Past simple	
will	

2 Reported questions
a Find five reported questions in Part two of the story. Which verb introduces them?
b What is the difference in the word order of reported and direct questions?
c In what type of questions do we use *if* and *whether*?

▶ Read Language summary B on page 152.

Part one

Michael and Harry Findlater were brothers, separated tragically when they were children. Michael had spent almost thirty years looking for Harry, who was sixteen years older than him. He only remembered one thing about his brother – he had an owl tattooed on the back of his hand.

One morning, Michael arrived at work to find that his secretary had phoned in sick. In order to check his appointments for the day, he looked at his secretary's diary. The first item was a seven-figure number with the name 'Bell' written next to it and URGENT written in red ink. He dialled the number, and a woman's voice answered.

Part two

On the phone ...

☐ The woman said that it was.

☐ The woman said she was sorry, but she had only just started working there, and she didn't know who Bell was.

☐ She told him that he had a tattoo of an owl on his hand.

☐ Michael asked if he could speak to Mr Bell.

☐ She asked him to ring back later when her boss, Mr Findlater, was there.

☐ Becoming excited now, Michael asked her whether she had ever noticed a tattoo on the back of Mr Findlater's hand.

☐ Michael said he would ring back later, and asked her if Mr Findlater's name was Harry.

The following day ...

☐ 10 Thanks to this amazing coincidence, Michael had found his brother at last.

☐ The secretary told him it wasn't a phone number, it was a bank account number for Mr Bell, one of their customers.

☐ When Michael's secretary came back to work, he asked her who had given her his brother's number.

Practice

1 a Decide who said these things after they met up: Harry or Michael.

1 'I can't believe I've finally found you.'
   Michael
2 'How did you get my phone number?'
3 'Will you show me your tattoo?'
4 'You're certainly taller than when I last saw you!'
5 'I spent nearly thirty years looking for you!'
6 'Did you ever try to look for me?'
7 'It's luck that your secretary was off sick that day!'
8 'I think I'll give her a pay rise!'

b Put the statements into reported speech.
Example:
Michael said he couldn't believe he'd finally found Harry.

2 Work in pairs. Student A: You are a journalist who is writing an article for a local newspaper about how the Findlater brothers were reunited. You are going to interview Michael Findlater. Prepare eight questions to ask him about what happened.

Examples:
Has Harry changed a lot since you last saw him?
Are you planning to do anything special now that you are reunited?

Student B: You are Michael Findlater. You are going to be interviewed by a journalist who is writing an article about how you were reunited with your brother. Try to guess what questions Student A will ask you and invent some appropriate answers.

3 When you have completed your interview, tell the class what happened using reported speech.

> I asked Michael if Harry had changed a lot since he'd last seen him.

> I told him that I hadn't seen him for nearly thirty years, so of course he had changed, but he was still …

Wordspot
say and *tell*

1 **T10.6** Complete the sentences with *say* or *tell*. Then listen and check.

a   Do you know how to _____ thank you, hello or goodbye in any other languages apart from English?
b   Do you have an elder brother or sister? Did he or she _____ you what to do as a child?
c   Do you often _____ jokes? Can you _____ a joke in English?
d   If your friend asked you if you liked her new hairstyle – and you thought it looked awful – would you _____ her the truth?
e   If you were in a minor car accident which you knew was your fault, would you _____ sorry to the other driver?
f   Can you _____ me something about your last holiday?
g   Do you think it's always wrong to _____ lies? When is it acceptable?
h   Why do teachers sometimes have to _____ children off at school?
i   In your family, do you usually _____ a prayer before meals?
j   Can you _____ the difference between British and American English?
k   If an attractive stranger asked you to dance, would you _____ yes or no?

2 Underline the phrases with *say* and *tell* and add them to the diagram below.

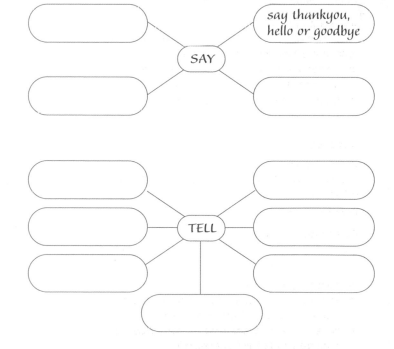

3 Work in pairs. Choose eight questions from exercise 1. Now ask and answer these questions with your partner.

Vocabulary
Adverbs for telling stories

1 Match the sentences in A with a sentence in B.

A

a   The audience were completely silent.
b   Mrs Brown was over eighty when she died.
c   The police searched the area for several days.
d   I realised I'd left my purse at home.
e   As the woman came round the corner, she was knocked off her bicycle by a passing car.
f   Robert really loves French food and culture.
g   Hannah found out today that she didn't get that job she applied for.
h   Marianne and Laura were great friends at university.

B

1   **Unfortunately**, she never saw her only grandchild, who was born in Australia.
2   **Surprisingly**, though, he's never visited France.
3   However, they **gradually** lost touch over the years.
4   I **immediately** ran over to see if she was all right.
5   **Suddenly**, a mobile phone rang and everyone turned and stared.
6   **Fortunately**, I had my credit card in my pocket.
7   **Obviously**, she was very disappointed.
8   **Eventually**, they found the piece of evidence they were looking for.

2 Complete the sentences in a logical way using both adverbs.

a   My aunt fell down the stairs the other day.
    Fortunately …
    Obviously …

b   My dad's been on a strict diet for nearly a month now.
    Unfortunately …
    Surprisingly …

c   I first met my wife at a party five years ago.
    Immediately …
    Surprisingly …

d   When I first came to live here, I didn't know anybody.
    Gradually …
    Eventually …

e   I spent an hour looking for the missing keys.
    Eventually …
    Suddenly …

f   The room was in complete darkness.
    Eventually …
    Suddenly …

Task: Tell a ghost story
Preparation: speaking

1 The pictures below come from a story called *The Guests*. Look at the pictures and find the following things.

a burned-out house	an isolated house
some ruins	an elderly couple
a newspaper headline	someone offering to pay
an envelope	a restaurant owner
thick fog	

2 Work in pairs. Decide what order the pictures should go in.

Pictures 7,4,6 …

Task: speaking and listening

1 Work in groups. Think about these questions.

a How does the story begin?
b How will you describe the characters and places?
c How does the story end?
d How can you make the ending more dramatic and interesting for listeners?

Then practise telling your story. Ask your teacher for any words or phrases you need.

▶ Useful language a and b

2 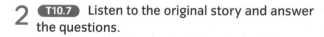 Listen to the original story and answer the questions.

a Where were the young couple going?
b Why did they decide to stop at the house?
c How did they spend the evening at the house?
d What did the young couple offer to do?
e What did the husband leave on the table?
f Why was the owner of the restaurant shocked?
g What had happened a month previously?
h Why did the woman scream?

What similarities and differences are there between your story and the original one?

Useful language

a Describing when things happen

One day/night ...

The following day ...

A few moments later ...

After a while ...

b Making the story more interesting

To their surprise/horror ...

Feeling tired/terrified, they ...

Suddenly ...

Eventually ...

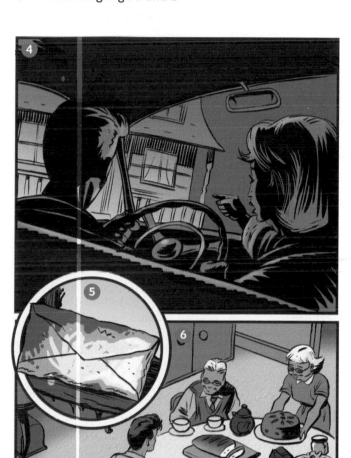

Writing
A narrative

1 Here are some time phrases we use to tell stories. Divide them into the following categories.

then	one day, many years ago	in the end
once there was a man	eventually	a few days later
at last	a few weeks passed	later that day
the following night …	finally	after a while

Probably from the beginning of the story

Probably from the middle of the story

Probably from the end of the story

2 Work in pairs or individually. You are going to tell a scary story like the one on page 108–109.

Either Think of a true story that happened to you or someone you know.

Or Invent a ghost story of your own.

Or Think of a story from a book, film, etc. that you know.

3 Spend a few minutes making notes about what happened. Write a first draft of your story. Ask your teacher for any words or phrases you need.

4 a Read through your first draft. Now try to make it sound more interesting by using the following:

– some of the time phrases from exercise 1.
– some of the adverbs from page 108.
– more dramatic words to tell the story (see page 65 and page 105).

b Check the tenses you have used. Underline any verbs you are unsure about and ask your teacher.

5 Write a final draft of your story. Hand it round the class for other students to read. Whose story is the scariest?

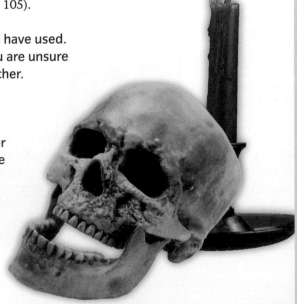

STUDY

Making the most of graded readers

Graded readers are simplified versions of real books – fact and fiction, biography, books based on popular films and TV series, and well-loved classics.

Here are some ways they can help you with your English:

- Improve your vocabulary or grammar by doing the exercises accompanying each graded reader.

- Improve your listening by listening to the accompanying recording.

- Improve your fluency and pronunciation by speaking along with the recording, following the text as you go.

- Improve your speaking by giving a spoken review of a reader to your classmates, or by choosing a scene from the book and acting it out as a radio play.

- Improve your written work by writing a review of a reader and sending it to www.longman.com/adult/students/reviews_form.html/.

You can find out more about graded readers by visiting the Penguin Readers website at www.penguinreaders.com.

PRACTICE

1 Past perfect ☐

In each sentence there are two verbs underlined. Circle the one which should be in the Past perfect and correct it.

a By seven o'clock, the place <u>was</u> completely empty – everyone <u>went</u> home.

b It <u>was</u> the first time I ever <u>spent</u> the night away from home.

c I <u>did</u> a lot of work on my assignment, so I <u>was</u> disappointed with the low mark.

d I <u>knew</u> Mark by sight for a long time before I actually <u>spoke</u> to him.

e As soon as our guests <u>left</u>, we <u>went</u> to sleep.

f He <u>threatened</u> to leave his job many times before he actually <u>did</u> it.

▶ **Need to check? Language summary A, pages 151–152.**

2 Reported speech ☐

Look at the sentences. Which four are incorrect?

a He told that he was coming to the party.

b He said he was coming to the party.

c He told me that he was coming to the party.

d He said me he was coming to the party.

e He said to me that he was coming to the party.

f He told to me he was coming to the party.

g He told that he was coming to the party.

h He said that he was coming to the party.

▶ **Need to check? Language summary B, page 152.**

3 Reported questions ☐

Put the words into the correct order to make reported questions.

a The / was / me / teacher / why / late / asked / I

_____

b us / home / He / were / if / we / asked / going

_____

c her / was / asked / going / where / They / she

_____

d brother / where / My / know / was / wanted / I / to

_____

e him / how / didn't / was / I / he / ask

_____

▶ **Need to check? Language summary B, page 152.**

4 Adverbs ☐

Match the adverbs in A with the conclusions in B. Can you remember any other adverbs used for telling stories?

A		B	
a	Fortunately	1	something bad happened
b	Surprisingly	2	something good happened
c	Unfortunately	3	something happened in the end
d	Gradually	4	something happened little by little
e	Immediately	5	something happened straight away
f	Eventually	6	something unexpected happened

▶ **Need to check? Vocabulary, page 108.**

5 Crime ☐

Choose the best explanation for the words in bold.

a The police **suspect** him. = They know / think / remember he committed a crime.

b He committed **fraud**. = He attacked someone. / He got money dishonestly. / He killed someone.

c He has decided to **plead** guilty. = He admits / denies / doesn't remember committing the crime.

d He was **arrested**. = He was taken to the police station. / stopped in the street. / sent to prison.

e He is going to be **sentenced**. = He is going to answer some questions / be arrested / find out his punishment.

▶ **Need to check? Reading, page 104.**

6 *say* and *tell* ☐

Which of these do you say and which do you tell? Can you remember any other phrases with say and tell?

a lie	yes	the truth	someone off
a joke	sorry	thank you	someone what to do

▶ **Need to check? Wordspot, page 107.**

Pronunciation spot

Pronouncing 'h'

a Count the number of /h/ sounds in the sentences below. Are there any /h/ sounds which are not pronounced?

1 My story has a happy ending.
2 If you see Harry, say hello.
3 He was arrested half an hour ago.
4 To their horror, there was a ghost in the house!
5 It was very honest of you to put your hand up.
6 How did you hear about us?

b **T10.8** Listen and check. Practise saying the sentences, paying attention to the /h/ sounds.

REMEMBER!

Look back at the areas you have practised. Tick the ones you feel confident about. Now try the MINI-CHECK on page 158 to check what you know!

Rules and freedom

▶ Obligation and permission in the present and past
▶ **Pronunciation:** Modal verbs
▶ **Listening:** Annoying rules
▶ **Task:** Present your opinions
▶ **Reading and vocabulary:** *To sue or not to sue?*
▶ **Writing:** Linking words
▶ **Wordspot:** *do*

Language focus 1
Obligation and permission in the present

1 What rules would you expect to find in the following places? Make a list of one or two rules for each place.

> airports bars and pubs beaches hospitals libraries
> roads museums nightclubs parks planes
> public swimming pools train stations

2 Look at the signs on pages 112 and 113. In which place(s) above would you see them? What do they mean?

3 Which signs on page 112 do the following relate to? Cross out the sentence(s) that are not true about each sign.

a You <u>can</u> use your credit card here.
   You <u>must</u> use your credit card here.
   You<u>'ve got to</u> use your credit card here.

b You <u>mustn't</u> smoke in the smoking area.
   You<u>'re allowed to</u> smoke in the smoking area.
   You <u>can</u> smoke in the smoking area if you want.

c You <u>mustn't</u> leave your mobile on.
   You <u>can't</u> use your mobile.
   You <u>shouldn't</u> leave your mobile on.

d Dogs <u>are allowed</u>.
   Dogs <u>are not allowed</u>.

e You <u>have to</u> be careful of the wet paint.
   You <u>don't have to</u> be careful of the wet paint.
   You <u>ought to</u> be careful of the wet paint.

Analysis

Put the underlined verbs from exercise 3 in the correct category.
1 It is necessary *have (got) to*
2 It is not necessary
3 It is OK/permitted *can*
4 It is not OK/permitted
5 It is a good idea / the correct thing
6 it is not a good idea / not the correct thing

▶ Read Language summary A on pages 152–153.

Signs labelled a–g: **Staff only** (a), **Please have your boarding card and passport ready for inspection** (b), (c), **NO DIVING** (d), **DRESS REGULATIONS FROM 7.00 PM TO 1130 PM SMART CASUAL NO DENIMS NO T-SHIRTS** (e), (f), **Cyclists and pedestrians only** (g)

Practice

1 a Find the signs on this page that the following sentences refer to. Then complete the gaps with the positive or negative form of the verbs in brackets.

1 The public _____ (allowed) to come in here.
2 Cyclists _____ (allowed) to use this path.
3 You _____ (have to) cycle on this path, you _____ (can) walk if you want.
4 You _____ (must) wear jeans or T-shirts.
5 You _____ (should) dress smartly, but you _____ (have to) wear a suit and a tie.
6 You _____ (should) swim here – it's dangerous.
7 You _____ (can) park your car here.
8 You _____ (ought to) have your boarding card ready for inspection.
9 You _____ (should) dive into the swimming pool.
10 You _____ (have to) show your passport.

b **T11.1** Listen and check.

Pronunciation

1 **T11.2** Listen to the pronunciation of each of the verbs in exercise 1.

aren't allowed to … the public aren't allowed to … the public aren't allowed to come in here.

2 Practise saying the verbs separately, then practise the full sentence.

---

2 Complete the gaps with a suitable verb from exercise 1 to make them true for your city/country.

In city centres …

a You _____ park in the city centre.
b Lorries _____ drive through the centre.
c You _____ pay to drive your car into the city centre.
d Cars _____ stop at pedestrian crossings.

On roads …

e You _____ wear a seat belt.
f You _____ pay to use the motorways.
g You _____ drive at 180 km/hr.
h You _____ take your driving test if you're seventeen years old.

On trains …

i You _____ buy your ticket in advance.
j You _____ buy your ticket on the train.
k You _____ pay a fine if you're caught without a ticket.
l You _____ smoke.

3 a Choose three of the places in exercise 1 on page 112 and make a list of the most important rules for each place.

b Work in small groups. Read your rules to your group, but do not say the place. Can they guess?

You have to get there two hours in advance.

You're in an airport!

Listening
Annoying rules

1 **a** Look at the photo. What rule do you think the driver has broken to have had his/her car clamped? Are cars clamped in your country?

b What rules and regulations can you think of connected with the following?

– driving – smoking – flying – ID cards

2 **T11.3** Listen to six people complaining about a rule they find annoying. Make a note about what each person is complaining about.

a *aeroplane safety announcements* d
b   e
c   f

3 **a** Match the two halves to make a phrase from the recording. Then listen again, or look at the tapescript on page 173 to check.

1 One rule I	social rule
2 totally	annoy me is …
3 I find	really annoying is …
4 A rule that does	in a hotel is …
5 One rule that really	this really annoying
6 an unwritten	annoys me is …
7 What really annoys me	find really annoying is …
8 One thing I find	unnecessary

b Which of the complaints in exercise 2 do you agree with? Which do you disagree with? Compare your ideas in small groups.

4 Work in small groups. Make a list of rules for the following places that you find annoying. Use some of the phrases from exercise 3a to help you.

– your place of work or study
– your town/city/country
– where you live

Language focus 2
Obligation and permission in the past

1 There have been some strange laws in the past. Match the examples below with the pictures.

a In the times of Peter the Great in Russia, noblemen weren't allowed to wear beards. If they wanted to keep their beards, they had to pay a special tax to the Tsar's government.

b In eighteenth-century England, people had to pay 'window tax' for each window in their house. However, this law was eventually changed because many poor people chose to live in houses without windows just so that they didn't have to pay!

c In the nineteenth century, female teachers in the USA couldn't get married, or even go out with men. If they got engaged, they had to resign from their job immediately. Male teachers, on the other hand, could get married and have children without any problem!

d If you travelled in any motor vehicle in nineteenth-century Britain, the law said that someone had to walk in front of you waving a red flag, or a red lamp at night time. This meant, in practice, that you couldn't travel at more than eight kilometres per hour!

e In the Midwest of the USA in the 1880s you were not allowed to eat ice-cream soda on Sunday. Restaurant owners solved this problem by serving ice-cream without soda, which became known as a 'Sunday' or a 'sundae'.

2 Work in pairs. Answer the following questions.

a What exactly were the laws in each case?

b Can you imagine any possible reasons for these laws?

c Which of these laws do you find the funniest / the strangest / the most unfair?

▶ Read Language summary A4 on page 153.

Analysis

1 Write the past forms of the following verbs, where possible. Which three verbs do **not** have past forms. Which form is used instead?

- can
- can't
- have to
- don't have to
- must
- mustn't
- have got to
- is/are allowed to
- isn't/aren't allowed to

2 Read the laws described in exercise 1 and underline any examples of these verbs.

Practice

1 **T11.4** Here are some more unusual laws from around the world. Complete the gaps with the past form of a verb from the Analysis. (In some cases there is more than one possibility.) Then listen and check.

a In the 1920s in the USA, 'prohibition' meant that you _____ produce or consume alcoholic drinks. Eventually, though, the government _____ change this law. Firstly because it was actually creating crime, and secondly because people were drinking more alcohol than ever before!

b During the French Revolution, you _____ use the polite form of 'you' (*vous*) because this was the word servants used to speak to their masters. Instead everyone _____ use *tu* – the familiar form.

c In Italy in the 1930s, Italians _____ use foreign words. That's why Italian is one of the few languages that doesn't use the word 'football'!

d In Switzerland, women _____ vote until 1971. In New Zealand, on the other hand, women _____ to vote from 1893 – making it the first country in the world to give women the vote.

e Seventy-five years ago, in Britain, anyone _____ drive a car on the open road without taking a driving test. People _____ take a test until 1935, when the first practical road test was introduced. From 1996, the test was changed and learners _____ take a theoretical test as well.

2 Discuss the following questions in small groups.

- Were your parents strict with you when you were a child? What rules did they have about the following?
  - clothes, jewellery and hairstyles
  - homework
  - household chores
  - staying out late

  What happened if you broke the rules?
- Did you have friends whose parents were stricter / more liberal than your own? In what ways did their rules differ?

Task: Present your opinions
Preparation: vocabulary

1 a Check the words and phrases in bold in your mini-dictionary. Which relate to having more rights and freedom, and which relate to having stricter laws and fewer rights?

> It should be against the law (to …)
>
> It should be **made legal** (for people to …)
>
> It should be made **illegal** (for people to …)
>
> It should be banned.
>
> People should **have the right to** do this.
>
> People shouldn't **have the right to** do this.
>
> People should be **fined / sent to prison** (for doing this.)
>
> There should be **capital punishment**.

b Are the sentences to describe laws in the box positive (+) or negative (–)?

It's **fair**.	It's **ridiculous**.
It's **too harsh**.	It's **sensible**.
It's **too liberal**.	It's **unfair**.

2 Read the controversial statements 1–14. Which of these ideas are already the law in your country?

3 a Mark the controversial statements in the following ways.
✓ if you agree
✗ if you disagree
? if you are not sure or think it depends

b Cross out the statements that you are not happy to discuss. Put a * next to the ones you are most interested in.

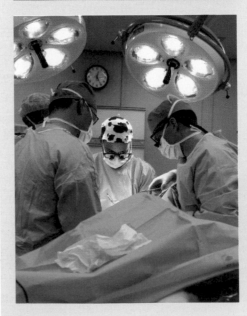

Controversy ...

1. All forms of hunting for sport (including fishing) should be banned.

2. It should be made illegal for parents to smack their children.

3. Terminally ill people who wish to die should have the right to do so.

4. People should not be allowed to work for more than thirty-five hours a week.

5. Everyone should have the right to carry a gun if they wish to.

Controversy ...

6. Young people should have the right to get married at sixteen without their parents' permission.

7. Smoking should be banned in all public places.

8. There should be capital punishment for anyone who commits murder.

9. Anyone who steals should be sent to prison, no matter how small the thing is that they steal.

10. It should be against the law to kill animals for food.

Controversy ...

11. Everyone should have the right to a free university education.

12. Military service should be compulsory for all young men and women.

13. Parents should have the right to choose the sex of their unborn child if they wish.

14. People who smoke should not have the right to free medical care from the state.

Task: speaking

1 **a** Work in small groups. Choose at least three topics from the controversial statements that you would like to discuss, but do not start discussing them yet.

b Work individually. Spend a few minutes planning how to express your ideas. Ask your teacher for any words or phrases you need.

▶ Useful language a

2 Work in small groups again. Discuss your views on each topic. Do you agree or not?

▶ Useful language b

3 Present your group's views to the class. Spend a few minutes deciding what to say. Do the rest of the class agree or not?

▶ Useful language c

Useful language

a Expressing your opinions

Personally, I think / don't think ...

It seems to me that ...

I think it's wrong to ...

Everyone should be free to ...

I don't really have any strong opinions about this.

b Agreeing and disagreeing

I completely agree.

Yes, you're right.

I agree in some ways but ...

I think it depends (on the situation/person)

I don't really agree.

I'm afraid I don't agree at all.

c Presenting the views of your groups

The topic we discussed most was ...

We all had different opinions about ...

Reading and vocabulary

1 Check the meaning of the title of the article in your mini-dictionary. What is the compensation culture? Which country do you associate it with? Do a lot of people make claims for compensation in your country?

2 Work in pairs. Check the words and phrases in your mini-dictionary. Then decide how they might be connected to the 'compensation culture'.

> big corporations greed an injury
> to slip on something to trip over something

3 Read the text and complete the table with information about each case.

Information about the person/ people suing	Name/Type of organisation sued	Amount of money they received	Reasons for suing
Roslyn Darch			Tripped over a child and broke her ankle
	Tobacco companies		
Overweight New York teenagers			
		€42,000	
	Restaurant in Philadelphia		

4 Discuss the following questions in small groups.

- Which of the people who sued do you think most deserved the money?
- Who do you think shouldn't have received anything?
- Do you think the compensation culture is something to worry about, or might it be a good thing?

TO sue
or not to sue?

The rise and rise of the compensation culture

Imagine on your way out of class today you trip on a loose piece of carpet and twist your ankle. As a result of the injury, you lose your place in the local sports team, and have to miss an important job interview. Bad luck? Just one of those things? Or an opportunity to get rich quick?

Perhaps it's not surprising that Roslyn Darch of Houston, Texas, USA felt annoyed when she tripped over a toddler running around a furniture store, and broke her ankle. But a few months later, she was $780,000 richer after successfully suing the shop. The owners were clearly surprised at the size of Roslyn's payout. Particularly since the toddler she tripped over was her own son.

Some argue that this is just greed – that the amount of money is far too much for the injury suffered – and it's not the shop's fault a mother can't control her child anyway. Others would say that it's good to see the law taking the side of the individual against the big corporations, for a change. Take the example of the hundreds of smokers who have received millions of dollars from the tobacco companies, after saying they were responsible for the terminal illnesses they had developed because of smoking. Whatever you think, the compensation culture which has grown up in the USA is spreading, and it will affect all of us.

And it's not only claims for physical injuries that are keeping the lawyers busy. A group of overweight New York teenagers sued a giant fast-food company claiming that they had not had enough warning that a diet of burgers, fries and milk shakes would make them fat. The parents of one nineteen-year-old English schoolgirl successfully sued her school  for €42,000 compensation when she failed to get a top grade in a university entrance exam: and in perhaps the most bizarre case of all, Sandra York received $113,000 from a Philadelphia restaurant after slipping on a spilt soft drink. However, the drink was on the floor because York had thrown it over her boyfriend thirty seconds earlier, during an argument.

If you think that going on holiday is a good way to get away from all this trouble, think again – millions of people complain to the British Tourist Authority every year, and many receive some form of compensation. Staff at British travel company Thomson Holidays are used to dealing with requests for compensation following poor weather, cancelled flights and lost luggage, but one spokesman revealed 'We recently had a claim from someone who said their holiday was ruined because they didn't get on with their travelling companion. And we regularly get complaints from holidaymakers travelling abroad who say the locals don't speak English!'

Who knows where it will end? Some say there should be penalties for excessive claims, or that there should be a limit on payouts. But one thing's for sure – in the end, the only certain winner is the lawyer!

Writing
Linking words

1 The words in the box are used to join sentences and link ideas. Put them in the correct category below. Then look at Language summary B on page 153 and check.

also although besides despite this for that reason
however as a result therefore what's more

similar meaning to *and*

similar meaning to *but*

similar meaning to *so*

2 The following sentences can be continued in two possible ways. Complete the gaps using a suitable word/phrase from the box in exercise 1 to link the two ideas. Add or change the punctuation as necessary.

a   Everyone knows that smoking is bad for you.
  • ___*What's more*___ it can be very expensive.
  • ___*Despite this*___ many young people start every year.

b   Regular exercise can prevent heart disease.
  • _____ experts recommend exercising three times a week.
  • _____ it can help to control your weight.

c   Many people nowadays believe that it is wrong to kill animals for food.
  • _____ they think eating meat is unhealthy.
  • _____ more and more people are becoming vegetarians.

d   Doctors agree that there is a strong link between alcohol and health.
  • _____ a small amount of alcohol may actually be good for you.
  • _____ it can make you depressed.

e   Doctors have found cures for many serious diseases in the last 100 years.
  • _____ the average person is living longer.
  • _____ there is still no cure for the common cold.

3 Write a few sentences about one of the topics in the Task on pages 116 and 117.

Wordspot
do

1 The diagram below shows the most common uses of *do*. Add the following phrases to the correct section.

do badly	do your homework	do the washing-up
do your best	do the ironing	do some work
do a course	do overtime (at work)	do yoga
do economics (at university)	do the shopping	

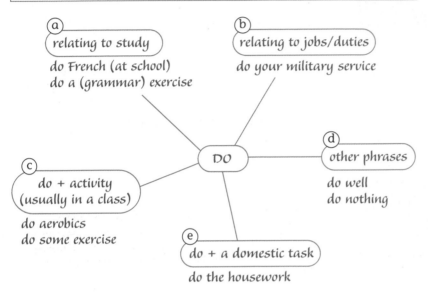

ⓐ relating to study
do French (at school)
do a (grammar) exercise

ⓑ relating to jobs/duties
do your military service

DO

ⓒ do + activity (usually in a class)
do aerobics
do some exercise

ⓓ other phrases
do well
do nothing

ⓔ do + a domestic task
do the housework

2 **a** **T11.5** Listen to twelve questions and make a note of your answers. Do not write complete sentences, just a word or phrase.

b Look at the questions in the tapescript on page 174. Memorise as many of the questions as you can in three minutes.

3 Close your books. Ask and answer as many questions as you can with a partner.

How often do you exercise?

I try to go to the gym three times a week.

Checking your written work

1 Before you give a piece of written work to your teacher, make the following checks:

- Read carefully to check if have missed out any words by mistake.
- Check that you have not forgotten the 's' on the third person (he, she, it) verbs.
- Check that the verb tenses are all correct.
- Are there any words where the spelling might be a problem? Use a dictionary to check.
- Check that all your sentences begin with capital letters, and that you have used full stops and commas correctly.

2 Look at the pieces of writing below and correct the mistakes. There are five in each one.

I'm just writeing to say thank you, for the lovely pullover you send me for Christmas. It fit perfectly, and the colour great.

Sorry I couldn't come to the ristorant tomorrow, but I have to make my homework and study for exam. I'm very worrying!

I am agree — peoples should be find for smoking in public place. I think it should made illegal.

CHECK YOUR WORK FOR MISTEAKS

PRACTICE

1 Obligation and permission in the present ☐

Match A and B to make logical sentences.

A
a You can do it
b You've got to do it
c You don't have to do it
d You're not allowed to do it
e You can't do it

B
1 if you don't want to.
2 if you want to.
3 because it's compulsory.
4 because it's forbidden.
5 because it's not possible.

▶ **Need to check? Language summary A, pages 152–153.**

2 Obligation and permission in the past ☐

Write the past forms of these sentences.

a We mustn't take our jackets off.

_____

b I can't understand every word.

_____

c We must leave early.

_____

d We're allowed to invite who we want.

_____

e I don't have to go to work.

_____

▶ **Need to check? Language summary A4, page 153.**

3 Rights and freedom ☐

Which pairs of sentences below have the same meaning?

a It's illegal. / It's against the law.
b It should be banned. / It shouldn't be permitted.
c You have the right to vote. / You have to vote.
d You can be fined for speeding. / You can be sent to prison for speeding.
e It's sensible. / It's fair.

▶ **Need to check? Task, page 116,**

4 Linking words ☐

Choose the correct alternative.

a He failed his final exam. As a result / Although he had to repeat the whole year.
b Even though / As a result we have different opinions about everything, we never argue.
c I'm very keen on skiing, and I also / too like ice hockey.
d We don't need a swimming pool in this house. Besides / Despite this we can't afford it.
e He's been refused several times already. In spite of this / Therefore he keeps applying.
f Sheila is clever, ambitious and however / what's more she really wants the job.

▶ **Need to check? Writing, page 119 and Language summary B, page 153.**

5 Presenting your opinions ☐

Cross out the extra word in each sentence.

a It is seems to me that he's right.
b I think it is depends.
c I am completely agree with you.
d One of the topics we discussed about was capital punishment.
e Everybody should be free for to do what they want.
f Yes, I think you are have right about that.

▶ **Need to check? Useful language, page 117.**

6 Phrases with *do* ☐

Cross out the words or phrases not used with *do*. Can you remember any other phrases with *do*?

the housework	nothing	a mess
overtime	a mistake	your best
a suggestion	some exercise	an arrangement
military service	someone angry	the ironing

▶ **Need to check? Wordspot, page 120.**

Pronunciation spot

Review

a Here are the sounds you have studied in the Pronunciation section of Study, Practise, Remember. Can you remember what the sounds are? (Look at the Pronunciation table of the mini-dictionary if you're not sure.)

/ə/	/ð/	/æ/
/ɪ/	/v/	/θ/
/ɒ/	/w/	/b/
/əʊ/	/iː/	/h/
/ʌ/	/ɔː/	

b Here are fourteen words from Module 11. Write the phonetic from above which matches each underlined sound in the words.

alth<u>ou</u>gh	l<u>i</u>beral
<u>c</u>ategory	li<u>b</u>rary
comp<u>e</u>nsation	m<u>u</u>st
d<u>og</u>s	<u>ough</u>t
gr<u>ee</u>d	pa<u>th</u>
<u>h</u>arsh	<u>th</u>ere
ha<u>v</u>e	<u>w</u>ashing

c T11.6 **Listen and check. Practise saying the words, copying the voices on the recording.**

REMEMBER!

Look back at the areas you have practised. Tick the ones you feel confident about. Now try the MINI-CHECK on page 158 to check what you know!

Dilemmas

▶ *could have, should have, would have*
▶ **Imaginary situations in the past with** *if*
▶ **Vocabulary:** Problems and solutions
▶ **Pronunciation:** Past modal forms, Vowel sounds
▶ **Song:** *Out of Reach*
▶ **Task:** Find solutions to problems
▶ **Wordspot:** *think*
▶ **Real life:** Saying goodbye

Language focus 1
could have, should have, would have

1 a Read about the journey Andrew and Debra Veal decided to make. Why was it challenging?

b Something went wrong in the middle of the Atlantic. Can you guess what?

2 **T12.1** Check the words in your mini-dictionary. Then listen to the first part of the story and answer the questions. (You can read the tapescript on page 174 as you listen.)

> an experienced rower   a violent storm
> a fear of the ocean   to make a tough decision
> abandon the race   to give up   a rescue vessel
> an oil tanker   a collision   sharks   rapturous applause

a   What experience did Debra and Andrew have of rowing?
b   What was the problem?

3 **T12.2** What do you think they decided to do? Listen to the rest of the story and answer the questions.

a   Did they agree about what to do?
b   What physical dangers did Debra face?
c   When did she feel particularly lonely?
d   Why was Day 74 especially good for her?
e   When did she arrive in Barbados?
f   How many days behind the winner was she?

The toughest decision of their lives

In October 2002, Debra and Andrew Veal, a married couple from south-west London, entered the Ward Evans Atlantic Rowing Challenge. They would race thirty-four other crews rowing 5,000 km from Tenerife, in the Canary Islands, to Barbados in the Caribbean – a journey expected to take sixty days. To do this, each team of two people rows twenty-four hours a day, in shifts of two hours.

4 Read what some people said about Andrew and Debra Veal. Which statement do you agree with?

a ❝Andrew shouldn't have left his wife alone. Either he should have persuaded her to come back with him, or he should have stayed with her. She could easily have died, and he would have been responsible.❞

b ❝Since Debra was determined to continue, Andrew couldn't really have done anything differently. It would have been wrong to force Debra to give up, too.❞

c ❝Debra should have gone home with Andrew. It would have been much more sensible, and more supportive of him. What she did was pretty stupid.❞

Analysis

Circle the correct alternatives and tick the best explanation a–c.

1 *She could have died out there.*
   This sentence refers to the past / present. It means:
   a She died.
   b She didn't die.
   c It was possible for her to die, but she didn't.

2 *He shouldn't have left her.*
   This sentence refers to the past / present. The speaker thinks:
   a He had to stay with her.
   b It was a good idea to stay with her, but he didn't.
   c He probably stayed with her.

3 *He would have been responsible.*
   This sentence refers to something that really happened /
   an imaginary situation.
   This sentence refers to the past / present.

▶ Read Language summary A on page 154.

Practice

1 **a** The sentences below give extra facts and opinions about the
   story of Andrew and Debra Veal. Complete them with *could have*,
   should(n't) have or *would(n't) have*.

1 Debra _____ (learn) to row much earlier – she was taking a
   huge risk.
2 I'm sure he _____ (enter) the race if he'd known about the
   phobia.
3 They _____ (enter) the race – it was far too risky!
4 Why did she decide to continue with the race? She _____ (die)
   out there!
5 The boat _____ (survive) a collision with a tanker.
6 She _____ (take) food from the people on the yacht – that's
   cheating!
7 Without her husband's support, I'm sure she _____ (find)
   things impossible.
8 I know I'm not as brave as Debra! I'm sure that in her position, I
   _____ (give) up!
9 A shark _____ (attack) the boat – fortunately it didn't happen!
10 The organisers _____ (give) her a special prize for bravery.

b T12.3 Listen and check.

Pronunciation

1 In speech, past modal forms are
   often pronounced as one word.

   Examples:
   could have — could've
   should not have — shouldn't've

2 T12.4 Listen to the examples
   on the recording. Practise
   saying the complete phrases.

2 **a** Read about Olivia and her
   husband's dilemma. What was
   the problem? How did Olivia deal
   with it?

Olivia and her husband were asleep
in bed one night when they heard
someone downstairs burgling their
house. Olivia's husband went down,
and after listening to their
conversation for a few minutes,
Olivia realised that the burglar had a
gun. There was a phone by Olivia's
bedside, but Olivia decided to go
downstairs herself, and managed to
hit the burglar over the head with a
vase. He was later arrested.

b Write some sentences about
Olivia's story.

She could have …
In my opinion, she should/
   shouldn't have …
In her position, I would/wouldn't
   have …
… could have happened …

3 Work in pairs. Student A: Read
   the story of Gill and George on
page 141. Be ready to tell Student B
the main points of your story.
Student B: Read the story of Jackie
and her children on page 143. Be
ready to tell Student A the main
points of your story.

4 Tell each other the main points
   of your story. Discuss what the
characters could/should have done,
and what you would have done in
their position.

Language focus 2
Imaginary situations in the past with *if*

1 Are you good at making decisions or not? If you find it hard to make a decision, what do you usually do?

a   Talk it over with a friend
b   Toss a coin
c   Make a list of pros and cons
d   Research expert opinion
e   Follow your instinct

2 Read about Luke Rhinehart and his novel *The Dice Man*. Answer the questions.

a   How does the main character in *The Dice Man* make decisions?
b   What about the author of the book? Give an example of an important decision he made in this way.
c   Why did he first start doing this?
d   What job did he do before he was an author?
e   What made him decide to write a book about throwing dice ('dicing')?
f   Who encouraged him to finish his book?
g   Why did Rhinehart say goodbye to his wife?
h   Who rescued them from the sea?

3 Match the beginnings of the sentences in A with the endings in B. Use the text to help you.

A

a   Luke Rhinehart probably wouldn't have started dicing
b   He wouldn't have met his wife
c   He wouldn't have started writing *The Dice Man*
d   He might not have finished the book
e   He wouldn't be alive today
f   He might still be a poor college professor

B

1   if the Scottish sailors hadn't rescued him.
2   if his students hadn't been so interested in dicing.
3   if his life had been more exciting when he was young.
4   if the book hadn't been so successful.
5   if he hadn't met Mike Franklyn.
6   if he had thrown an even number.

The Dice Man is a novel about a man who throws dice to decide his every action – and it's based on fact. The author, Luke Rhinehart, has made some of his best and worst decisions that way. When he was twenty-one, he was driving on Long Island when he saw a pretty nurse walking along the road. 'I took out the die and said to myself: If it falls on an odd number (one, three or five), I will turn around and offer her a ride. And it came out odd. So I did. I arranged to play tennis with her the next day. These many years later, I am still married to the same woman.'

Rhinehart first started making decisions by throwing dice when he was at college because he didn't like the kind of person he was: a person who always made very 'safe' and 'boring' decisions. Throwing the dice was a way of making himself take more risks. Years later, when he himself was a college professor, he told his students about his 'dice philosophy'. They were so fascinated that he decided to write a book about it.

However, the book – and the rest of his life – almost didn't happen. Five years later, Rhinehart was living on the Spanish island of Majorca teaching English, but he had still only written two hundred pages of the book. He met an English publisher, Mike Franklyn, and showed him the manuscript of *The Dice Man*. Franklyn knew it would be a big success, and encouraged Rhinehart to finish it.

Then, when the book was done, the author and his wife bought a sailing boat and set off from the south of France to Majorca. Along the way, they met a fierce storm and lost their engine. 'I said goodbye to my wife. We assumed we were going to die.'

However, the couple were pulled from the ocean by some Scottish sailors, the book was published and Franklyn sold the rights all over the world.

Analysis

1 a Are the sentences in exercise 3 on page 124 true or hypothetical?
  b Look at the 'conditions' in B. Do they refer to the present or the past? What form of the verb is used to talk about past conditions?
  c Look at the hypothetical situations in A. Which ones refer to the past? Which refer to the present?

2 Notice the verb forms.

Past condition →	Past result
If **he hadn't been** bored,	**he wouldn't have started** dicing.

Past condition →	Present/general result
If the book **hadn't been** successful	he **would/might** still **be** a college professor.

Underline these forms in the exercise.

▶ Read Language summaries B and C on page 154.

Practice

1 **T12.5** Look at the photos and listen to the three people describing a big decision in their life. Answer these questions about each person.

a What was the decision?
b Why did they make it?
c How are their lives different now?

Would you have made the same decisions in their position?

2 Complete the sentences about each person. Use *might* where appropriate.

a If Erin _____ (not have) a baby, she _____ (continue) working.
b If she _____ (not leave) her job, she _____ (spend) a lot of time away from her children.
c The family _____ (have) a lot more money now, if she _____ (stay) in her old job, but she _____ (not be) happy with the situation.
d Kieron _____ (become) a top class footballer, if he _____ (not break) his leg.
e If he _____ (be able) to play for a big club, he _____ (not become) a coach.
f He _____ (be) happier now, if he _____ (fulfil) his ambitions.
g If Margot _____ (not go) to Greece for her holidays that year, she _____ (not meet) Nikos.
h She _____ (forget) about Nikos, if he _____ (not follow) her home.
i If she _____ (not marry) Nikos, she _____ (still live) in England.
j If she _____ (not move) to Greece, she _____ (still be) a nurse now.

3 Complete the following sentences to make them true for you.

a I wouldn't have met ... if ...
b I would have studied ... if ...
c I wouldn't have studied ... if ...
d I wouldn't have gone to ... if ...
e I would have more money now if ...
f I'd feel better now if ...

4 Think about a big decision or event in your life. How would your life have been different if things had happened differently? Write sentences about it, then tell your partner.

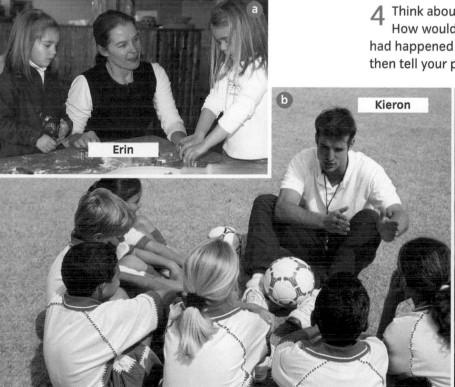

a

Erin

b

Kieron

c Margot

Vocabulary
Problems and solutions

1 The sentences below tell the story of Frank's problem, but they are in the wrong order. Check the words in bold in your mini-dictionary. Then work in pairs. Put the sentences in the same order as the pictures.

a   In the end, he **made up his mind** – he knew exactly how to **sort** the problem **out**. ☐

b But things got no better, he began to feel a little **concerned**. ☐

c   He **suffered** several **sleepless nights thinking it over**. ☐

d   Frank's life was **trouble-free** – he **didn't have a care in the world**. ☐1☐

e   Until one day a problem **came up**. ☐

f   He even phoned a **helpline** to ask for some **expert advice**. ☐

g   At first, Frank thought he should **ignore** the problem, hoping it would just **go away**. ☐

h   He **talked** it **over** with a friend, who was very **sympathetic**. ☐

2 Match the words or phrases in bold in exercise 1 with the definitions below.

a   disappear   *go away*
b   without problems
c   solve (a problem)
d   had nothing to worry about
e   was unable to sleep at night
f   kind and willing to listen
g   help given by people who know a lot about a subject
h   a number you call for help or advice
i   appeared unexpectedly
j   decided
k   pretend you can't see or notice something
l   discuss something seriously
m   worried
n   think about something carefully

3 **a** Work in pairs. Choose one of the topics below. Imagine Frank's problem was related to this topic.

– his health
– his love life
– his job or studies
– money
– a secret in his past

b Re-tell the story and invent extra details.

> Frank had a carefree life until a slight problem came up.

> The problem was that his girlfriend didn't seem to like him anymore …

Wordspot
think

1 Match a phrase in A with an ending/response in B.

A		B	
a	What do you **think**	1	about twenty years old.
b	My brother is **thinking**	2	**don't think so.**
c	Mrs Potts **thinks the world**	3	some time to **think it over.**
d	**Just think!**	4	I can't **think straight!**
e	We'd better try and **think**	5	**of going** abroad for a year.
f	I can't decide now: give me	6	Marta's in New York now!
g	A: Is Paul coming this evening?	7	**of** her grandchildren.
	B: Yes, **I think**	8	**of** the new boss?
h	There's so much noise in here	9	**so.**
i	It's important that parents	10	**think back.**
	encourage their children	11	to **think for themselves.**
j	Where were you on the night of	12	**up** a good excuse for being
	the robbery? Try to		so late.
k	A: Can Karl speak French?		
	B: I		
l	**I should think** she's		

2 The diagram below shows the most common uses of *think*. Add the phrases from exercise 1 to the correct section.

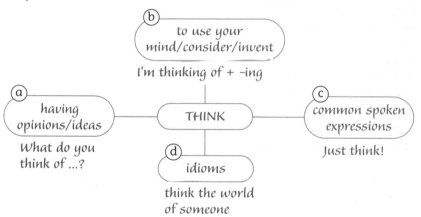

3 Replace the words and phrases in bold with an appropriate phrase with *think*.

a 'Is Sydney the capital of Australia? '**Probably not.**'
b **What's your opinion of** Louise's new hairstyle?
c Apparently John and Lucy **are considering** selling their flat.
d They're trying to **invent** a name for the new hairspray.
e If we win, we'll be millionaires!! **Imagine it!**
f 'Is Martin coming this evening?' '**Probably.**'
g 'What time will we get there?' 'About nine, **I suppose.**'
h All the students in the class **respect and admire** their teacher.
i I was so tired I couldn't **concentrate.**
j He's always encouraged his employees to **have their own ideas.**
k When I **remember**, it seems the happiest time of my life.
l Katie didn't agree to the idea straightaway, but asked for some time to **consider it carefully.**

Task: Find solutions to problems
Preparation: reading and vocabulary

1 **a** Read the titles of five letters on an Internet problem page, without reading the letters. What do you think each letter is about? Compare your opinions in small groups.

b Read each letter and check. Use your mini-dictionary, if necessary.

2 Read the letters again. In which letter (1–5):

a has someone's husband and best friend had a huge argument? **1**

b does a couple live hundreds of kilometres apart?

c is someone unable to cope without her mother?

d does someone's boyfriend pretend that they are just friends?

e has someone been offered a fantastic opportunity?

f does someone insist on seeing a solicitor?

g has someone never had a romantic relationship?

h does someone's boyfriend come from a very traditional culture?

i does someone have some minor health problems?

3 Work in pairs. Summarise each person's problem.

---

shareyourdilemmas.com

The forum where everyone's views are welcome.

Read this week's top-five problems, then click to send your advice.

❶   My husband and my best friend have fallen out

My problem concerns my best friend of twenty years. (We have been friends since we were three.) I got married a year ago and, unfortunately, a few months ago my friend and my husband had a huge argument. It started about politics, but both my husband and my friend are quite strong, argumentative people and they ended up shouting and calling each other names. Since then, my friend and I have hardly spoken, and she refuses to pay back the $3,000 that I lent her (using my credit card). She says that she didn't borrow that much, and that my husband had been using my credit card. He says that I must go to a solicitor to get the money back. What should I do? I know if I go to a solicitor she will make things really hard for me (she can be extremely difficult) and it will be impossible ever to be friends again.

SEND YOUR ADVICE – CLICK HERE

❷   Why won't he introduce me to his family?

My boyfriend and I are twenty-one and have been going out for a year. We live in a big city where there are people from many different races and cultures. He comes from a culture that is much more religious and traditional than mine. This is not a problem for me or my family: they have always welcomed him into our home. However, he refuses to introduce me to his family, and when his brother (who I know) is around, he pretends we are just friends. Apart from this we love each other very much. Should I insist that he introduces me to his family?

SEND YOUR ADVICE – CLICK HERE

❸   Can we leave my mother?

I am forty-four years old and have looked after my elderly mother for a number of years. She has a few small health problems and is rather lonely since my father died. Recently, my husband was offered a new job in the United States, a once in a lifetime opportunity. My husband is desperately keen to go, and both our children would enjoy the experience, but I know that my mother would not consider moving to the USA, and I am terribly worried about her coping on her own, as she has no other relatives nearby. Should I persuade my husband to refuse the job offer?

SEND YOUR ADVICE – CLICK HERE

Done

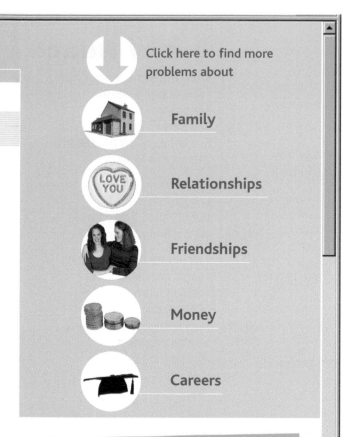

Click here to find more problems about

Family

Relationships

Friendships

Money

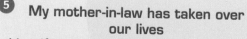

Careers

4 **Love online?**

I have got to know a woman through the Internet and have been e-mailing her nearly every day for the last year. We have become very close and she now says she is in love with me. I have never really had a girlfriend before, but she has been married and has a baby (she is twenty-four, I am twenty-one). We have not yet met, as we live three hundred kilometres apart, but she wants to meet up, and is talking about moving to my town to be near me. What should I tell her?

SEND YOUR ADVICE – CLICK HERE ◯

5 **My mother-in-law has taken over our lives**

My wife and I are twenty-five and have just had a baby. The problem is my mother-in-law. She is helping my wife and has completely taken over the house. My wife and I feel as if it is no longer our own home or our own baby. I have asked my wife to speak to her mother, but although she agrees with me, she says she can't cope without her mother. Should I speak to her mother? I can't live like this much longer.

SEND YOUR ADVICE – CLICK HERE ◯

Internet

Task: speaking

1 Work individually. Make a list of all the options for the people who wrote the letters (whether or not you think they are a good idea).

► Useful language a

2 Work in groups. Discuss each problem and try to agree on the best solution. Ask your teacher for any words or phrases you need.

► Useful language b

3 Present your conclusions to the class. Do they agree or not? Which is the most difficult problem, in your opinion?

► Useful language c

Useful language

a Suggesting possibilities

He/She could …

On the other hand, he/she could always …

Another possibility is to …

b Giving your opinion

I think/don't think he/she should …

In his/her position, I'd/wouldn't …

If she …, her mother/husband/boyfriend might …

Personally, I would (never) …

c Presenting your conclusions

We thought the best solution would be to …

We couldn't agree about what he should do …

Follow up: writing

Choose the problem you find most interesting.

Either Write a dialogue between two of the people as they discuss the problem.

Or Imagine what happened in the end. Write the full story from the point of view of one of the people involved (not necessarily the writer of the letter).

Song
Out of Reach

1 a Look at the photo. What difficult decision do you think the woman has made? What do you think the letter says?

b You are going to listen to a song called *Out of Reach*. Check the words and phrases in the box in your mini-dictionary. Do you expect this to be a happy or a sad song?

> bruised keeping busy swept away we were meant to be
> out of reach to be over someone/something

2 a Read the words of the song. In the lines written in red, there is one word missing. Can you guess what it is?

b **T12.6** Listen and check.

3 Add some words or phrases from the song to the categories below. Do you think the song is mainly optimistic or mainly pessimistic?

Words/Phrases connected with sadness	*feel like a fool*
Words/Phrases connected with happiness	

Pronunciation

1 **T12.7** The words below are from the song. Put them into pairs according to the vowel sound in bold. Then listen and check.

okay bruised far fool see heart
mind pain reach confused sign you

2 Practise saying the words, paying attention to the vowel sound.

Out of Reach

Knew the signs, wasn't right
I was stupid a while
Swept away by you
And now I feel a fool
So confused, my heart's bruised
Was I loved by you?

Out of reach, so far
I never had heart
Out of reach, couldn't see
We were meant to be

Catch myself from despair
I could drown if I stay
Keeping busy every day
I know I will be
But I was so confused, my
heart's bruised
Was I loved by you?

CHORUS
So much, so much pain
Takes a while to regain what is
lost inside
And I that in time, you'll be out
of my mind
And I'll be over you
But now I'm so confused, my
heart's bruised
Was I loved by you?

Out of reach, so far
You never your heart
In my reach, I can see
There's a life there for me

130

Real life
Saying goodbye

1 a Look at the pictures below. What do you think is the relationship between the people shown?

b [T12.8] Listen and check.

2 Complete the gaps with a word or phrase from the box. Which picture does each phrase belong to?

> around better do come dreams I wish I'd like
> in touch it's been great off night safe see you take

a   Sweet _____ .
b   Night _____ .
c   _____ you all the very best of luck.
d   I'll be _____ then.
e   _____ care.
f   _____ to thank you all …
g   _____ in the morning.
h   I'll see you _____ .
i   _____ working with you.
j   _____ journey!
k   Keep _____ .
l   _____ and see me.
m   I'd _____ be going.

3 a Work in pairs. Choose some characters and a setting. Then prepare a short dialogue (about twelve to fifteen lines) where people are saying goodbye. Use some of the phrases from exercise 2.

Characters	Setting
classmates	an airport
family members	your school
friends	an office
people who have just met	in the street
teacher and students	at home
work colleagues	a leaving party

b Take it in turns to present your dialogue to the class. Can they guess the characters and the setting?

> Thanks for coming to see me. Safe journey home.

> Thanks. Hope you feel better soon.

CONSOLIDATION

A Past perfect / Reported speech

Complete the gaps in the text with the correct form of the verb in brackets.

Possibly the world's least successful tourist is Mr Nicholas Scotti, an Italian living in San Francisco. Some years ago, he (1) _____ (decide) to fly back to Italy to visit relatives. During the journey, the plane (2) _____ (make) a one-hour stop at Kennedy Airport. Thinking he (3) _____ (arrive) in Italy, Mr Scotti (4) _____ (get) out of the plane and (5) _____ (spend) the whole day in New York thinking he was in Rome. The great traveller (6) _____ (notice) that modernisation (7) _____ (destroy) many of Rome's ancient buildings and he later (8) _____ (tell) friends that he (9) _____ (be) surprised so many people (10) _____ (speak) English. In fact, Mr Scotti's English is rather limited, but when he (11) _____ (ask) a police officer for directions, he (12) _____ (manage) to choose an officer who (13) _____ (emigrate) from Italy several years before, and so (14) _____ (be able) to answer in fluent Italian.

After Mr Scotti (15) _____ (spend) several hours riding around on a bus, the driver (16) _____ (decide) to hand over his passenger to another police officer, who (17) _____ (try) to explain to Mr Scotti that he (18) _____ (not be) in Rome, but in New York. Mr Scotti (19) _____ (refuse) to believe him, but told the officer how surprised he (20) _____ (be) that the Rome Police Department (21) _____ (hire) a policeman who (22) _____ (not speak) Italian. Eventually, the officer decided that Mr Scotti's adventure (23) _____ (go on) long enough, so he (24) _____ (drive) Mr Scotti back to the airport at top speed in order to catch the San Francisco plane. Mr Scotti then told his interpreter he now (25) _____ (know) he was in Rome as only Italians (26) _____ (drive) that way.

B Possibility, obligation and permission

Choose the best alternative.

1   You look really tired. I think you **must / ought / should** to take a few days off.
2   The hours of work are quite flexible – you **can / have to / should** do a minimum of thirty hours per week, but you **don't have to / mustn't / shouldn't** start till 10 a.m. if you don't want to.
3   I'm sorry, but it's too late to change your plans now – you **had to / should have / would have** told me earlier.
4   The children **aren't allowed / can't / don't have to** run in the corridors – it's a school rule.
5   It seemed that everyone in Amsterdam spoke perfect English, so we **could have spoken / didn't have to speak / shouldn't have spoken** any Dutch.
6   The transport system may **likely / probably / well** get worse before it gets better.

C Listening: Hypothetical forms

1 [C1] Listen to three people. Which person is talking about:

a   living in Britain?
b   a business venture that failed?
c   a tennis tournament?

2 Make notes about what each person says. Then check the tapescript on page 175.

3 Each person ends with a half-sentence with *if*. Think of two different ways to complete each conditional sentence. Compare sentences with a partner.

D *make / do / say / tell / think*

1 Match a word or phrase in the box below with *make, do, say, tell* or *think* to make phrases from the Wordspots in Modules 9–12.

back	a course	the difference
some exercise	hello	the housework
lies	a prayer	a profit
someone what to do	something over	sorry
straight	a suggestion	sure
tthe world of someone	the truth	up your mind
yes	your best	

2 Write a short dialogue (six to eight lines) using two or three of the expressions above.

E Speaking: Agreeing and disagreeing

1 Read the ten statements below and decide whether you agree or disagree with each.

a   New technology is making our lives easier.
b   In another fifty years, everyone will work from home and there will be no offices, etc.
c   It should be compulsory for everyone to continue studying until the age of twenty-one.
d   My life wouldn't change if I were a millionaire.
e   Children should be made to do household chores – boys as well as girls.
f   The world would be a better place if we were all vegetarians.
g   It's always wrong to tell lies.
h   Men and women are basically equal nowadays.
i   Crime doesn't pay.
j   There is no such thing as a ghost.

2 Choose four of the topics and prepare to talk about them for one minute. What are your reasons for agreeing/ disagreeing with each statement? Spend a few minutes thinking about what you would say about each one.

3 Work in groups. Compare which topics you chose, and take turns to talk about each of the topics. Do you agree/disagree with the other students?

F Vocabulary: Word puzzle

Read the definitions below and complete the puzzle. The words all come from Modules 9–12. When you have completed the puzzle, read the hidden message in the shaded column.

1   the opposite of *come here* is go … (*adverb*)
2   linking word with a similar meaning to *so* (*adverb*)
3   if something happens like this, it happens slowly (*adverb*)
4   get better (*verb*)
5   it will probably happen – it is … to happen (*adverb*)
6   this type of children's story is one where magical things happen (*adjective*)
7   the opposite of *fall* (*adverb*)
8   if you decide something, you make up your … (*noun*)
9   the opposite of *innocent* in a court of law … (*adjective*)
10   if things deteriorate, they get … (*adjective*)
11   to remain in contact – to keep in … (*noun*)
12   the opposite of *decrease* (*verb*)
13   prohibited (*adjective*)
14   frightening (*adjective*)
15   if you discuss a problem at length you … it over (*verb*)
16   if something is prohibited, it's not … (*adjective*)
17   when someone deceives people to get money (*noun*)
18   the police are going to … the suspect (*verb*)
19   if you deal with a problem you … it out (*verb*)

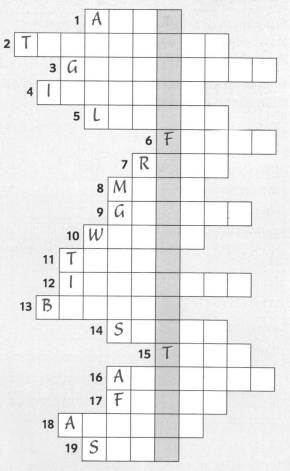

Module 2: Task, exercise 1, page 22

Memory quiz for Student A

1 What was the mobile phone number you had to memorise?

2 What can you remember about your first day at school as a small child? Give as much detail as you can.

3 This is one of your new classmates. What is his name?

4 What can you remember about your last English lesson? Give as much information about it as you can, for example:
- What did you study?
- Where were people sitting?
- What did you talk about?
- What was your teacher wearing?
- Who was absent?
- What homework did you receive?

5 What are the Past simple forms of *bite, throw* and *hit*?

6 What was the date of the father-in-law's birthday in the memory task?

7 What was the last film you saw at the cinema? Give as much information about it as you can, for example:
- Who starred in / directed it?
- Where was it set?
- What was the story about?
- How did it end?

8 What were the five things on the shopping list in the memory task?

9 Who did you phone yesterday? What did you talk about?

Module 3: Real life, exercise 5b, page 34

Student A

You want to fly return from Paris to Tokyo in May. Decide which dates you want to travel. Student B is the travel agent.

Then swap roles. You are the travel agent. Listen to Student B and complete the form below.

Personal details

Mr ☐   Mrs ☐   Miss ☐   Ms ☐

Surname

First name

Contact number

Flight details

Flying from

Stopover at

Departure details

date

time

airport

Module 5: Task, exercise 1, page 54

Peter Krajeck

Age: 28
Nationality: Slovak
Mother tongue: Slovak
Marital status: single

Skills/Background
- Ex-professional skier
- A lot of experience with small children – ski instructor in summer camps
- Speaks good French, some German
- Driver
- Good computer skills

Interview notes
- Retired from skiing because of knee injury
- Plans to open own hotel in ski resort – wants to get experience in all aspects of hotel work
- Very friendly, enthusiastic, seems hard-working

Module 3: Practice, exercise 1, page 31

Find these things in the pictures.

> a cash point   a kiosk   a pavement café   a phone box
> a post box   a souvenir shop   a tour bus   the church roof
> a tourist information office   some steps

Module 2: Task, exercise 1, page 23

Memory quiz for Student B

1 What was the date of the mother-in-law's birthday in the memory task?

2 What can you remember about your last birthday / name day? Give as much information about it as you can, for example:
   - Where did you go?
   - Who did you see?
   - Did you get any presents?
   - Did anything special happen?

3 What are the Past simple forms of *hold, eat* and *win*?

4 What was the e-mail address you had to remember in the memory task?

5 What and where did you eat last Sunday? Give as much information about it as you can.

6 This is one of your new classmates. What is her name?

7 What can you remember about your last important journey? Give as much information about it as you can, for example:
   - Where did you go?
   - Who did you go with?
   - What happened before/during/after the journey?

8 What is the first verse of the song on page 18? (You don't have to sing it!)

9 What were you doing exactly a month ago? Give as much information as you can about what happened on that day. (Don't look in your diary!)

Module 3: Real life, exercise 5b, page 34

Student B

You are a travel agent. Listen to Student A and complete the form below.

Personal details

Mr ☐   Mrs ☐   Miss ☐   Ms ☐

Surname _____

First name _____

Contact number _____

Flight details

Flying from _____

Stopover at _____

Departure details

date _____

time _____

airport _____

Then swap roles. You want to fly return from New York to Melbourne in July. Decide which dates you want to travel. Student A is the travel agent.

Module 5: Task, exercise 1, page 54

Brenda MacDonald

Age: 46
Nationality: British
Mother tongue: English
Marital status: widow

Skills/Background
- Several years' experience as hotel receptionist/secretary, has not worked for fifteen years
- French good, but not used for a long time
- Driver
- No experience of computers
- No knowledge of skiing
- Very good cook

Interview notes
- Husband died fifteen years ago so stopped work to bring up three sons, all now grown up
- Wants to do something different and adores France
- Very friendly – good fun!
- Seems capable and flexible

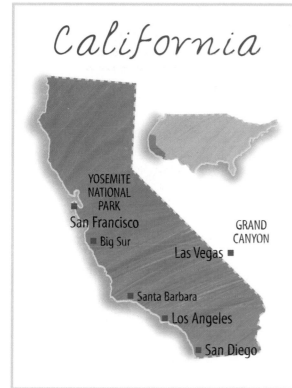

California

Yosemite National Park
Walk and swim amongst the incredible cliffs and mountains, visit the amazing waterfalls, see the giant trees or just relax and enjoy the scenery.

San Francisco
Enjoy the sightseeing and shopping. See the famous bay and the Golden Gate Bridge, walk through Chinatown or take a boat to the old prison on Alcatraz Island. Take an old-fashioned tram through the steep streets.

Big Sur
Enjoy the beautiful coast and cliffs, and the empty beaches in this part and see the Redwood Forests.

Santa Barbara
Visit southern California's prettiest little coastal town.

Los Angeles
You can visit the world-famous Universal Film Studios, take a walk down the streets of Hollywood, do a tour of the stars' homes in Beverly Hills, visit Disneyland or relax on some of the many beautiful beaches such as Santa Monica, Venice or Marina del Rey.

San Diego
For those who love animals, you can see dolphins at Seaworld Adventure Park and visit San Diego Zoo or just relax on one of the beautiful beaches in Mission Bay.

Las Vegas
Visit the casinos, experience the fantastic shopping and enjoy the entertainment and nightlife.

Grand Canyon
You can walk, travel by donkey or go white-water rafting on the Colorado River.

Scotland

Isle of Lewis and the Callinish Standing Stones
Experience magnificent beaches and the old world serenity of this island and visit the mysterious Callinish Standing Stones – believed to be about 4,000 years old.

Isle of Skye
An island full of romance and history and famous for its towering mountains and spectacular sea views. You can visit the Talisker distillery and sample the famous liqueur Drambuie.

Inverness and the Highlands
Take a long walk in some of Europe's most spectacular scenery or visit the ancient city of Inverness, 'Capital of the Highlands'.

Spey Valley
Scotland's main all-year-round holiday location. Numerous activities include mountain biking, riding, adventure parks, go-carting, skiing and golf all within the Cairngorm National Park.

Loch Ness
Explore the village of Fort Augustus and go monster spotting for 'Nessie' in Scotland's most famous stretch of water.

Ben Nevis
The highest mountain in the UK – although anyone can climb to the top via a long, safe path or visit Aonach Mor and take Britain's only mountain gondola to Scotland's highest restaurant (914 metres).

Stirling
Visit this historic town and discover the truth behind the legend of William Wallace, the Scottish hero made famous in the film *Braveheart*.

Edinburgh
Visit the art galleries, museums and historic buildings of Scotland's ancient capital, dominated by its medieval castle. Shop in Princes Street or just walk through streets rich in history. If it's August, sample the delights of Edinburgh's famous festival.

Glasgow
A bustling city which is home to Scotland's two most famous football clubs, Celtic and Rangers.

Module 3: Practice, exercise 3, page 27

	Area	Population density (people per km²)	Number of tourists (per year)	Main city (population) Main airport (number of users)
France	550,000 km²	Medium (107 km²)	75 million	Paris (2.1 million) Charles de Gaulle (39 million)
Ireland	69,000 km²	Low (52 km²)	5.5 million	Dublin (500,000) Dublin International (12 million)
UK	241,000 km²	High (241 km²)	26 million	London (6.3 million) Heathrow International (65 million)

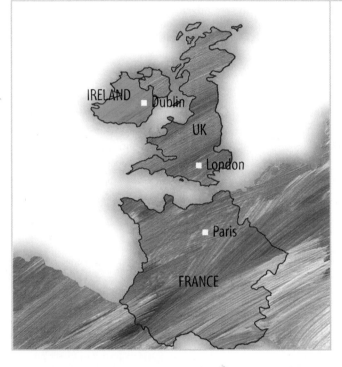

Module 4: Practice, exercise 3, page 39

- meet a famous person
- see a famous singer / group perform live
- play in a group
- sing in a choir
- learn a musical instrument
- be on TV / in the newspaper / in a play
- win a prize / a competition / any money
- go to the ballet / the opera / a classical concert
- visit a country / a city / a famous monument
- climb a high mountain / building
- go parachuting / skiing / sailing
- drive a bus / a lorry / a sports car
- ride a horse / a camel / a motorbike
- break your arm / leg / something very valuable
- lose a lot of money / a credit card / an important document / your mobile phone
- steal anything!

Module 4: Vocabulary 1, exercise 3, page 40

LIFE EVENTS QUIZ

1 Which phrases need *a*? (7 points)

buy house   get degree   get job   move house
go to university   leave home   start school

2 Which doesn't take *get*? (2 points)

children   divorced   engaged   promoted

3 Match the verbs with the noun/adjective they were used with on page 40. (7 points)

a	become	an exam
b	bring up	an exam
c	fail	children
d	lose	a house
e	make	money
f	pass	your job
g	rent	very successful

4 Complete the sentences with *to, with* or *from*. Use your mini-dictionary to help you. (4 points)

a He got married _____ his son's ex-wife!
b Unfortunately, he's just split up _____ his girlfriend.
c She's been engaged _____ her boyfriend for over four years.
d She got divorced _____ her first husband after just six months.

TOTAL ── 20

Module 4: Writing, exercise 5, page 45

Pavel Cizek is from the Czech Republic, and is about to continue his studies in the UK. He is looking for summer work in the travel, tourism or translation industries before continuing his studies. Read the notes and write out his Curriculum Vitae.

Pavel was born in the Czech Republic, on 23rd April 1981. He is not married. His present address is 61 Wilmslow Gardens, London NW9 4DG (telephone 0205 849 7594). His mobile telephone number is 07316 5924897 and his e-mail address is p.cizek@mailshot.com.

He has just obtained a Master's degree in Computer Science at Charles University, Prague and he intends to continue his studies in the UK by doing a postgraduate course in Computer Science. Apart from his studies, he has worked extensively in the areas of travel, tourism and translation. He has worked as an interpreter and tour guide in his native city of Prague, and has an official Tourist Guide Certificate awarded by the Business and Travel Institute, Prague. He has done work translating and interpreting for various language agencies and magazines in the Czech Republic since 2000.

His mother tongue is Czech. He is fluent in English and German, and speaks some Russian. He is computer literate and has good mathematical and personal skills. He has a full clean driving licence.

Module 4: Wordspot, exercise 3, page 44

Student A

Read through the questions below and check you understand them. Then take turns with Student B asking and answering questions. Make a note of his/her answers to these questions.

a Who do you **take after** more – your mother or your father?
b Do you always **take notes** in your English lessons?
c When was the last time you were **taken out** for a meal? Who paid? What was the meal like?
d Are there any sports you would like to **take up**? What are they?
e Have you ever **taken part in** a public performance or concert? Where was it? What happened?
f If the leader of your country fell ill, who would **take over**?

Module 5: Task, exercise 1, page 54

Brigitte Schumann

Age: 33
Nationality: Austrian
Mother tongue: German
Marital status: divorced

Skills/Background
- Eight years as assistant manager of hotel in a ski-resort
- Speaks good French and English
- Good skier
- Driver
- Good computer skills

Interview notes
- Recently divorced and wants a complete change in her life
- Has seven-year-old daughter and four-year-old son – she will bring them with her if she gets the job
- Seems very efficient (a bit cold?)
- Obviously has very strong personality and opinions

Module 5: Reading, exercise 3, page 48

Scores		
1 a 0	b 1	c 2
2 a 2	b 1	c 0
3 a 1	b 2	c 0
4 a 0	b 2	c 1
5 a 0	b 1	c 2
6 a 1	b 2	c 0
7 a 2	b 0	c 1
8 a 1	b 0	c 2
9 a 0	b 2	c 1
10 a 0	b 2	c 1
11 a 2	b 1	c 0
12 a 1	b 0	c 2

Assessment

20–24 If you are not already a success, there is no doubt that you will be one day. You have got all the qualities necessary for success, including ambition, determination and imagination. Take care not to become a workaholic – if you do, it will affect your family, yourself and, in the end, your happiness.

8–19 You want to be successful and have got many of the necessary qualities. But perhaps you need a little more self-confidence to believe that you can and will succeed. Perhaps you dream about success, but do not really believe it will happen. Making those dreams come true is not easy, but it is certainly possible.

0–8 You need a lot of hard work to make a success of your chosen career, but is this really what you want in life? Perhaps you believe that happiness is more important than success. Maybe you prefer a happy family life, a steady job and a regular salary. Remember everyone is different and happiness does not come from trying to become something that you do not really want to be.

Module 4: Wordspot, exercise 3, page 44

Student B

Read through the questions below and check you understand them. Then take turns with Student A asking and answering questions. Make a note of his/her answers to these questions.

a   Can you remember the last time someone **took your picture**? Who was it? Where were you?

b   Have you ever **taken care of** a small baby? Who was it?

c   What do you think is the best month to **take a holiday**? Why?

d   How old do you have to be to **take your driving test**? Have you taken yours yet?

e   Which shoe do you usually **take off** first – the right one or the left one?

f   When was the last time you **took a train**? Where did you go? What happened?

Module 8: Practice, exercise 3, page 83

Team A

a)   Choose eight words or phrases and write questions for the words using relative clauses.

air traffic controller	answering machine
beach	call centre
cartoon	chain of restaurants
colleague	costumes
hero	neighbour
rainforest	shopping mall
slippers	temporary job
trainee manager	

Example:
What do you call a person who ...?

b)   Now take turns to test team B. Your teacher will give you two points for a good question and two points for a correct answer to Team B's questions. The team with the most points at the end wins.

Module 5: Practice, exercise 3, page 51

1 Write down three arrangements or appointments that you have got for the next week or two.
2 Tell your partner about your hopes or plans for your next holiday.
3 Write down how you think you'll spend next Sunday morning.
4 Tell your partner two domestic tasks you are planning to do this weekend.
5 Write down where you are due to be after this lesson.
6 Write down one good intention you have got for this week.
7 Tell your partner about two things that you are hoping to buy in the next few months.
8 Tell your partner about your family's plans for the next year or so.
9 Write down two ambitions you have got that are not connected with work.
10 Tell your partner what you think your teacher is about to do.
11 Guess your partner's plans for this evening.
12 Predict two things you'll do in your next lesson.

Module 5: Task, exercise 1, page 54

(John Bailey)

Age: 55
Nationality: Canadian
Mother tongue: English
Marital status: single

Skills/Background
• Thirty-five years in hotel business (including fifteen years as assistant manager of Toronto Hotel)
• Excellent French
• Good skier
• Driver
• Computer experience

Interview notes
• Retired from Hilton two years ago because of nervous problems (doctor's letter says now fine)
• Has never worked with children but has many nephews and nieces and loves children
• Seems friendly and considerate

Module 9: Real life, exercise 3a, page 100

Student A

	China	United Arab Emirates
Area	9,326,410 km²	
Population	1.3 billion	
Average number of visitors (per year)	23.7 million	
Minimum/Maximum temperature	-25°C – 33°C.	
Ethnic groups	93% Han Chinese 7% other	
Kilometres of road	1,530,000 km	
Number of full-time students	5.8 million	

Module 10: Practice, exercise 2a, page 103

Solution to puzzle B
Before the party began, someone had put some poisoned ice cube into the punch. The man who left early had been the first person to try the punch. At this time, the ice hadn't melted so the poison hadn't got into the punch. Everyone else drank the punch when the ice had already melted.

Module 12: Practice, exercise 3, page 123

Student A

Gill and George

Gill, a widow in her fifties, was devoted to her seven year-old cat, George. However, one day, George was run over by a car. When she took him to the vet she was told that the operations to save him would cost €2,000, but that they might not be successful. As Gill did not have that much money, her twenty-five-year-old daughter agreed to pay with her credit card. Gill said she would pay her daughter back month by month.
Unfortunately, George died.

Module 7: Practice, exercise b, page 73

a) Read the situations. Write two or three things you might say in each one, using *I'll* and the phrases in the box.

babysit …	go and buy some …
phone the …	call you a …
help you with …	phone you …
carry … for you …	lend you my …
put on some …	come with you to …
look after …	take you …
cook the …	make you a …
take you out for …	

1   Your friend calls to say he can't go to a party tonight because he's got a lot of homework to do. You've already finished yours. What do you say to your friend?

2   You are having dinner in a restaurant with a group of friends. Suddenly the person next to you tells you she feels really ill. What do you say to her?

3   You are at a friend's house with a group of people, but nobody seems to be enjoying themselves. Your friend looks more and more worried. What do you say to him/her?

4   You find you've won €500 in a competition. What do you say to your friends?

5   Your sister and her husband have been invited to a party, but can't go because they can't find a babysitter. What do you say to them?

6   You see your teacher in the corridor carrying a big pile of dictionaries. What do you say to him/her?

7   Your mum comes home from work with a really bad headache. What do you say to her?

b) Give your sentences to another pair. Which do they think is the best answer for each situation?

Module 10: Practice, exercise 2a, page 103

Solution to puzzle A

The man had been out fishing and had caught an unusually large fish. He was so excited that he'd phoned his wife to tell her about it. Unfortunately, as he was describing the fish, he stretched out his arms to demonstrate how large the fish was, and had smashed through the glass on either side of the phone box, and had tragically bled to death as a result.

Module 8: Practice, exercise 3, page 82

Team B

a)   Choose eight words or phrases and write questions for the words using relative clauses.

advert	harbour
songwriter	acquaintance
identical twins	stranger
bill (in a restaurant)	karaoke bar
wallpaper	firefighter
laptop	monument
graduate	market
theme park	

Example:
What do you call a person who …?

b)   Now take turns to test Team A. Your teacher will give you two points for a good question and two points for a correct answer to Team A's questions. The team with the most points at the end wins.

Module 9, Real life, exercise 3a, page 100

Student B

	China	United Arab Emirates
Area		83,600 km²
Population		2,400,000
Average number of visitors (per year)		1.8 million
Minimum/Maximum temperature		15°C – 40°C
Ethnic groups		50% Asian 42% Arab 8% other
Kilometres of road		3,000 km
Number of full-time students		10,641

Module 9: Wordspot (*make*), exercise 4, page 98

1. What could you do if you suddenly feel hungry in the middle of the day? (4,1,8)
2. Shoes are usually more comfortable if they're ... (4,2,7)
3. If you drop your food all over the floor, you will ... (4,1,4)
4. A lot of cars and electrical equipment are ... (4,2,5)
5. You can use the 'delete' button on a computer or typewriter if you ... (4,1,6)
6. When children are playing they usually ... (4,1,5)
7. A successful businessman has to ... (4,1,6)
8. Sometimes very sad films ... (4,3,3)
9. If you are studying some difficult grammar, your teacher tries to ... (4,2,5)
10. If you want to go to the doctor's or dentist's, you usually need to ... (4,2,11)
11. If a friend comes round to visit you, you might ... (4,1,3,2,6)
12. If someone in the street shouted something rude at you, it would probably ... (4,3,5)

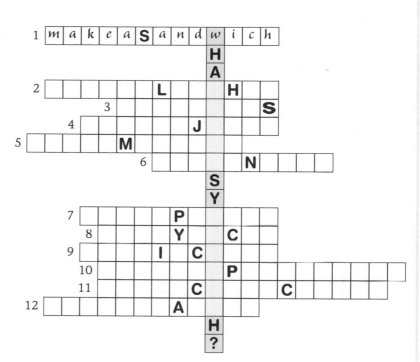

Module 5: Task, exercise 1, page 54

Anne-Sophie Martin

Age: 21
Nationality: Swiss
Mother tongue: French
Marital status: single

Skills/Background
- Two years as nanny
- Two years as receptionist in a hotel in Geneva
- Good skier
- Very good German, good English
- Computer experience
- Doesn't drive

Interview notes
- Rather quiet (shy?), but very nice
- Experience with small children
- Excellent references from previous employers

Module 12: Practice, exercise 3, page 123

Student B

Jackie and her children

Jackie and her three children, eight-year-old Lucas, and eighteen-month-old twins, were driving to visit a friend on a remote country farm. In the middle of nowhere, Jackie's car broke down. Her mobile had run out, and she had not brought the twins' pushchair with her. She knew that she had passed a pub less than a kilometre before. After waiting half an hour for someone to go past, she locked the car and left Lucas to look after the sleeping twins, while she ran to get help. When she returned thirty minutes later, all three children were crying, but perfectly safe.

Module 1

(A) Verbs *be*, *have* and *do*

Be, *have* and *do* can all be used as the **main verb** in a sentence.
*My brother **is** still at school.*
*We **have** lunch at about one o'clock.*
*I usually **do** my homework in my bedroom.*

1 Auxiliary verbs to form tenses

We also use *be*, *have* and *do* to form tenses, questions and negative forms, and on their own (in short answers, question tags, etc.). In this case they are called **auxiliary verbs**.

a   We use *be* (+ verb + *-ing*) to form **continuous** tenses.
Present continuous: *He**'s studying** to become a doctor.*
Past continuous: *I **was talking** to Charles the other day.*

b   We use *have* (+ past participle) to form **perfect** tenses:
Present perfect: *We**'ve been** here for three months.*
Past perfect: *The film **had started** when we got there.*

c   We use *do* in **simple** tenses (in the question and negative forms).
Present simple: ***Does** all your family live round here?*
Past simple: *I **didn't** get your e-mail.*

> **REMEMBER!**
> 1   **Third person singular forms**
>   do → he / she / it does
>   have → he / she / it has
>
> 2   **Contractions**
>   She **is** waiting → She**'s** waiting
>   You **are** joking → You**'re** joking
>   He **has** left → He**'s** left

2 Auxiliary verbs in questions and negatives

a   In continuous and perfect tenses, **questions** are formed by inverting the subject and auxiliary verb.
***Is he** studying to become a doctor?*
*How long **have your brother and sister** lived here?*

b   **Negatives** are formed by adding *not* to the verb. We often shorten this to *n't*.
*She **is not** working → She **isn't** working.*
*He **has not** come home → He **hasn't** come home.*

> **REMEMBER!**
> 1   With modal verbs, we form questions by inverting the subject and the verb.
>   ***Can I** come in?*
> 2   We form negatives with *not*.
>   *I **mustn't** stay long.*

3 Auxiliaries used on their own

a   **Short answers**
These can make the speaker sound more polite/interested.
A: *Have you been here before?*
B: *Yes, I **have**.*

We also use auxiliaries to avoid repeating long sentences.
A: *Does your family live in Paris?*
B: *My father **does**, but my mother **doesn't**.*

b   **Short questions and question tags**
A: *My brother's gone to live in Australia.*
B: ***Has he?***

*You were at home last night, **weren't** you?*

(B) Present simple and Present continuous

1 Present simple

Positive form	Negative form	Question form
I / you / we / they **work**	I / you / we / they **don't** (= do not) **work**	**Do** I / you / we **work**?
he / she / it **works**	he / she / it **doesn't** (= does not) **work**	**Does** he / she / it **work**?

We use the Present simple for:
a   repeated actions or habits.
*We **go** out every Saturday night.*

b   something we see as permanent.
*My sister **works** in a bank.*

c   describing a state that doesn't change.
*I **look** like my mother.*

2 Present continuous

Positive form	Negative form	Question form
I**'m** (= I am) **working**	I**'m not** (= am not) **working**	**Am** I **working**?
you / we / they**'re** (= are) **working**	you / we / they **aren't** (= are not) **working**	**Are** you / we / they **working**?
he / she / it**'s** (= is) **working**	he / she / it **isn't** (= is not) **working**	**Is** he / she / it **working**?

We use the Present continuous for:
a   things in progress now, at the moment of speaking.
*The sun **is shining** and it's a beautiful day!*

b   temporary actions or situations that are happening 'around now'.
*I**'m reading** a very good book at the moment.*

c   describing a situation which is changing.
*People **are working** longer hours nowadays.*

3 Present simple versus Present continuous

Sometimes either form is possible. Compare the following pairs of sentences.
•   *Paola is the student who **sits** at the back of the class. (= she always does this)*
*Paola is the student who **is sitting** at the back of the class. (= she is there now)*
•   *My parents **stay** at the Metropole Hotel. (= every time they visit the town)*
*My parents **are staying** at the Metropole Hotel. (= they are there at the moment)*

4 'State' versus 'action' verbs

Some verbs are rarely found in continuous forms. These are verbs which describe 'states' (things which stay the same) rather than 'actions' (things which can change). Some of the most common are verbs:
a   connected with emotions: *hate, like, love, want.*
b   connected with understanding: *believe, know, prefer, understand.*
c   connected with possession and unchanging qualities: *belong, cost, weigh.*
d   connected with the senses: *hear, smell, sound, taste.*

Module 2

A Past simple

Positive form	Negative form	Question form
I / you / he / she / it / we / they **worked**	I / you / he / she / it / we / they **didn't work**	**Did** I / you / he / she / it / we they **work?**
I / you / he / she / it / we / they **left**	I / you / he / she / it / we / they **didn't** (= **did not**) **leave**	**Did** I / you / he / she / it / we / they **leave?**
Regular verbs: base form + **-ed** **Irregular verbs:** see list of irregular verbs on page 155	**Regular and irregular verbs:** subject + **didn't** (= **did not**) + base form	**Regular and irregular verbs:** **did** + subject + base form

1 We use the Past simple for states and actions which happened in the past. We often say **when** the action happened.
*I **saw** someone famous **yesterday**.*

2 The action can be short or long, single or repeated.
*I **dropped** the glass and it **broke** on the floor.*
*He **took** the train to work **every day**.*

3 We also use the Past simple to talk about states in the past.
*When I **was** young, I **loved** playing with my toys.*

B Past continuous

Positive form	Negative form	Question form
I / he / she / it **was working**	I / he / she / it **wasn't working**	**Was** I / he / she / it **working?**
you / we / they **were working**	you / we / they **weren't** (= **were not**) **working**	**Were** you / we / they **working?**

1 We use the Past continuous for actions **in progress** at a time in the past.
*I **was living** in London then.*

Sometimes this includes a specific time or another (completed past action).
*We **were having** breakfast at eight o'clock.*
*I **heard** the news on the radio while I **was driving** home.*

2 The Past continuous often describes the situation or the background to a story. We use the Past simple for the main events.
*The sun **was shining** and I **was walking** along the road. Suddenly someone **shouted** to me ...*

3 Sometimes the Past continuous action is interrupted.
*They **were talking** about me when I **walked** in the room. (= they stopped talking)*

4 We use the Past continuous for actions we see as incomplete.
*I **read** a book about Italy. (= I read it all)*
*I **was reading** a book about Italy on the plane. (= I probably didn't read it all)*

Similarities with other continuous forms

1 Continuous forms describe activities in progress.
*He**'s reading** the newspaper. (= he's in the middle of it)*
*He **was reading** the newspaper. (= he was in the middle of it)*

2 We use continuous forms to emphasise that situations are temporary.
*She**'s staying** with us at the moment. (= temporary in the present)*
*I **was sleeping** on a friend's sofa. (= temporary in the past)*

3 We do not use continuous forms with state verbs.
*I **hated** vegetables when I **was** young.*
not:
I was hating vegetables when I was being young.

C Contrasting past and present

1 used to

Positive form	Negative form	Question form
I / you / he / she / it / we / they **used to** work	I / you / he / she / we / they **didn't use to** work	**Did** I / you / he / she / it / we / they **use to** work?

a We use *used to* for habits and states in the past.
*I **used to go** to the gym every day.*
*My sister **used to** have really long hair.*

There is no equivalent form in the present.
*I **usually go** to my parents' house on Sundays.*
not:
I use to go to my parents' house on Sundays.

b We can always use the Past simple instead of *used to*.
*I **went** to the gym every day.*
*My sister **had** really long hair.*

2 not ... any longer / not ... any more

These phrases mean that an action or state was true in the past, but is not true now.
*I **used to** play volleyball, but I don't any longer.*
*Andrew **doesn't** drink coffee **any more** – it gives him a headache.*

3 still

We use *still* when we want to emphasise that an action or state has not stopped or changed, but continues up to the present.
*I **still** remember how frightened I was.*

D Short questions to show interest

1 These are formed by inverting the auxiliary verb and the subject in the first sentence.
A: *Shirley's having a baby!*
B: ***Is she?***

2 In Present simple and Past simple affirmative sentences where there is no auxiliary verb, we use *do, does* or *did* with the appropriate pronoun.
A: *Her parents went to China last year for their holidays.*
B: ***Did they?***

Module 3

A Comparative and superlative adjectives

1 One-syllable adjectives and two-syllable adjectives ending in -y

adjective	comparative adjective + **-er**	superlative the + adjective + **-est**
old	old**er**	the old**est**
big	bigg**er**	the bigg**est**
large	larg**er**	the larg**est**
friendly	friendli**er**	the friendli**est**

2 Other two-syllable adjectives and longer adjectives

crowded	more crowded	the most crowded
boring	more boring	the most boring
interesting	more interesting	the most interesting
polluted	more polluted	the most polluted

3 Irregular forms

bad	**worse**	the **worst**
good	**better**	the **best**
far	**further/farther**	the **furthest/farthest**

> **REMEMBER!**
> 1 With short vowels the final consonant doubles.
> thin → thi**nner** → the thi**nnest**
>
> 2 If the adjective ends in -e, we only add -r or -st.
> fine → fine**r** → the fine**st**
>
> 3 -y changes to -ier and -iest.
> busy → bus**ier** → the bus**iest**

B Large and small differences

1 If there is a large difference between two objects, we can use *far*, *much* and *a lot*.

Russia is | **far** / **a lot** / **much** | **bigger** than Belgium.

2 For small differences, we can use *a little (bit)* or *slightly*.

France is | **a little** / **a little bit** / **slightly** | **bigger** than Spain.

C Common phrases with superlatives

1 by far the most ... / -est

Brazil is **by far the largest** country in South America.

2 one of the most ... / -est

Baghdad is **one of the oldest cities** in the world.

3 the second / third most ... / -est

Birmingham is **the second biggest** city in England.

4 the least

The coach is **the least expensive** way to get to the airport.

> **REMEMBER!**
> The superlative phrases are often followed by *in* + place.
> Buenos Aires is the biggest city **in** Argentina.

D Other ways of making comparisons

1 not as ... as

Silver **isn't as** expensive **as** gold.

If there is only a small difference, we can use *quite*.
Linda **isn't quite as** tall **as** her sister.

2 Comparing two things which are the same

Susan is **as** tall **as** her mother.

3 less

Less is the opposite of *more*.
Petrol is **less expensive than** it is in Europe.

4 Making comparisons with nouns

Rome has **more historic buildings** than any city I know.
There's **less space** in this room than in the other one.
There were **fewer** people in my old class.

We use *fewer* with countable and *less* with uncountable nouns.

5 Other useful expressions for comparing things

a If two things are nearly the same:
Their new car is **very similar** to their old one.
The train times are **about the same as** before.

b If there is no difference between two things:
His watch is **exactly the same as** mine.

c If there is a small difference between two things:
The new timetable is **slightly different from** the previous one.

d If there is a big difference between two things:
The new stadium is **completely different from** the old one.

Module 4

A Present perfect simple

Positive form	Negative form	Question form
I / you / we / they**'ve** (= **have**) worked	I / you / we / they **haven't** (= **have not**) worked	**Have** I / you we / worked?
he / she / it**'s** (= **has**) worked	he / she / it **hasn't** (= has not) worked	**Has** he / she / it worked?
subject + **have / has** + past participle	subject + **haven't / hasn't** + past participle	**Have / Has** + subject + **past participle**

We use the Present perfect to talk about the **past and the present together**. The past action or situation is connected to the present in various ways.

1 The state or action continues from the past to the present.
I've known her for many years. (= I still know her now)

2 The results of the past action are important in the present.
He**'s lost his key**. (= he doesn't have it now)

3 The time reference in the sentences includes the present.
He**'s been** ill all this week. (= this week isn't finished)

4 When we mean 'in my whole life': we do not give a specific time.
I've been to Spain lots of times. (= in my whole life)

B Present perfect versus Past simple

1 We use the Past simple for **completed actions** that are in the past.
*Marilyn Monroe **was** married three times.* (= she is dead)
*As a child, I **spent** a lot of time with my grandparents.* (= I am an adult now)

Compare these to similar Present perfect sentences.
*My friend **has been married** three times – and she's only thirty!* (= her life is not finished)
*I**'ve spent** a lot of time abroad this year.* (= this year is not finished)

2 Whether or not we use the Present perfect or Past simple often depends on **how we see the action**. If we see it as related to the present, we use the Present perfect. If we see it as finished and in the past, we use the **Past simple**, even if we do not mention the time.
Compare the following sentences.
*John**'s had** an accident! – they've taken him to hospital.*
*John **had** an accident – but he's okay now.*

C Time words with the Present perfect and Past simple

1 Time words often found with the Past simple

a ago: *five minutes ago, three months ago, a thousand years ago*
b questions with *when*: ***When** did you see him?*
c specific times in the past: *yesterday, last night, last week*

2 Time words often found with the Present perfect

a periods of time which are still in progress: *all my life, this week, this year*
b *already, yet* (= before now)
c *ever* (= any time in the past until now)
Have you ever met anyone famous?

> **REMEMBER!**
> We use *yet* in questions and negatives to talk about actions that haven't happened in the past, but we think could happen in the future.
>
> Compare the following sentences.
> *Maria **hasn't phoned**.* (= and maybe she won't)
> *Maria **hasn't phoned yet**.* (= but she probably will later)

There are many words or phrases which can take either the Present perfect or the Past simple according to the context.
*I **spoke** to Robert **this morning**.* (= it is afternoon/evening now)
*He **was** in prison **for many years**.* (= he is not in prison now)
*I**'ve never** been to China.* (= in my life until now)

D Present perfect continuous

Positive form	Negative form	Question form
I / you / we / they**'ve been** (= have been) working	I / you / we / they **haven't been** (= have not been) working	**Have** I / you / we / they **been** working?
he / she / it**'s been** (= has been) working	he / she / it **hasn't** (= has not been) working	**Has** he / she / it **been** working?
subject + **have / has** + **been** + -*ing*	subject + **haven't / hasn't** + **been** + -*ing*	**Have / Has** + subject + **been** + -*ing*

The Present perfect continuous is like the Present perfect simple in all the ways mentioned in part A. However, we use the Present perfect continuous if:

1 we want to emphasise that the action is long or repeated.
*She**'s been trying** to pass her driving test for years.*

2 the action is in progress / not complete.
Compare the following sentences.
*I**'ve been doing** some work.* (= perhaps it is not finished)
*I**'ve done** my homework.* (= it is finished)

3 the action is temporary.
*He**'s been working** in a bar this summer.* (= but afterwards he's going to university)
Like other continuous forms, we do not use it with 'state' verbs.
*I**'ve known** Anne all my life.*
not:
I've been knowing Anne all my life.

> **REMEMBER!**
> We often use *for* and *since* with the Present perfect and Present perfect continuous.
>
> We use *for* to talk about a period of time. (= how long?)
> *I've known him **for several years**.*
> We use *since* to talk about a point of time. (= when?)
> *I've known him **since 2002**.*

Module 5

A Future plans and intentions

1 *going to*

am / is / are + going to + verb		
Positive form	Negative form	Question form
I**'m** / you**'re**, etc. **going to help**	I**'m not** / you **aren't** etc. **going to help**	**Is** he / **Are** you **going to help?**

We use *going to* to talk about present intentions about the future. This can be the near future, or the more distant future.
*I**'m going to have** a bath in a few minutes.* (= the near future)
*Lucy says she**'s going to be** a ballet dancer one day.* (= the distant future)

2 Present continuous

a We use the Present continuous to talk about things we have already arranged for the future.
*I**'m meeting** Tony this weekend.* (= I've arranged this)
*What **are** you **doing** tonight?* (= asking about your plans)

b In some cases, it doesn't matter whether we use the Present continuous or *going to*.
*I**'m playing** football this evening.*
*I**'m going to play** football this evening.*
*I**'m going** shopping this afternoon.*
*I**'m going (to go)*** shopping this afternoon.*
* Some people think it is bad English to repeat *go* like this.

In other cases, there is a clear difference in meaning.
*We**'re going to get** married one day.* (= an intention)
*We**'re getting** married soon.* (= the wedding is arranged)

147

3 *will*

Positive form	Negative form	Question form
I / you / he / she, etc. **'ll** (= will) **+ verb**	I / you / he / she, etc. **won't** (= will not) **+ verb**	**Will** I / you / he / she, etc. **+ verb?**
I'll see her.	*I won't see her.*	*Will I see her?*

We use *will* for talking about things that we think will happen **without** any special plan or arrangement. We predict they will happen or see them as a future fact.

> *I can give it to her – I'll see her at work.* (= I don't need to arrange this)
>
> *I know I'll forget if I don't write it down.* (= this is a future fact / I predict this will happen)

> **REMEMBER!**
> We can use *shall* for *I* and *we*. We normally use this in the question form to make offers or suggestions.
>
> Compare the following pairs of sentences.
> * **Will I** meet you at the station? (= asking about a future fact)
>   **Shall I** meet you at the station? (= an offer)
> * **Will we** have dinner at the hotel? (= asking about a future fact)
>   **Shall we** have dinner at the hotel? (= a suggestion)

4 Other ways to talk about the future

a Verbs
* *hope: We**'re hoping to buy** a flat later this year.*
* *plan: I**'m planning to sell** my scooter.*
* *think: We**'re thinking of having** a party soon.*
* *want: I **want to finish** this by tonight.*

b Phrases
* *due to:* We use *due to* for something that is formally arranged.
  *The plane**'s due to take off** in about twenty minutes.*
* *(be) about to:* when something will happen very soon or immediately.
  *Jill**'s about to** have a baby.*

B Future clauses with if, *when*, etc.

Even when we are talking about the future, we use a present verb form after *if, unless, when, before, after, as soon as, until, once, next time,* etc.

> **If** she **fails** her exam again, she'll be really upset.
> I won't do anything **unless** you **phone**.
> **When** I **find** it, I'll bring it for you.
> Remember to turn off the lights **before** you **leave**.
> **As soon as** we **get** home, I'm going to have a shower.
> I'm going to stay here **until** I **find** somewhere to live.
> **Once** we finish the decorating, we'll invite you round for dinner.

Notice that in the other part of the sentence, a future verb form is used (*will, going to,* etc.)

Module 6

A -ed/-ing adjectives

1 *-ing* adjectives

Adjectives ending in *-ing* describe the thing or person that has an effect on us.

> *Today's lesson was very **interesting**.* (= the lesson interested me)

2 *-ed* adjectives

Adjectives ending in *-ed* describe our feelings about something or someone.

> *I felt **bored** at the party.* (= I found the party boring)

B The passive

Simple tenses

	Positive form	Negative form	Question
Present	It**'s** (= is) **made**	It **isn't** (= is not) **made**	**Is** it **made?**
Past	It **was made**	It **wasn't** (= was not) **made**	**Was** it **made?**
Present perfect	It**'s** (= has) **been made**	It **hasn't** (= has not) **been made**	**Has** it **been made?**
Future	It**'ll be made**	It **won't** (= will not) **be made**	**Will** it **be made?**
	subject + verb 'to be' + past participle	verb 'to be' + not + past participle	verb 'to be' + subject + past participle

Continuous tenses

	Positive form	Negative form	Question form
Present	It**'s** (= is) **being made**	It **isn't being made**	**Is** it **being made?**
Past	It **was being made**	It **wasn't** (= was not) **being made**	**Was** it **being made?**
	subject + verb 'to be' + *being* + past participle	subject + verb 'to be' + *not being* + past participle	verb 'to be' + subject + *being* + past participle

1 The difference between the active and passive

In active sentences, the subject is the 'doer' of the verb (the person who makes the action happen).

> The firefighter **rescued** the child.
> (subject)   (verb)

In passive sentences, the 'doer' of the verb is not the subject.

> The child **was rescued** by the firefighter.
> (subject)   (verb)

> **REMEMBER!**
> If we mention the 'doer' of the verb we use *by* + the person.
> *The building was designed **by Sir Andrew Rowley**.*

2 Reasons for using the passive

a to focus on the main topic of the sentence
The beginning of the sentence normally tells us what the sentence is mainly about. Compare the following sentences.
Jackson won the Olympic gold medal. (= the sentence is mainly about Jackson)

The Olympic gold medal was won by Jackson. (= the sentence is mainly about the Olympic gold medal)

b **if the person who does the verb is unknown or unimportant**
*My handbag **has been stolen**.* (= we don't know who did this)
*The Petronas Towers **were built** in 1996.* (= we are interested in **when** they were built, not who built them)

c **the doer of the verb is obvious, or 'people in general'**
*Dozens of people **were arrested**.* (= it is obvious that the police arrested them)
*Spanish **is spoken** in more than twenty countries.* (= it is not necessary to say 'by people')

> **REMEMBER!**
> We often use the passive in more **formal** contexts (e.g. news reports), and less when we are speaking informally. Compare the following sentences.
>
> *A new parking scheme **is being introduced** in the town centre.* (= from a news report)
> *I hear **they're introducing** a new parking scheme in the town centre.* (= from a conversation)

3 Verbs often used in the passive

a verbs related to accidents/injuries, etc.
was injured / was killed / was damaged / was destroyed, etc.

b verbs related to crime
was arrested / was sentenced / was found guilty / was sent to prison, etc.

c verbs related to inventions, books, films, etc.
was invented by / was discovered by / was produced by / was directed by / was written by, etc.

C Extreme adjectives

1 *Absolutely* can only be used with extreme adjectives
absolutely freezing not: ~~absolutely cold~~

2 *Very* can only be used with non-extreme adjectives
very cold not: ~~very freezing~~

3 *Really* can be used with both types of adjectives:
really freezing, really cold

Module 7

A Polite requests

1 Asking if you can do things (asking for permission)

Asking	Saying yes	Saying no
Can I ...? Could I ...? Could I possibly ...?	Yes, sure. Yes, of course. That's fine. Certainly.	Well, I'm afraid (+ reason) ... Well, the problem is that ...
Is it all right if I ...? Do you think I could ...?		
Do you mind if I ...?	No, not at all. Of course not.	Sorry, but ...

2 Asking other people to do things (making requests)

Asking	Saying yes	Saying no
Can you ...? Could you ...? Is it all right if I ...? Do you think you could ...?	Yes, sure. Yes, of course. That's fine. Certainly.	Well, I'm afraid (+ reason) ... Well, the problem is that ...
Will you ...? Would you ...?		Sorry, but ...
Do you mind -*ing*? Would you mind -*ing*?	No, not at all. Of course not.	

- We use *Do you mind if I ...?, Could I possibly ...?, Could you possibly ...?, Do you think you could ...?* when we want to sound particularly polite.
- *Could/Would you?* are a little more polite than *Can/Will you?* In all these questions, however, intonation is more important than the words you use if you want to be polite.

> **REMEMBER!**
> 1 After *Would you mind ...?* we use the -*ing* form of the verb.
>
> 2 *Would you mind ...?* and *Do you mind ...?* mean 'Is it a problem for you?' so the polite answer is no!
>
> A: **Do you mind getting** some bread on your way home?
> B: **No, not at all.**

B *will* for instant decisions and responses

1 If we make a decision at the moment of speaking we use *will*.
*I suddenly feel a bit tired ... I think I**'ll stay** in tonight.*

2 Very often these decisions are offers.
*Don't worry – I**'ll give** you a lift.*

This use of *will* is often contrasted with *going to* (used if you've already decided). Compare the following pairs of sentences.

A: *Do you want to play squash tomorrow sometime?*
B: *Sorry, I can't – we**'re going to paint** the living room this weekend.* (= they've already decided do this)

A: *Do you want to go and have a quick coffee?*
B: *Good idea ... I**'ll finish** this later.* (= speaker decides at that moment)

3 For instant decisions and responses, we always use the contracted form *'ll* and not the full forms *will/shall*.

C Making generalisations

1 Impersonal or 'empty' *it*

We often use *it* + adjective + infinitive to describe a general situation or experience.
> *It's **normal to** have lunch around twelve.*
> *It's **difficult to** study in such hot weather.*

In this pattern, we talk about people using *for*.
> *It's common **for people** to eat outside in summer.*
> *It's difficult **for young people** to find accommodation.*

2 *tend to* + verb

We use *tend to* + verb to say that something often happens.
> People in the country **tend to** be very friendly.

Notice that the negative form is *tend not to* + verb.
> Older people here **tend not to** go out in large groups.

3 *most people, a lot of people, not many people, very few people*

Notice that *people* is a plural noun.
> **Most people** live in flats rather than houses.
> **A lot of people** go to the coast at the weekends.
> **Not many people** stay in the city in August.
> **Very few people** speak a foreign language.

Module 8

Ⓐ Defining relative clauses

Defining relative clauses give us information about things, people, possessions, places and times using a **relative pronoun**.

1 Things (*that, which* or –)

> A machine **which** converts information.
> A calculator is a little machine **that** does arithmetic.

> **REMEMBER!**
> What is not possible here.
> A calculator is a machine ~~what~~ does arithmetic.

2 People (*who, that* or –)

> A person **who** doesn't use technology.
> A newsreader is a person **that** reads the news.

The pronoun *that* is less common than *who* here.

> **REMEMBER!**
> Notice that in all the examples above, *which, who* and *that* are the **subject** of the relative clause, so they cannot be left out.
>
> We can leave out *which, who* and *that* if they are the **object** of the relative clause.
> There are people (**who** / **that**) you can phone if you have a problem.
> Gloves are things (**which** / **that**) you wear in cold weather.

3 Possessions (*whose*)

> He's a person **whose** life is dominated by computers. (= his life)
> An orphan is a child **whose** parents have died. (= his/her parents)

4 Places (*where, which / that* + preposition)

We can refer to places in the following ways:
> This is the house **where** I grew up.
> This is the house (**which** / **that**) I grew up in.

Notice that if we have a preposition at the end of the sentence, the relative pronoun can be omitted.

5 Times (*when*)

> The evening's a time **when** we can all relax.
> Saturday's the day **when** I tidy the flat.

Ⓑ Quantifiers (*a few, a lot of,* etc.)

With uncountable nouns only	With countable nouns only	With both uncountable countable nouns
(too) much a bit of a little	(too) many one or two several a couple (of) a few loads of	(not) any (not) enough a lot of / lots of no plenty of some

1 *some* and *any*

Some means 'a limited quantity or number of something'. It is often used in positive sentences.
> I like **some** pop music. (= but not all)

We can also use *some* in the question form when we make requests and offers.
> Can you give **some** information about excursions? (= request)
> Would you like **some** more soup? (= offer)

Any is often used in negatives and questions.
> We haven't got **any** milk in the fridge.
> Are there **any** questions?

2 *a lot of* and *much / many*

A lot of is usually used in positive sentences. It is common in speech or informal writing.
> We sell **a lot of** imported goods.

In informal speech and writing, *much* and *many* are generally used in questions and negatives.
> We'd better hurry – we haven't got **much** time.
> Are there **many** clothes shops in your town?

3 *too much / many*

We use *too much* and *too many* when there is more of something than we need.
> Let's go somewhere else. There are **too many** people in here. (= it's too crowded)
> Do you want some of my pizza? There's **too much** for me. (= I can't eat it all)

4 *enough*

We use *enough* to mean 'as much as we need'.
> Have we got **enough** chairs for everyone?

5 *plenty of*

We use *plenty of* to mean 'more than enough'. It has a positive meaning.
> Don't worry – we've got **plenty of** time before your train leaves.
> We've got **plenty of** sandwiches for everyone – we don't need any more.

Module 9

(A) Making predictions

1 Using *will* or *won't*

We often use adverbs with *will* and *won't* to show how certain we are about something.

> Our team **will probably lose** on Saturday.
> I think he'**ll almost certainly** pass the exam.
> We **definitely won't** be there on time.

These adverbs (*probably, almost certainly, definitely*, etc.) come **after** *will* but **before** *won't*.

2 Using *may (not) / might (not) / could*

These modal verbs all mean that something is possible in the future. We add *well* if we are more sure it will happen.

> It **may / might / could** snow tomorrow. (= it is possible)
> It **may / might / could well** snow tomorrow. (= we are more sure)

We can use *may* and *might*, but not *could*, in the negative form.

| He | **may not** **might not** **could not** | phone this weekend. |

3 *likely to*

We use *likely to* when we think something will probably happen. We can also use the negative form.

> People **are likely to** live longer in the next century.
> Computers **are not likely to** replace teachers.

(B) Hypothetical possibilities with *if*

1 Hypothetical (imaginary) possibilities

a If we are talking about an imaginary/hypothetical situation, we use *would/wouldn't* + verb. Notice the contracted form *I'd*.
> **I'd** never **lie** to my friends.
> I **wouldn't like** to be famous.

b If we talk about a hypothetical situation or condition, we use *if* + Past simple or Past continuous. This type of sentence is often referred to as the 'Second conditional'.
> If I **found** a wallet in the street, **I'd** take it to the police.
> **I'd** go for a walk if I **wasn't feeling** so tired.

> **REMEMBER!**
> 1 It is not correct to use *would* in the *if* clause.
> If I **had** enough money, I'd go abroad on holiday.
> not:
> If I ~~would have~~ enough money ...
>
> 2 In *if* sentences, we can use *were* instead of *was*. This is especially common in the phrase *If I were you* ..., used to give advice.
> **If I were you**, I wouldn't trust him.
>
> 3 We can change the order of the sentence.
> I wouldn't trust him **if I were you**.

c Instead of *would*, we can also use *might* or *could*.
> If you didn't talk so much, people **might** listen to you more.
> I **could** help you if I had more time.

2 Real and hypothetical possibilities

a To talk about a real possibility in the future, we use *will*.
> **I'll** be worried if he **doesn't phone** me.

This type of sentence is often referred to as the 'First conditional'. For more on future sentences with *if* and *when*, see Language summary 5B.

b Sometimes the difference between a real and an imaginary possibility is very clear.
> I'll be very disappointed if we lose. (= a real possibility)
> I'd be absolutely terrified if I saw a ghost. (= an imaginary situation)

Sometimes, whether we use the First or the Second conditional depends on *how we see the situation*.
Compare the following sentences.
> If I **have** enough time, **I'll** help you. (= it is possible I'll have time)
> If I **had** enough time, **I'd** help you. (= I don't have time)

Module 10

(A) Past perfect

had + past participle		
Positive form	Negative form	Question form
I / you / he / she, etc. **'d (= had) done** it	I / you / he / she, etc. **hadn't (= had not) done** it	**Had** I / you / he / she, etc. **done** it?

The Past perfect links one time in the past to another time further in the past.

When we **got** there, everyone **had left**.

1 Similarities with the Present perfect

The Present perfect is 'the past of the present'.
*It **isn't** Jane's first visit to Australia: she**'s been** here twice before.*

The Past perfect is 'the past of the past.'
*It **wasn't** my first visit to Australia: I**'d been** there twice before.*

2 Time words with the Past perfect

With the Past perfect, we use many of the same time words that we use with the Present perfect.
> We had been in Cairo **for two months / since August**.
> I'd **already / just / recently** passed my driving test.
> It was the **first / second / third time** I'd met her.

The following words and phrases are also often used with the Past perfect.

a *by / by the time*
   By 5.30 everyone **had left**. (= they left before this time)
   By the time we arrived, the film **had finished**.

b *when / after / before / as soon as*
   With these words, we use the Past perfect for the first action to happen.
   When I got up, the others **had** already **left**.
   We **did** the washing-up **as soon as** our guests **had left**.

3 Cases where the Past perfect is optional

We do not usually use the Past perfect when the sequence of events in the past is clear.
   I **had** a shower and **went** to bed.

If we use *when* with the Past perfect, it means that the first action was finished when the second action happened.
   The game **had** already **started** when we **arrived**.

With two Past simple verbs, the two actions happened at more or less the same time.
   The game **started** when we **arrived**.

Ⓑ Reported speech and reported questions

1 Change of tenses

When we report someone's words afterwards, the verb forms often move into the past. This is because what they said is now in the past.

Direct speech (actual words)	Reported (indirect speech)
Years ago, John said …	A few years ago, John told me that …
'**I want** to get away from here.' Present simple	he **wanted** to get away from there. Past simple
'**I had** an awful time last year.' Past simple	he **had had** an awful time the previous year. Past perfect
'**I've found** a new job in Canada.' Present perfect	he **had found** a new job in Canada. Past perfect
'**I'm leaving** tomorrow.' Present continuous	he **was leaving** the next day. Past continuous
'**I'm going to start** a new life.' is / are going to	he **was going to start** a new life. was / were going to
'**I'll write** to you when I get there.' will / won't	he **would write** to me when he got there. would / wouldn't
'**You can** come and see me ' can / can't	I **could** come and see him. could / couldn't

Notice:

a the changes in place and time references in the reported statements.
   here → there
   last year → the year before

b that other modal verbs (*would, could, should, ought, might*) do not change in reported speech.

c the changes in pronouns used in reported speech.
   I → he

2 Verbs and conjunctions used for reporting

a In statements, *say* and *tell* are the most common reporting verbs. Look at how they are used.
   He **said** it was true. not: ~~He told it was true~~.
   He **said** it was true. not: ~~He said me it was true~~.
   He **said to me (that)** it was true. not: ~~He told to me (that) it was true~~.

   These verbs can be followed by *that*, but it is not necessary.

b In questions, *ask* and *want to know* are common reporting verbs.
   In *yes / no* questions the verb is joined to the reported words with *if* or *whether*.

   She **asked/wanted to know** | *if* / *whether* | it was true (or not).

   In *Wh-* questions, we do not need *if* or *whether*.
   '**What** do you think?'
   He asked me **what I thought**.

3 Word order in reported questions

The word order in reported questions is the same as in normal statements.
   '**Can you come** early?' → She asked if **I could come** early.
   '**Did you see** anything suspicious?' → The police officer wanted to know if **we had seen** anything suspicious.

Module 11

Ⓐ Obligation and permission

Positive forms			
	You	can must should	go
	You	're allowed have have got ought	to go
Negative forms	You	can't mustn't shouldn't 're not allowed to don't have to haven't got to	go
Question forms	Can Should	I go?	
	Am I allowed Do I have Have I got	to go?	

1 Talking about what is necessary / not necessary

a We use *must*, *have to* and *have got to* + verb to talk about something that is necessary or important.
*We **must be** at the airport by seven.*
*He **has to take** medicine every day for his asthma.*
*I**'ve got to** find a telephone – it's urgent!*

The meaning is very similar, but:

* *must* often shows that the obligation comes from the person speaking.
*We **must be** more careful.* (= I, the speaker, say it's important)

* *have to* and *have got to* show that the obligation comes from another person, not the speaker.
*All young men in this country **have to** do military service.* (= the government says)
*Jake**'s got to do** his exams.* (= his teacher says)

There are differences of formality. *Must* is often written down, for example on public notices.
*All visitors **must** report to reception.*

Have to and *have got to* are more common in speech.
Must is rarely used in question forms – *Do I have to?* is more common.
~~*Must I*~~ / *Do I have to* sign here?

b We use *don't have to* and *haven't got to* + verb to talk about something that is not necessary.
*People **don't have to** vote if they don't want to.*
*We **haven't got to** be there till ten.*

2 Talking about what is permitted / not permitted

a We use *can* and *be allowed to* + verb to talk about things we are permitted to do.
*You **can** park here after 6.30 p.m.*
*My brother's **allowed to** borrow my father's car.*

b We use *mustn't*, *not allowed to* and *can't* + verb to talk about things which we are not permitted to do (= prohibited).
*Members of the audience **must not** take photographs during the performance.* (= written notice)

*You**'re not allowed to** / **can't** take photos during the performance.* (= spoken)

c *Can't* has the idea that it is not possible or permitted to do something.
*You **can't** take photographs in here.*

3 Talking about what is / isn't a good idea / the correct thing

a We use *should* to say something is a good idea, or if it is correct / right.
*You **should** try this ice cream – it's delicious.*
*Those books are in the wrong place: they **should** be in the fiction section.*

Should is weaker than *have to* or *must*. It is often used to give advice or make suggestions.

b *Ought to* has the same meaning as *should*. It is not usually used in the question or negative forms, where *should* is more common.
*You **ought to** be more careful.*

4 Past forms

Present form	Past form
*I **must** / **have to** / **'ve got to** go home.*	*I **had to** go home.*
*I **don't have to** go home.*	*I **didn't have to** go home.*
*They **can** / **can't** vote.*	*They **could** / **couldn't** vote.*
*We're **allowed to** / **not allowed to** / **mustn't** speak.*	*We **were** / **weren't allowed to** speak.*

B Linking words (*although, however*, etc.)

1 Meaning

a Words with a similar meaning to *and*
*My cousin's a professional footballer. He's **also** an excellent tennis player.*
*I haven't got time to go on holiday. **Besides,** I can't afford it.*
*Yoga is excellent exercise: **what's more,** it really helps you to relax.*

b Words with a similar meaning to *but*
***Although** she's much younger than me, we get on very well.*
*The economy seems to be improving. **Despite this**, unemployment is still high.*
*Her father was very angry with her. **However**, he didn't say anything.*
Other such phrases include *though*, *even though* and *in spite of (this)*.

c Words with a similar meaning to *so*
*More and more people are moving to the city. **As a result**, housing is terribly expensive.*
*At least you haven't lied to me. **For this reason**, I'm not going to punish you.*
*He received just five percent of the votes, and **therefore** he has been eliminated.*
Other such words and phrases include *that's why* and *consequently*.

2 Word order

a *Although* is a conjunction – it joins two clauses (smaller sentences). There are two possible positions.
***Although** I don't like him, I respect his opinion.*
*I respect his opinion, **although** I don't like him.*
Though and *even though* can be used in the same way.

b All the other words and phrases are adverbials. There are three possible positions for them in the sentence or sentences:

1 at the beginning of the second sentence.
*She loved him very much. **However**, he knew they could never marry.*
All the adverbials on page 119 can be used in this position.

2 in the middle of the second sentence.
*She loved him very much. He knew, **however**, they could never marry.*
Also, *despite this*, *what is more* and *therefore* can be used in this position.

3 at the end of the second sentence (although many people consider this rather formal / old-fashioned).
*She loved him very much. He knew they could never marry, **however**.*
Therefore can be used in this position.

> **REMEMBER!**
> *Also* comes before the main verb and after verb *be* and auxiliary verbs.
> *Adam is a very keen golfer. He **also** likes tennis.*
> *Adam is a very keen golfer. He is **also** very keen on tennis.*

Module 12

A Past modal verbs (*could have* / *should have* / *would have*)

1 *could have* + past participle

This is used for events which were possible in the past, but didn't happen.

> *He could've drowned.* (= it was possible for him to drown, but he didn't)

Compare the following sentences.

> *Ruby **could walk** before she was a year old.* (= she was able to do this)
> *Ruby **could have walked** to work, but she took a taxi instead.* (= it was possible for her to walk, but she didn't)

2 *should have* / *shouldn't have* + past participle

This means it was a good idea to do something in the past, but you didn't do it. We often use this to **criticise** other people, or to talk about **past regrets**.

> *You **shouldn't have** been so rude.* (= criticism: you were rude, and it wasn't a good idea)
> *I **should've looked** in the mirror before I went out.* (= past regret: it was a good idea to look, but I didn't)

3 *would* / *wouldn't have* + past participle

We use this for imagining something in the past that didn't happen.

> *In his position, I **would have waited** for help.* (= I wasn't in his position – I am imagining the situation)

B Talking hypothetically about the past with *if*

If you are imagining possibilities in the past, we often use *if* to describe the hypothetical situation.

> *If he**'d stayed** at home that day, he **wouldn't have met** his wife.*
>   (condition)   (result)

Notice that after *if* we use the Past perfect. This form is often called the 'Third conditional'.

> **REMEMBER!**
>
> We can also use *might have* or *could have* if we are less sure about what would have happened.
>
> *If he'd (= he had) worked harder, he **might have** got into university.*
>
> *We **could've** won the competition if our best player hadn't got injured.*

C Talking hypothetically about the past and present together

Notice the difference between these two forms:

a imaginary situations generally / in the present
> **if + Past simple + would + verb**
> *If I **wasn't** an actor, I**'d be** a musician.*

b imaginary situations in the past
> **if + Past simple + would have + past participle**
> *if I**'d gone** to the party, I **would have seen** her.*

Sometimes we want to talk about the past and present together. In this case, we can 'mix' the two forms.

> *If she **had stayed** in her job, she **would be** richer now.*
>   (past)   (present)

> *If I **didn't trust** you, I **wouldn't have lent** you the money.*
>   (present)   (past)

Verb	Past Simple	Past Participle
be	was / were	been
beat	beat	beaten
become	became	become
begin	began	begun
bend	bent	bent
bite	bit	bitten
blow	blew	blown
break	broke	broken
bring	brought	brought
build	built	built
burn	burned / burnt	burned / burnt
burst	burst	burst
buy	bought	bought
can	could	been able
catch	caught	caught
choose	chose	chosen
come	came	come
cost	cost	cost
cut	cut	cut
dig	dug	dug
do	did	done
draw	drew	drawn
dream	dreamed / dreamt	dreamed / dreamt
drink	drank	drunk
drive	drove	driven
eat	ate	eaten
fall	fell	fallen
feed	fed	fed
feel	felt	felt
fight	fought	fought
find	found	found
fly	flew	flown
forget	forgot	forgotten
forgive	forgave	forgiven
freeze	froze	frozen
get	got	got
give	gave	given
go	went	gone / been
grow	grew	grown
hang	hung	hanged / hung
have	had	had
hear	heard	heard
hide	hid	hidden
hit	hit	hit
hold	held	held
hurt	hurt	hurt
keep	kept	kept
kneel	knelt	knelt
know	knew	known
lay	laid	laid
lead	led	led
learn	learned / learnt	learned / learnt
leave	left	left
lend	lent	lent

Verb	Past Simple	Past Participle
let	let	let
lie	lay	lain
light	lit	lit
lose	lost	lost
make	made	made
mean	meant	meant
meet	met	met
must	had to	had to
pay	paid	paid
put	put	put
read / riːd /	read / red /	read / red /
ride	rode	ridden
ring	rang	rung
rise	rose	risen
run	ran	run
say	said	said
see	saw	seen
sell	sold	sold
send	sent	sent
set	set	set
shake	shook	shaken
shine	shone	shone
shoot	shot	shot
show	showed	shown
shut	shut	shut
sing	sang	sung
sink	sank	sunk
sit	sat	sat
sleep	slept	slept
slide	slid	slid
smell	smelled / smelt	smelled / smelt
speak	spoke	spoken
spend	spent	spent
spill	spilled / spilt	spilled / spilt
spoil	spoiled / spoilt	spoiled / spoilt
stand	stood	stood
steal	stole	stolen
stick	stuck	stuck
swim	swam	swum
take	took	taken
teach	taught	taught
tear	tore	torn
tell	told	told
think	thought	thought
throw	threw	thrown
understand	understood	understood
wake	woke	woken
wear	wore	worn
win	won	won
write	wrote	written

MINI-CHECKS

Module 1

A Complete the sentences with a suitable word.

1 Paul's got a great _____ of humour.

2 _____ your parents born here?

3 Anne doesn't work _____ – she only works mornings.

4 I'm not very good at _____ in touch with old friends.

5 _____ is the new car going?

6 _____ care of Mum while I'm away!

7 What time do you _____ lunch?

B Correct the sentences which have mistakes.

8 Her husband is a taxi driver, so he's getting home very late.

_____

9 Are you like my new shoes?

_____

10 She wants to find a job where she looks for children.

_____

11 You can't use the bathroom – Alice is having a shower.

_____

12 Excuse me, what is this word mean?

_____

13 I must go to the hairdresser's – my hair gets very long.

_____

14 In my job, I spend a lot of time driving.

_____

15 Sorry, but I'm thinking you're wrong.

_____

C Choose the correct alternative.

16 Three of my cousins / nieces are boys and three are girls.

17 At Christmas all my parents / relatives come to stay.

18 I don't know Alex very well – he's just an acquaintance / a stranger.

19 We're visiting my wife's family this weekend. I really like her father, but my mother-in-law / stepmother drives me mad.

20 Richard is having / has got a little chat with the boss.

/20

Module 2

A Complete the sentences with the Past simple or continuous of the verbs.

The last time I [1]_____ (see) them, they [2]_____ (play) football in the park.

I couldn't sleep because my neighbours [3]_____ (argue) very loudly last night.

When I [4]_____ (walk) into the room, everyone [5]_____ (stop) talking.

The exam [6]_____ (last) nearly three hours.

B Cross out the extra word in each sentence.

7 My mother didn't remember me to send grandad a birthday card.

8 Michael was helped us to get everything ready.

9 I am still remember what she said to me.

10 They are used to walk to school every day.

C Complete the sentences with a suitable word.

11 I'm not very good _____ remembering people's names.

12 When did you learn _____ to cook so brilliantly?

13 My sister used to have long hair, but she doesn't _____ more.

14 I didn't know you were interested _____ motorbikes!

15 Does that girl in the corner remind you _____ anyone?

D Choose the correct alternative.

16 Did you notice anything strange about / at / for his appearance?

17 'I felt so ridiculous. They were all laughing at me!' 'Are / Did / Were they? How awful!'

18 If you realise / recognise / remind anyone in the picture, please tell us.

19 I still / usually / used to take my dog for a walk every evening.

20 I was looking out of the window because / when / while someone called my name.

/20

Module 3

A Complete the sentences with the correct form of the adjectives.

1 Which airport is _____ (far) from London – Heathrow or Stansted?

2 That was one of the _____ (bad) meals I've ever eaten.

3 I'm not as _____ (tall) as you.

4 The situation is actually much _____ (good) we thought.

5 Because we didn't have much money, we chose the _____ (expensive) form of travel – the local bus.

B Choose the correct alternative.

6 There's fewer / the least / less space in the new flat than in the old one.

7 For a beach holiday, I'd experience / find / recommend Thailand.

8 The square is more or less the same as / like / than it was fifty years ago.

9 This hotel is best / the second best / the better in the city.

10 I can't see any difference – to me they're a little bit / exactly / slightly the same!

C Complete the sentences with a suitable word.

11 The tram is probably _____ easiest way to get around the city.

12 The climate here is very similar _____ the climate in England.

13 The city has got _____ historic buildings than anywhere else I know.

14 This is the tallest building _____ the whole city.

15 Szechuan is a province of China, famous _____ its delicious food.

16 There are several attractive resorts _____ the east coast.

D Choose the correct alternative.

17 People have been trying to cross the border / edge / front / side into India.

18 The old market is one place that's really worth see / seeing / to see / to be seen.

19 It's a twelve-hour flight / fly / travel / plane from New York.

20 The scene / scenery / sight / view from the top of the hill is absolutely fantastic!

/20

Module 5

A Complete the sentences with the correct form of *go*.

1 I _____ to Paris last Sunday.

2 We're planning _____ to the beach this afternoon.

3 I'm thinking of _____ to Paul's barbecue on Saturday.

4 As soon as my parents _____ out, we'll put on some music.

5 The band is due _____ on at nine o'clock.

6 If you give me money, I _____ to the shops for you.

B Complete the table.

Noun	Adjective
imagination	7
8	jealous
success	9
10	ambitious

C Choose the correct alternative.

11 To do this job well, you need good people ability / skills / training.

12 Our manager has agreed to make / run / take up a computer course for new employees.

13 Mr Irvine isn't here at the moment. Shall I ask him to call you back / return to you / ring again?

14 The train is due / hoping / planning to arrive in twenty minutes.

15 This job will give me more opportunities of travelling / to travel / travel.

D Complete the sentences with a suitable preposition.

16 Bye. Thank you _____ calling.

17 I need to concentrate _____ my work more.

18 My parents have agreed to pay _____ my computer.

19 I'm doing a degree _____ art.

20 I've applied _____ a job.

/20

Module 6

A Complete the sentences with the correct form of the adjectives.

1 It's not _____ (surprise) you're cold – you need a warmer coat!

2 I was very _____ (disappoint) when I failed my driving test.

3 After reading the instruction manual, I was even more _____ (confuse)!

4 It was one of the most _____ (excite) matches I've ever seen.

5 After the divorce, Frank became more and more _____ (depress).

B Complete the sentences with the active or passive form of the verbs.

6 Every year, 1,200 people _____ (injured) in road accidents.

7 The search for the missing man continues. Up until now, no clues _____ (find).

8 At the moment, a new shopping centre _____ (build) in the town centre.

9 My coat _____ (cost) €250.

10 Nearly €1 million _____ (steal) during the robbery.

11 The council say they _____ (complete) the work next year.

C Complete the phrases with a suitable preposition.

12 It was made _____ the 1990s.

13 The best thing _____ the film is the music.

14 I'd recommend this film _____ anyone.

15 It was written _____ William Shakespeare.

16 I'm not worried _____ the exam.

D Write an adjective with *very* that means the same as these extreme adjectives.

17 delighted   very _____

18 furious   very _____

19 boiling   very _____

20 amazed   very _____

/20

Module 7

A Cross out the extra word in each sentence.

1 Most of people nowadays don't dress up when they go out.

2 Could you mind wait here, please?

3 'Can I look at your newspaper?' 'Yes, of course not.'

4 I usually go to home immediately after class.

5 Do you mind if helping with the washing up?

B Choose the correct alternative.

6 Could / Will / Would I borrow a pen, please?

7 'Oh no! I've forgotten my purse.' 'Don't worry. I'm going to lend / I'll lend / I'm lending you some money.'

8 Are you going to / Do you / Will you turn off the lights before you leave, please?

9 Are / Do / Would you like to come to the cinema with us?

10 It's hard to decide … hmm … OK, I'll have / I'm going to / I'm having the red one, please.

C Complete the sentences with the correct form of *close*.

11 Would you mind _____ the door?

12 He offered _____ the door.

13 It's usual for people _____ the curtains at night.

14 Is it all right if I _____ the curtains?

15 How about _____ the window?

D Cross out the extra word in each sentence.

16 I went to the bed early, but I found it hard to sleep.

17 I think I'll become go mad if I stay here any longer.

18 It's ten o'clock … I think it's time for us to go to home.

19 We usually go for having a coffee after class – would you like to come too?

20 Julia went on for studying English even when her exams were over.

/20

Module 9

A Put the word in brackets in the correct place in the sentence.

1 There will certainly be a storm tonight. (almost)

_____

2 The situation is to get worse. (likely)

_____

3 There won't be any news until tomorrow. (definitely)

_____

4 We may get home till late. (not)

_____

5 You well have to do the test again. (may)

_____

B Complete the sentences with the correct form of the verbs in brackets.

If he ⁶_____ (not start) studying soon, he ⁷_____ (definitely fail) his exams in June.
If someone ⁸_____ (give) you a huge amount of money, what ⁹_____ (you do) with it?
If I ¹⁰_____ (be) you, I ¹¹_____ (not lend) any money to someone like that.

C Complete the table.

Noun	Verb	Adjective
economy		12 _____
education	educate	13 _____
prediction	14 _____	
15 _____		unemployed

D Choose the correct alternative.

16 Hello. I'd like to do / make / take an appointment to see Dr Lee, please.

17 There are over five million / millions / million of people living in this city.

18 The number of people applying for courses is still raising / rising / risen.

19 I think you're doing / making / taking a big risk by doing that.

20 I'd stay if I had / have / would have the time, but I really must go now.

/20

Module 10

A Complete the sentences with the correct form of the verbs.

When I finally ¹_____ (arrive) home, my parents asked me where I ²_____ (be) all that evening.
We ³_____ (not have) a proper meal for several days, so we ⁴_____ (eat) everything hungrily.
Most of the people who ⁵_____ (be) on the plane ⁶_____ (not fly) before.

B Complete the sentences with a suitable word.

7 The prisoner was _____ guilty of robbery.

8 People are always asking him _____ he's planning to make another film.

9 When I see your brother, I'll tell _____ about the party.

10 We waited ages for a bus. _____ the end, two came together!

C Put the sentences into reported speech.

11 'Where do you live?' she asked the boy.
She asked _____
_____ .

12 'I'm leaving tomorrow,' she told me.
She said _____
_____ .

13 'I've never eaten snake before,' I said to the waitress.
I told _____
_____ .

14 'Did you enjoy the film?' asked my friend.
My friend asked _____
_____ .

15 'I've just got engaged,' she said to her friends.
She told _____
_____ .

D Choose the correct alternative.

16 He made me cry / crying / to cry.

17 I could see that I'd have to ask / say / tell the truth.

18 By / By the time / When the middle of the afternoon, the sun had gone.

19 My teachers were always telling me away / down / off for talking in class.

20 The prisoner decided to plead / say / tell guilty to the crime.

/20

Module 11

A Replace the phrase in bold with an appropriate modal verb or phrase.

1 **It wasn't not necessary for us to** buy a ticket in advance.

_____

2 Members of the public **can** see inside the castle at weekends.

_____

3 **It's a good idea to** check the train times before you travel.

_____

4 **Is it necessary** to fill in both forms?

_____

5 **It's forbidden** to smoke here.

_____

6 **It is permitted for you** to learn to drive when you are seventeen.

_____

B Choose the correct alternative.

7 It hasn't rained for two months. As a result / However / In spite of this the ground is very dry.

8 I like the country very much although / consequently / therefore I wouldn't want to go and live there.

9 Despite / Even though / However he's young, he's very mature.

10 It's much too early to go home now. Besides / For this reason / That's why you haven't met everyone yet.

11 As well as being fluent in French and English, Nadine also / besides / what's more understands German.

C Cross out the phrase in each group which does not belong with _do_.

12 your homework / the housework / the ironing / a mess

13 badly / your best / a mistake / well

14 aerobics / some exercise / yoga / a suggestion

15 a profit / military service / overtime / some work

D Complete the sentences with the correct form of _make_.

16 People ought _____ up their own minds about this.

17 We must _____ plans for every possibility.

18 I think all forms of hunting should _____ illegal.

19 You can be fined for _____ too much noise late at night.

20 It's a great opportunity _____ some money.

/20

TAPESCRIPTS

Module 1

Recording 1
1 What's your full name?
2 Where do you come from originally?
3 Are you married?
4 Have you got any children?
5 Where were you born?
6 What's your date of birth?
7 Where exactly do you live?
8 Does all your family live round here?
9 Where did you learn English before this?
10 How was your weekend?

Recording 3
1 What's the English word for this?
2 How do you pronounce this word?
3 How do you spell it?
4 Which page are we on?
5 What's tonight's homework?
6 Can you say that again, please?
7 Can you write it on the board, please?
8 Can you explain that again, please?

Recording 4
1 Choose a shape and write the name of your oldest relative.
2 Choose a shape and write the name of a neighbour or colleague.
3 Choose a shape and write the number of aunts you've got.
4 Choose a shape and write 'yes' if you've got any nieces and 'no' if you haven't.
5 Choose a shape and write how many years you've known your best friend.
6 Choose a shape and write the number of cousins you've got.
7 Choose a shape and write 'yes' if you've got a mother-in-law and 'no' if you haven't.
8 Choose a shape and write the name of someone who's an acquaintance, but not really a friend.

Recording 5

K = KARINA; C = COLLEAGUE

C: So who are the people with you in this photo, then?
K: Well, this is my friend Nikita. She lives in the flat upstairs from us, and actually she's going out with my brother Danny ...
C: Oh, right, is this Danny then?
K: Yeah.
C: And does he live with your parents, too?
K: Usually he does, but at the moment he's staying with my aunt and uncle in Edinburgh. He's doing a design course at Edinburgh College of Art.
C: Really, so he wants to be a designer?
K: Hmm, not sure to be honest. He's enjoying the course, but he doesn't really know what he wants to do.
C: Mmm, and is this your sister? She really looks like you, it's incredible!
K: No. Actually that's my cousin, Holly, but everyone thinks we're sisters!
C: And this is your gran, I suppose?
K: Yeah. She's getting old now, poor thing. She needs more help these days so she comes and stays with us every weekend. She doesn't usually go out much. She loved my birthday party though. She had a fantastic time!
C: Aah, that's nice. And who's this with her then?
K: That's my little brother Richard – you know Richard ...
C: Wow, is that Richard? He looks really grown up ... he's getting really tall.

K: I know! My little brother's taller than me – it's really weird!

Recording 6

(answers only)

a lunch b look c headache d humour e problem f rest g family

Recording 7
Conversation 1

K = KATIE; PH = PHILLIP; P = PETRA

K: Phillip, can I introduce you to Petra, a friend of mine from Prague?
PH: Hi, Petra. Nice to meet you.
P: Nice to meet you, too.
K: You were in Prague last year, weren't you, Phillip?
PH: The year before last, yeah. It's an absolutely beautiful city. The architecture is amazing! I loved it.
P: Oh yes, I do, too. Were you there for a holiday?
PH: Yes and no. I actually went over to watch Scotland play football. I'm a big football fan.
P: So am I! I was at that match too with my brother and father. They're crazy about football. It was a good game; a shame there were no goals!
PH: Yeah. There are never any goals when I go to matches! Anyway, what are you doing here in Edinburgh?
P: I'm working as an au pair with a Scottish family for a few months to improve my English.
PH: So you look after the children and do the housework?
P: Well, really I just look after the children. I'm terrible at housework; I don't like it all!
PH: Oh, it's the same with me. I hate it, I'm terrible.
P: Yeah, and they've got four children, so I'm pretty busy!
PH: Gosh! I can't think of anything worse than spending my day with four children!
P: Oh, don't you like children? I really enjoy it; they're lovely children.
PH: Oh, not for me, thank you! Anyway, so ... erm ... which part of Edinburgh are you staying in?
P: I'm near the university; Dalkeith Road. Do you know it?
PH: Yes, as a matter of fact I live very near there too, Clerk Street. It's very nearby.
P: No, I don't know it.
PH: Well, perhaps I could come round and see you some time, and we could go and watch some football together?
P: Yeah, that would be great. I really want to go and watch ...

Conversation 2

A = ANDREW; C = CARRIE

A: Hi, Carrie. How are things with you?
C: Oh, Hi, Andrew. Okay, I suppose, not too bad.
A: Hm-mm. How's your job going?
C: Oh, don't talk about it! I've moved to a new office and I just hate it. The people are so unfriendly! Actually, I'm looking for a new job!
A: Oh, really? Me too! I'm just so bored with my job. I've been there far too long!
C: So what kind of thing are you looking for?
A: Mmm. I don't know really. Maybe something in the travel industry. I'd love to work somewhere nice and hot; somewhere like Spain.
C: Oh, I know! It would be lovely to go and live abroad, wouldn't it? Hey, we ought to go out there together, you and me, set up a travel business.
A: The only problem is, I don't speak Spanish, so I don't know if that would count against me.
C: No, I don't speak Spanish either. Don't speak any foreign languages for that matter. It's terrible, isn't it?
A: Mmm. Oh well, one day, maybe. Anyway, how are your family? Are your Mum and Dad still ...?

Module 2

Recording 1

past.

Sung

In 1972, when I was, um maybe seven years old, the President of the United States, President Nixon came to my country, came to China. And one of the places he visited was Datong, which was my city. And I was very good at dancing when I was young so I was chosen from my school to dance, to dance in front of the President. And at the end, we were all standing in line and he stopped when he came to me and I remember he smiled and said 'Hello', which was the only English word I knew. And I just said 'Welcome', in Chinese, of course. I still remember it very clearly.

Andy

past continu

I met my girlfriend while I was working as a barman in a disco. And there was this really gorgeous girl in the club and I really wanted to talk to her, but I couldn't because I was working. Anyway as luck would have it, I was carrying a … a bucket of ice and I dropped it, accidentally, of course, just next to where she was sitting. And well, I said 'Oh, I'm so sorry. I'm really, really sorry.' And we started chatting and I found out her name was Karen, and in the end she gave me her phone number. We started going out and we've been together for nearly two years.

Raul

A few years ago, there was a football match in my country against Italy, and my friend and I were walking past the hotel where the Italian team were staying. I wasn't thinking about that, I was just talking to my friend. Anyway, we were just walking along when I bumped into someone. I suppose I wasn't really looking where I was going. He was a big man, wearing a tracksuit and I said 'Oh sorry, sorry,' and I looked and I saw that it was Vieri, the Italian footballer. And I was so surprised, I just didn't know what to say. Then I said 'Do you mind if we take a photo?' and he said 'Yes, OK,' and I've still got the photo to this day, at home.

Recording 2

(answers only)

a met	g arrived	l was
b went	h were still tidying	m asked
c was staying	i offered	n seemed
d was visiting	j started	o liked
e invited	k were preparing	p was wearing
f was helping		

Recording 5

(answers only)

1 had	5 remember	9 laughed
2 had	6 cry	10 needed
3 laughed	7 had	11 remember
4 needed	8 had	

Recording 6

Justin

Okay, so one of the things I remember about my childhood was when I was at primary school. I suppose I was about eight or nine. Well, first of all I ought to tell you about this boy who used to bully me. Carl Foster his name was, and he was really like a big kid, who used to bully smaller kids, like me, and, you know, he called me names and threatened to beat me up and horrible things like that. So I really didn't like this guy, at all. And anyway, we used to have our lunch in the dining hall, and we weren't really meant to be there after we'd had lunch, because there was a big marble floor and what people used to do was run along and dive onto the floor and slide right to the other side of the room. And one time I was a bit over-enthusiastic I suppose, and jumped onto the floor and went sliding along at high speed and hit my head and cut my head open. And I kind of ran out, you know, blood everywhere and er … spoke to a teacher. And the kind of slightly embarrassing thing about it was that I said to the teacher that Carl Foster had hit my head against the wall and so … erm, he got the blame for it and I got some care and attention. So it was a bit unfair, but it serves him right, I suppose!

Helen

When I was a child we used to go on holiday to the same place every year. It was a seaside town in England, and there was a fairground kinda place with all kinds of amusements and slot machines and things like that. And we went along with our pocket money and there was a machine where you put some money in and if it landed in the right place you won a prize. And I was sure I'd dropped my money in the right place, but I didn't win a prize and I was very upset and furious. So I hit the machine to try to make sure that I won a prize, but the alarm went off and when the alarm went off the manager came out of his office so I ran away with my brother and we ran all the way back to where we were staying … and I was absolutely terrified … and when we got back my brother told me that the police were going to come and arrest me and for about three days afterwards, right until the end of the holiday, I didn't dare go out or go to the beach or anything, 'cause every time I saw a policeman I thought I was going to be arrested and maybe sent to prison which didn't happen actually. So you should never believe anything your brother tells you basically!

Recording 7

T: TOM; K: KIRSTIN

T: … and I realised we were completely lost, but at least we got there in the end.

K: Funny you should say that, because … er a similar thing happened to me one time when I was abroad. We were actually doing a concert in this bar in Germany …

T: Really?

K: I was actually about to appear on stage, y'know with the band, and I just thought well, y'know, I'll just go out for a little walk …

T: Yeah, yeah.

K: Get some fresh air, as I had about half an hour before we had to go on …

T: Uh-huh.

K: And I went outside, y'know, had a look around, walked around for a bit and then I decided to go back, and I was … er, I couldn't find it. I'd taken a wrong turn or something and I was walking round. It was about two minutes before we were supposed to start …

T: No! You're joking!

K: Yeah, I thought 'Argh! What am I going to do?'

T: Couldn't you ask for directions?

K: Well, I tried. I asked this old woman, but she didn't speak English and I don't speak German …

T: Don't you? Oh, right.

K: And then I realised I couldn't remember the name of the bar, or the street it was in, or anything. So, y'know, I was in the middle of a town I didn't know, not knowing the language …

T: So what … what happened? How did you get back?

K: I mean I was just standing thinking 'What am I gonna do?' and luckily I saw someone wearing one of our T-shirts. He was obviously going to the gig, to the concert, so I sort of followed him back to the bar …

T: Wow! That was lucky! Thank goodness.

K: And when I got there the guys were like 'Where've you been? We thought you'd run out on us.' Anyway we managed …

Recording 8

Really? Yeah, yeah. Uh-huh. No! You're joking! Don't you? Oh, right. Wow! That was lucky!

Module 3

Recording 1

1 Russia is by far the biggest country by area in the world – it is over 17 million square kilometres. But China has a much bigger population, with nearly 1.4 billion people.

2 The longest river in the world is the Nile at 6,995 kilometres, but it is only slightly longer than the Amazon – the second longest river in the world, at 6,750 kilometres.

3 Seoul, in South Korea, is the most populated city in the world with a population of about 10.3 million people. The second most populated is Mumbai, in India (formerly Bombay). It's only a little bit bigger than São Paulo, in Brazil. Both cities have about 9.9 million. Jakarta, in Indonesia, is next, with about 9.3 million, and Moscow in Russia, is in fifth place with approximately 9 million people.

4 Canada has by far the longest coastline in the world – it is approximately 244,000 kilometres long. The second longest is Indonesia, but it is a long way behind at only 55,000 kilometres.

5 Chicago is the furthest north, although it is only slightly further north than New York. San Francisco and Los Angeles are both in California, but Los Angeles is a lot further south – about 900 kilometres.

6 Surprisingly it is China, not the USA, that has the most fast food restaurants in the world. The nation that drinks the most tea is not the Indians, or the English as you might think, but the Irish, who drink around five cups a day! India has by far the most universities in the world with nearly 8,500. It also has the biggest university in the world – the Kameshwar Singh Darbhanga Sanskrit University has over half a million students!
London Heathrow is the busiest airport in the world with around 65 million passengers a year. While France is by far the most popular country with tourists, with nearly 75 million visitors a year. The second most popular, the USA, is a long way behind with just 53 million.
And the most popular theme park in the world isn't in the USA either – it's actually Disneyland Tokyo, which attracts around 18 million visitors a year.

Recording 2

1 Write the name of one of the hottest places in the world.
2 Write the name of one of the coldest places in the world.
3 Write the name of the second biggest city in your country.
4 Write the name of one of the most beautiful cities in your country.
5 Write the name of one of the oldest parts of your town.
6 Write the name of one of the busiest streets in your town.
7 Write the name of one of the ugliest buildings you've ever seen.
8 Write the name of the nicest beach you've ever been to.

Recording 3

1 The UK is by far the largest of the three countries.
2 France is slightly more crowded than the UK.
3 Ireland is much more popular than the UK with tourists.
4 Dublin has by far the smallest population.
5 Heathrow International is a lot busier than Dublin International Airport.
6 Charles de Gaulle is the busiest of the three airports.

Recording 4

Michael Tang

I: So is Hong Kong very different from before, from when it was British?

MT: On the surface, no. I mean you still find all the same groups of people here and daily life is very similar to how it was before. We still do the same things and Hong Kong people still run around all the time, we never relax! The pace of life is still very fast, very frantic. But I think people feel slightly different nowadays. Of course, we have Chinese passports and we use the Chinese language more. We just feel more Chinese, and I think that's good.

I: Are there any bad things?

MT: Well, I think people worry more about the government, and the economy. But actually, there are economic problems everywhere in Asia at the moment.

I: Mmm. Has this affected your standard of living?

MT: Uh, actually, I think our standard of living is more or less the same; and a lot of things are cheaper. We can go shopping to mainland China where things are a lot cheaper.

I: Does the place look the same?

MT: Mmm, yes and no. There are Chinese flags everywhere now, and we don't have the red British post boxes any more; actually I miss those! But we still have the same British street names; uh, Queen's Road and Victoria Park, and we still drive on the left, like in Britain. Strangely, I think Hong Kong is even more western and modern than before.

I: Mmm, that's interesting.

Irina Solokova

I: So is Moscow very different from how it was in the early nineties?

IS: Completely different. Sometimes you feel as if you're in a different city.

I: In what way?

IS: It used to be very dirty and shabby. Even the beautiful historical monuments were very dirty, and there was rubbish everywhere in the streets. It's much cleaner now. They've repaired the old buildings, and a lot of attractive new ones have appeared. There are luxury hotels now. Before we didn't have five star hotels, just hotels. And there are lots of new shops. You can buy anything you want in Moscow now, if you've got the money, of course!

I: Uh-huh.

IS: Another thing that's very different. There are a lot more churches; old ones and new ones too, and there are a lot more foreigners around. Russian people really need to learn English now, to communicate with all the tourists.

I: Is there anything you miss?

IS: Mmm. Somehow it feels less Russian. I mean, before it was a very traditional place. Now sometimes you feel as if you are in Disneyland, everything is so clean and bright. It's not like a real place where people work and live.

I: That's interesting.

IS: One thing that is definitely much worse than before is the traffic. It's terrible. There are thousands of cars everywhere – often it's faster to travel on the underground! And the cars are very different too. In the old days it was really rare to see any foreign cars, like a Ford or a BMW. That was something really special. The men and boys used to stop and discuss them, if they saw one! These days you hardly see any Russian cars any more.

I: So is the standard of living better, do you think?

IS: For some people yes, of course, but actually I think for most people life is harder, especially old people. Everything is much more expensive – food, transport, houses. It's difficult to imagine when you see this bright new city, but really it's true, believe me!

Tapescripts

Recording 5

1 The church in picture A is more or less the same as the one in B.
2 The church window in picture A is exactly the same as the one in B.
3 The church roof in picture A is slightly different from the one in B.
4 The tour bus in picture A is completely different from the one in B.
5 The bus driver in picture A is very similar to the one in B.
6 The café window in picture A is exactly the same as in B.
7 The kiosk in picture A is very different from the kiosk in B.
8 The telephone box in picture A is slightly different from the one in B.

Recording 6

1 The city centre's a lot busier than it used to be.
2 The shops are completely different from before.
3 The traffic's a bit better than it was.
4 Public transport's worse than it used to be.
5 This is one of the biggest parks in the city.
6 The square looks about the same as before.
7 This part of town is exactly the same as it was before.
8 This is one of the nicest areas of town.

Recording 8

E = ELAINE; M = MARCO

E: So you're flying to Melbourne, right?
M: Yeah, I've got some distant cousins there so I'm visiting them first for a few days, just to say hello. What's Melbourne like?
E: Well, I'm from Melbourne so, of course, I think it's great … but no, seriously, I think you'll really like it. It's quite cosmopolitan, so you get nice bars and cafés, and great food from all over the world.
M: And is it an attractive city?
E: Oh, yeah! There are some lovely old buildings and some really nice modern buildings, too. There's the cathedral and the Parliament House and it's got loads of parks … the Royal Botanic Gardens … so yeah, it's a really nice place to walk around. And you're going in January, so the weather should be really nice. There's a lot of wine growing round Melbourne too, so you can do some wine tasting if you like that sort of thing … and there are lovely beaches nearby.
M: Great! Well, I'll probably stay there three or four days, but then I want to see as much of Australia as I can, but you know without rushing around too much.
E: And you're flying back to Europe from Sydney, right?
M: Yeah, that's right.
E: Mmm. So you want to travel around and end up in Sydney then?
M: Mmm. Any ideas?
E: Well, I don't think you'll have time to go over to Perth and see Western Australia, not if you want to see Sydney and the Great Barrier Reef and that area, and you've got to do that!
M: Okay. So where should I go after Melbourne?
E: Well, personally I'd fly from there to Alice Springs and go and see Ayer's Rock. Look, it's here on the map. I think it's the biggest single rock in the world, and it's this reddy-orangey colour. It's just amazing. If you're feeling energetic you can climb it! And you'll also get the chance to see the Outback while you're there, and the desert scenery, and find out a bit about the Aboriginal culture, so it's really worth going.
M: It sounds great.
E: I'd recommend staying for about two days or so; that's probably enough. Then from there I think you can fly straight up to Cairns.
M: Where is Cairns, exactly?

E: It's here, look, in North Queensland, right up by the Great Barrier Reef.
M: Yes, I see. There are beautiful beaches up there, aren't there?
E: Yeah, some of the best beaches in the world, supposedly. It's just paradise! Except for the jellyfish. You need to be careful of those when you go swimming! But there's loads to do, too. You've got to stay at least four or five days. You won't want to leave!
M: So should I stay in Cairns?
E: You could do. It's a really nice place, but personally I'd go and stay on an island or by the beach. There's rainforest up there and you can find beaches near the rainforest like Kewarra Beach just to the north of Cairns. That's gorgeous.
M: It sounds amazing, and of course, I have to see the Great Barrier Reef.
E: Yeah, of course! You can take day cruises out there and go snorkelling. It's really easy to arrange, so it'll be no problem. You can even stay on the Reef if you want to.
M: And then from there, I can fly to Sydney?
E: Yeah. You should have at least four or five days in Sydney, because it's a great place, too. Obviously there's the Opera House, the Harbour, the Bridge, Bondi Beach – all the famous places. And if you can, it would be great to visit the Blue Mountains just outside Sydney. They're really worth seeing, too!
M: I don't know how I'm going to have time for all this, perhaps I need to go for longer!
E: Yeah, change your flight and stay three weeks, you'll love it, I'm absolutely sure you will!
M: Well, thanks, this has been great.

Recording 9

(answers only)

a like
b you'll have time
c I'd fly
d recommend staying for
e four or five days
f Personally
g should have
h great to visit; really worth seeing

Recording 10

TA = TRAVEL AGENT; R = RACHAEL

TA: Hello, I'm Jude. What can I do to help?
R: I'm interested in return flights to Buenos Aires, travelling on the fourth of April.
TA: Coming back when?
R: Around the seventeenth or eighteenth.
TA: Okay, I'll just check availability for you. Umm, it's looking pretty busy. Yeah, it's completely full, I'm afraid. It's because it's a Friday. The fifth and sixth are full, too.
R: Oh no! Can you try the third instead?
TA: Okay. Yes, that's fine. Let's just check the return date. The eighteenth is full but the seventeenth is fine. Is that okay?
R: Yeah, that sounds fine. How much will it be?
TA: Erm, just a second. I can do it for €979 return including taxes. It's with Iberia.
R: Okay. That sounds fine. Is it a direct flight?
TA: No, there's an hour stopover in Madrid. You leave London Heathrow at 1915 on the third, and arrive in Buenos Aires at 0650 on the fourth.
R: So how many hours is that?
TA: It's a twelve-hour flight from Madrid basically – two hours to Madrid from London.
R: Okay, and what are the times of the return flight?
TA: It leaves Buenos Aires at 1335 and arrives in Madrid at 0610, then leaves Madrid at seven and arrives at London Gatwick at 0820.
R: Just a minute, that was a bit fast for me. Could you say that again?

TA: Sure. It departs Buenos Aires at 1335 on the seventeenth of April and arrives in Madrid at ten past six in the morning. Then it departs Madrid at seven and you arrive back at London Gatwick, not Heathrow, at eight twenty on the morning of the eighteenth.

R: Okay, that sounds fine. Can I reserve that for a few days, while I just check everything with my friends in Buenos Aires?

TA: I can hold it for two days. After that I'll need the payment in full or you might lose it.

R: Okay.

TA: Okay, just a few details. Are you Miss, Mrs or Ms?

R: Er, Miss.

TA: And the surname?

R: Stewart.

TA: That's S-T-E-W-A-R-T?

R: That's right.

TA: And your first name?

R: Rachael ... R-A-C-H-A-E-L.

TA: And a phone number where I can contact you?

R: Yeah, my mobile is O7711 737385.

TA: Okay great. So I'll hold it for you for two days then. This is my direct number if you need to call me ... 0207 887 9345. So either come in or give me a call with your credit card details when you're ready to pay.

R: Okay, thanks a lot then.

Module 4

Recording 1

(answers only)

1 were	6 finally ended	11 have also produced
2 have been	7 have become	12 have built up
3 appeared	8 published	13 were
4 started	9 have sold	
5 appeared	10 have made	

Recording 2

1 A: What's the matter?
   B: It's my glasses. Have you seen my glasses anywhere?
   A: I don't know if I have. I can't believe you've lost them again!
   B: Okay, so I've lost my glasses! Will you help me look for them, please?
   A: Have you looked under the ... look! They're just there on the table.
   B: Well, who put them there?

2 A: ... didn't even recognise you for a minute. You look so different. You've changed your hair. It's really nice, I like it.
   B: Oh, thanks, and you look really well too. You've lost weight, haven't you?
   A: Well, yes, a bit. I've been on a diet for about three months, and I've joined a gym.

3 A: John, is Daniela still here?
   B: Well, she was here. Perhaps she's just gone out for a minute.
   C: If you're looking for Daniela, she's gone home. She left about ten minutes ago.
   A: Oh, never mind. I'll talk to her tomorrow.

4 A: Barbara? Catherine? What are you two doing?
   B: We've finished. Can we go now?
   A: Well, just wait a minute. Frank, how about you? How are you getting on?
   C: Sorry, I haven't finished yet ... just a minute.
   A: Well, hurry up, then.

5 A: Let me see ... er ... George... have you met Silvina, Silvina Ramos?
   B: Yes, I think we have. We met at the conference last year, didn't we?
   A: That's right, I remember. Nice to see you again.

Recording 4

S = SARA; I = INTERVIEWER

S: Well, I was born in 1979 in a small town near Rome.
I: What's the name?
S: The name is Alatri.
I: Alatri?
S: Alatri, yes, and I spent my childhood there. I went to school in Alatri, primary and secondary school. While I was at school when I was, maybe, sixteen? Sixteen, yes, so it was 1995, I started playing volleyball, and I've been playing since then. It's still my favourite sport. I play as often as I can.
I: What was your first job?
S: My first job was in 1997. I worked for a radio station, my local radio. The name was Radio Comunità. I was an announcer on the radio, and I did that for about a year.
I: But you live in Rome now?
S: Yes, I moved to Rome in 1999, that's when I started university. I was twenty years old.
I: What do you study?
S: Medicine. I'd like to be a doctor. The course is six years. I haven't finished yet. I'm still doing it. I'm still studying.
I: And how long have you been learning English?
S: I started learning English in 1998, I think. Before that I studied French.
I: What else?
S: I've got a boyfriend, Gianluigi. I met him when I was at school. I was seventeen when I met him. In 2001, I bought my first car. It's a Nissan, a Nissan Micra. I've still got it now! It's quite old now, but it's OK. 2003, yes, that's the year I bought my first house in Rome. My parents helped me, of course! I'm very happy. It's a little house, but I like it very much. And I live there with my cats. I have many, many cats.
I: How many?
S: Eleven!
I: Eleven?!
S: Yes, I love cats!

Recording 6

1 He passed his driving test about a year ago.
2 We haven't had a holiday since October.
3 They got married a few weeks ago.
4 They've been married for ages and ages.
5 She hasn't been well for a long time.
6 He's been working here since about 1990.

Recording 7

1 How long have you been studying with your present teacher?
2 When did you first start learning English?
3 When did you leave home this morning?
4 How long were you at primary school?
5 How long have you known your oldest friend?
6 When did you last go to the cinema?
7 How long have you had your present hairstyle?
8 When did you last have a holiday?
9 How long have you had your shoes?
10 How long have you been doing this exercise?

Recording 8

1 The person I admire most in the world is Nelson Mandela. He was the President of South Africa during the 1990s, but before that he spent more than twenty-five years, I think, in prison. He was put in prison because of his political beliefs. He wanted to get equal rights for black people in South Africa, and the government put him in prison because of his political views … um … he was a lawyer before he went to prison and he represented himself at his trial. Some of the things he said during his trial were amazing. They're still famous speeches, I think.

The reason that I admire him is that in spite of the fact that he spent such a long time in prison he never changed his views. It would've been quite easy for him to perhaps stop campaigning for the rights of black people, but he never did that. Right until the end of his time in prison, he was still campaigning. When I went to South Africa, I met somebody who was in prison with him and it was amazing to hear about how they were. They found it so easy to forgive the government and the people who'd put them in prison, they weren't bitter or angry about it.

I think he's really influenced the way people think about how they can make changes, political changes, by standing by what they believe in and stating their beliefs very clearly.

2 Okay, the person I admire is my father actually … and um … he was a civil engineer for thirty-three years and he was very successful in his job. And after thirty-three years of working quite happily, he was suddenly made redundant. And at the age of fifty-two it was actually very, very difficult for him to get another job. So he started thinking about what he could do, and he remembered that he'd actually been very good at um … teaching me maths when I was younger, and I'd had a lot of problems with maths and he'd got me through my exams. So what he did was he went back to university, and he trained as a maths teacher. And now I have to say that whenever I go back to my town to visit my dad, I bump into a lot of people in our road who he teaches and they say he's one of the best teachers that they've ever had, so that's great!

The reason I admire him so much is because, you know faced with that kind of situation it would be very easy to be depressed and feel sorry for yourself, and my dad showed just how strong he was and how flexible and creative he can be and that makes me very proud.

Consolidation Modules 1–4

Recording 1

a A: Do you speak any other languages?
 B: Yes … French.
b A: How long have you been here?
 B: Only about a week.
c A: What are you doing at the moment?
 B: I'm working in an advertising agency.
d A: Did you have a good holiday?
 B: Oh, yeah, it was great – the scenery, the food, the weather … fantastic!
e A: So where were you born?
 B: In Caracas. It's the capital of Venezuela.
f A: How often do you go swimming?
 B: Oh, about once a week. I'd like to swim more often, though.
g A: Where are you staying while you're here?
 B: I'm staying in St Paul's Square – right in the centre of town.
h A: Have you got any brothers or sisters?
 B: Yes. I've got an older brother and two younger sisters.

Recording 2

I'd say I've changed quite a lot in the last ten years actually … um mostly to do with my personality. I think I used to be quite serious and worry a lot about things and now I don't so much. Um, my friends are the same. Something that has changed is what I do in my free time. I used to go out to clubs and go out dancing and I smoked and I drank … uh … and now I usually stay home on a Friday night and watch television or read a book. Um … my appearance has changed a bit too. I used to spend lots of time on my hair and lots of time on make-up and clothes, and now I'd rather sleep and spend less time on it … uh than I used to.

Module 5

Recording 2

Nora
I've just done a degree in Drama and education, so I'll probably end up teaching drama in a secondary school, I suppose, but I'm not going to apply for anything this year. Right now, I want to get away from education and do some travelling, probably to the West Indies. I've got family in Trinidad, so I'm hoping to go there for a few months, and maybe find some kind of job there.

Oliver
I've just finished a degree in Ancient History and I'm about to join the army for five years! I've applied and been accepted, and I'm starting my training in September, assuming I pass my medical.

Dino
I'm just finishing my final exams in fashion, and it's been incredibly hard work. So first I'm having a holiday with my family back home in California. I'm leaving in five days, I'm so excited! After that I'm planning to do a master's degree in Fashion design, I've applied for a course, and I've been accepted if I get good grades in my exams, so I'm hoping!

Caroline
I'm about to graduate in modern languages, Spanish and Russian and I've already been accepted for a job as a trainee manager with an international clothing company. I'm due to start work at the beginning of September, so I'm having a couple of months' break over the summer. I'm going to find a beach somewhere nice and hot for a couple of weeks in August, hopefully, and then after that I'll start work. I'm really looking forward to it.

Zak
My degree is in Business studies, but I'm thinking of applying for a course in journalism, but I'm not sure yet. It's a bit of a change, but I think that's what I want to do.

Alice
I've just finished a law degree, but I'm definitely not going to be a lawyer. I've realised I hate the law! I've basically got no idea at all what I want to do. I suppose I'll do some kind of temporary job for the next few months; work in a shop, or do telephone sales or something, and then see what happens. Hope that I get some ideas!

Recording 4

Clare

I'd been working as a geography teacher in a big secondary school for about three years and I was getting really fed up. The kids were really badly behaved and rude, and it was really hard to control them. Every day was really stressful and awful. I was working every evening marking homework and preparing lessons and I just went to bed exhausted and really depressed every night. It just wasn't the right job for me.

Then one day I read in the newspaper that there aren't enough plumbers in the country. Too many people are going to university and not enough people are training to be plumbers! And I said jokingly to my boyfriend, 'I'll be a plumber. I'll earn more money and I won't have to deal with those kids every day! And I'll never have to worry about finding a job!'

And at first it was just a joke, but then I started thinking about it seriously and well here I am, and so far I'm really enjoying it. You have practical problems to solve every day, which I like. You start work early, which I don't like I must say, but when you go home at four or five o'clock that's it, you can forget about it until the next day. No more nights lying awake worrying about it!

I'm the only woman on the course. My colleagues are all male, but they're fine. They make a few jokes, mostly because I used to be a teacher, but it's all very friendly. Sometimes you meet older people who think you can't do the job because you're a woman, and that's a real pain, but compared to my classes at the school where I used to work it's really no problem at all!

Kevin

I lost my job when the company where I worked closed down, and it was terrible. All these men unemployed and no jobs for them anywhere. And so my wife, Sally decided to go back to work. She's a legal secretary and there's always lots of that kind of work, but she has to work long hours.

So basically we changed places. I look after the baby and take the other two to school, and do the shopping and the cooking and the housework. And I must say it's the hardest work I've ever done! Before I used to think my wife had an easy time while I was working. Now I see mums and housewives in a different way!

At first I hated it. I was desperate to get back to work, but now I've started to enjoy it. I never used to see much of the kids and now I'm watching them grow up, and I'm part of everything they do. I still feel a bit lonely sometimes. Em, I miss the people I worked with, but at least the other mothers at school talk to me now, and I've even met some other 'house-husbands' at the school gate. But I don't want to do it for ever. I'm still looking for another job.

Lorna

Ian and I were both doing well in our careers in the city, but we were working really long hours, often twelve hours a day and travelling two hours a day as well – and still living in a tiny flat, because flats are so expensive in London. And when we decided to get married and start a family, we just realised we didn't want to bring our children up with that kind of life, that kind of stress.

We came down here for a holiday and just fell in love with this place. It just seemed like the ideal place for children to grow up, and when we found the hotel, it was perfect – like a dream come true.

I must say, it's been a lot harder than I thought. Running a hotel is a twenty-four hour job, and we've had lots of problems that we didn't really expect. The people in the village weren't that friendly at first, though it's getting better now, and we had quite a lot of money problems and things like that. After the baby's born it's going to be difficult too. Ian will have to work even harder, because I'll have the baby to look after.

But even with all those problems I still really love it. I really enjoy meeting new people all the time. It's still the place where I want to bring up my children, and I don't miss my life in London at all! At the end of a long day, I just look out at the view and listen to the sea. I still think we're really lucky to be here.

Recording 5
(answers only)

1 I'd like to speak
2 put you through
3 could I speak
4 who's calling
5 a message
6 her to call you
7 just phoning because
8 I'll pass on
9 she can contact you on
10 is there a mobile number
11 leave a message
12 for calling

Recording 7

d Can I take a message?
e Shall I ask her to call you back?
f Have you got a number she can contact you on?
g Is there a mobile number?
h I'm just phoning because …
i I'll pass on the message.

Recording 8
(answers only)

a dream	e Monday	i Monday	m time
b stream	f Sunday	j train	n wear
c paid	g fun day	k nine	o there
d made	h run day	l aeroplane	

Module 6

Recording 1

1 A: Tallinn is the capital city of which Baltic state?
  B: Is it Lithuania?
  A: No, I'll have to pass it over. Come on, we need an answer…
  C: Could it be Latvia?
  A: No, it could not. You're both wrong. The answer is Estonia. Fingers on buzzers for the next question. Art: Which French painter, born in 1848, spent several years on the Pacific Island of Tahiti, where he painted many of his most famous works including …

2 A: Welcome back, it's 5.25 here on Sports Talk and it's day four of the World Athletic championships in Berlin. The afternoon session is now underway and we'll go over now to our reporter Tom Ashton over there at the Olympic Stadium for the live coverage of the 400 metres final. Tom, what are the prospects for the British hope Joe Rawlings? Has he got a realistic chance of a medal?
  B: Well, he's been injured, but he was in terrific form previous to that. He's clearly a very talented runner. He's run well so far. He must have a chance, but when you look at the calibre of the opposition, there's the Frenchman Kedar, the very powerful Russian Valeriy Koznetsov, he'll be one to watch …

3 A: … you can have your say with me, Bob Barrett, here at radio South-West, 630 2525. That's the number to call if you want to air your views. We're talking about the huge open-air rock concert at the weekend. Were you there?

What did you think of it? Our first caller is Kerry, Kerry you're on Radio South-West. What's on your mind?

K: Hello?

A: Hello, Kerry.

K: Well, yes, about the rock concert, just in answer to your previous caller. I think it's really unfair that people are always trying to criticise young people, and there were I dunno how many, but something like three, four thousand people there and there was such a good atmosphere. There was no trouble whatsoever and okay, so you have a few problems with people dropping litter and that, but overall …

4   … and there are reports of long delays on the M4 Motorway Westbound, that's between Junctions 8 and 9. This is due to a broken-down lorry blocking the central lane, so motorists are advised to find alternative routes or to avoid the area if at all possible. Meanwhile an update on the M6 Northbound: the earlier accident near Longbridge has been cleared and traffic is now moving, although you can expect some delays due to the build up of traffic in the Birmingham area. Up in Scotland now and in Fife, the A92 remains …

5   M: … well maybe I can explain it better. When I was away, there was only one person I missed … you.

W: That's very nice, but why?

M: Uh … because I've come to appreciate you. Because no other woman's got what you've got.

W: Oh, right family, right age, right income …

M: No! Stop, just listen. Maybe I haven't been using the right words. Maybe I haven't told you the most important thing: I love you.

W: People usually say that before they propose, they usually say it many, many times.

M: Yes, I know, I know …

Recording 2

1   Mmm, I suppose they should show more good news on TV. Yeah, we always hear the bad stuff, and not the good things that are happening in the world. But I suppose good news isn't so exciting, is it? It doesn't make such a good story. It's an awful thing to say, but if we just had good news on TV all the time, we'd probably all get bored and switch it off!

2   I don't know if there's exactly too much sex and violence, but I do think dramas and soap operas these days deal with topics that can be quite upsetting and confusing for young children. You know, family break-ups and domestic violence, and so on. And often it's on very early in the evening when children are still up. Sometimes it's very difficult to avoid. I get quite worried about it sometimes.

3   I do think the quality of TV programmes has gone down in the last ten years or so. It's all reality TV, and these stupid game shows, and there are far more adverts than there used to be, I'm sure. Personally, I think it's a bit depressing. The TV producers must think we're all morons!

4   I certainly don't believe most of what I read in the newspapers. Often they make a story out of nothing. I find it really annoying. These so-called newspapers are full of silly unimportant gossip about famous people when there are really important things happening in the world, like wars or whatever, and the only thing they ever write about is some TV personality who's having an affair with someone or other. Personally, I'm not interested!

Recording 3

1   The very first newspapers were produced in Ancient Rome around 59 BC, but these were written by hand of course. Newspapers were first printed around 1615 in Germany.

2   The answer is Baywatch, which in the late 1990s was watched by over 1.1 billion people every week. The series has been translated into 142 languages.

3   CCTV is watched regularly by around 750 million viewers, around 85% of all Chinese TV viewers, making it the most watched TV network in the world. The TV network with the biggest international audience is CNN, which is watched by around 150 million households in 212 countries across the world.

4   Although earlier radios existed, the radio was first used for communication by Guglielmo Marconi, an Italian electrical engineer in 1895. He was awarded the Nobel prize for his work in 1909.

5   The cartoon The Simpsons was created by Matt Groening in 1986. The characters were named after members of Groening's own family.

6   The answer is a. The twentieth Bond film, Die another Day was released in 2002. The Bond films have made more money than any other series of films in history, so far over $13 billion dollars.

7   The answer is Shakespeare. Around 400 films have been based on his plays.

8   It is estimated that around 70 million TVs are manufactured in the world every year. The smallest TV in the world was made in Japan in the 1980s. It was a wristwatch TV and measured just three centimetres across.

Recording 4

astonished, boiling, brilliant, delighted, dreadful, freezing, furious, hilarious, ridiculous, terrible, terrific, terrified, tragic

Recording 5

1   I'd like to talk to you about a book that um … I just read while I was on holiday and it's called 'Behaving Badly' and it's by an English writer called Isabel Wolff. Her stories are always about women … and women in their twenties in London at the moment which is why I like them. Erm … this book is … erm … this book stars … a, a lady called Rose who is actually a pet therapist. It's a love story and erm … it's about how Rose has been having a bit of a hard time with men and how slowly she meets somebody and rebuilds her confidence and falls in love again. The book's very, very, very easy to read and erm … one thing I really liked about it was the humour. It's written with a fant– it's just got so many lines in it that are really witty and they make you laugh out loud. Erm … a weak point about it could be that the story is possibly a little bit predictable. I'd recommend it to anyone who likes to really switch off when they read so it was great for a holiday it was nothing too challenging. it was just pure escapism.

2   I think the best film I've seen, ever, probably is 'Moulin Rouge'. It was directed by an Australian man called Baz Luhrmann and it stars Ewan McGregor and Nicole Kidman. It's based in Paris … Moulin Rouge is a club and it's basically the story of a poet and an actress who er … fall in love and have a lot of problems and finally end up together. I think it's er … what I really like about the film is the way it's like theatre in the cinema. The songs are absolutely fantastic. The … er … the staging … the staging's marvellous, the dance routines are absolutely um … are inspiring quite frankly. And one of the things I didn't really like about it was, mostly at the beginning of the film, which is extremely fast-moving, and frankly if you look at the screen it gives you a headache. I know a lot of people don't like films with

songs in but this … this is done … this does that really, really absolutely fantastically I'd recommend it to anyone.

3 About two weekends ago, I went to see a concert um … in Earls Court in London. Um … it was Justin Timberlake. Er …it was called *Justified*. Er … I'm not the biggest fan of Justin Timberlake, but my friend got me a ticket so I went along with her. And actually I was really impressed by him. Um … he writes all the stuff himself. He is an amazing singer, which was good to find out. He was incredible singing live. Um, the best thing I thought about the concert was his dancing and the dancers. They were just absolutely fantastic … and the lighting was amazing. The musicians were incredible and erm … it was really loud and fun and the atmosphere was brilliant. Um … the only bad thing about it was that I was sitting quite far back so I couldn't really see his face very well but I didn't have anything in the way of my view so it was OK. Um … I'd definitely recommend going to see Justin Timberlake because it is a big erm … and exciting show. Um … yeah, I really enjoyed myself.

Recording 7

1 The match has begun.
2 I rang lots of times.
3 They ran away.
4 We've drunk the whole bottle!
5 He swam every day this summer.
6 I've sung in public many times.

Module 7

Recording 1

1 Could I have the bill, please?
2 Is it okay if I take this chair?
3 Excuse me, can I get past, please?
4 Could you pass me the water, please?
5 Do you mind if I borrow your mobile, really quickly?
6 Could you possibly change this five-pound note for me?
7 Would you mind watching the children, just for a second?
8 Is it all right if we sit here?
9 Can you tell me the time, please?

Recording 2

1 A: Could I have the bill, please?
   B: Certainly, sir.
2 A: Is it okay if I take this chair?
   B: Sorry, but someone's sitting there.
3 A: Excuse me, can I get past, please?
   B: Sure.
4 A: Could you pass me the water, please?
   B: Here you are.
5 A: Do you mind if I borrow your mobile, really quickly?
   B: I'm afraid the battery's flat, sorry.
6 A: Could you possibly change this five pound note for me?
   B: Sorry, but we've got no change ourselves mate.
7 A: Would you mind watching the children, just for a second?
   B: Of course not, dear!
8 A: Is it all right if we sit here?
   B: Sure, go ahead.
9 A: Can you tell me the time please?
   B: Certainly. It's three minutes past eleven.

Recording 4

1 A: I'm off home now. See you tomorrow.
   B: Oh, Tony says he needs to speak to you urgently.
   A: Ohh! Thanks, I'll go and see what he wants.
   B: I think he's still in a meeting.

A: Urr! I really need to go. I'm taking Mandy out tonight. We're going to see that new film at the Ritzy and I've got to pick her up in an hour. Look, tell Tony I'll come in early tomorrow. He … he can talk to me then.
2 A: Oh no! Is that the time? I think I've missed the last bus.
   B: Don't worry, I'll give you a lift home.
   A: No, there's no need for that. It's too far and anyway, you must be tired.
   B: Yeah, yes, I am a bit. I tell you what, Andy'll take you. Andy??
   A: No, really. I'll phone for a taxi. Have you got a number?

Recording 5

1 I carry those for you.
2 I'll come with you, if you like.
3 I take you all out for a pizza!
4 I'll help you with those.
5 Don't worry, I'll baby-sit.
6 What a shame! I cook the dinner if you like.

Recording 6

I = INTERVIEWER, N = NIKAM NIPOTAM

I: So what kind of things would a visitor to Thailand need to know about? Are there any er … social customs that are very different from a European country, say?
N: Well, er … there are a lot of things that are different … um … for example, the names, er … the way you address people is different.
I: How's that?
N: Well, you always call people by the first name. The polite way to address people is by their first name.
I: What, even in a formal situation?
N: Yes, you say 'khun' – it's like 'Mr' or 'Miss' or 'Mrs'.
I: Oh, you mean it's the same for men and women?
N: Yes, 'khun' is for men and women. It's the same. You say 'khun' and the first name; and also, when you meet people, you don't shake hands usually. There's a traditional greeting called a 'wai'.
I: A 'wai'? And what's that exactly?
N: Well, you put your hands together, like when you pray, er … when you say a prayer, and you bow your head forward slightly, and the other person does the same. But it's not usually for friends, uh … you don't need to do it. You just do it for people older than you.
I: I see. And in public are there any things that you find different? Is it true that it's not acceptable for a young couple to hold hands in public?
N: Well, uh … nowadays some of them do; maybe because of the influence of Western society, but it's not so common. I think, um, twenty years ago you couldn't do this. You couldn't hold hands in public, and even now, a couple kissing in public. Oh, no, you wouldn't see that.
I: Uh-huh.
N: Another thing that people might find very different is that the head is very important for Thai people. You can't touch another person's head. You have to respect people and in the same way as the head is the most important part, the feet is the lowest part. It's very rude to point at anything with your feet. If you want to open a door with your foot, you can't do that!
I: Right. So if someone invites you to their home, is there anything you should know about how to behave?
N: Yes, you have to take your shoes off! Don't forget!
I: You have to?
N: Oh, you have to, and if you're invited to eat in someone's house, it's a little bit different. When we eat a meal, we always put the food in the middle, for sharing. You have a big bowl for the rice and everyone helps themselves to the

other dishes with a spoon and fork. Mm, we don't have salt and pepper, and we have something, something called 'nam pla' on the table. It's ... er it's a ... fish sauce. It's got a very strong taste. It's typical of Thailand. For me, Thai food is very good. It's delicious!

I: Right. Okay ... anything else, any other 'dos', 'don't forgets' and don'ts'?

N: Mmm ... ah, let me see ... erm ... maybe one thing you should know is about the royal family, the Thai royal family. It's not the same as in England. In England, you can say anything about the royal family, but in Thailand you can't talk about them like that. You always have to show respect.

I: That is very different from England. Well, thank you very much for your help. I'll try to remember everything you've told me!

N: You're welcome.

Recording 7

Amy
If a couple go out on a date here, they definitely split the bill. Well, maybe not on the first date, or if the guy has a job and the woman doesn't, but generally you pay fifty-fifty for everything, and you always offer to pay.

Pawel
Men usually shake hands when they greet each other, not only the first time they meet, or if they haven't seen each other for a long time, like people do in England, but every day. When a man enters a room, it's quite common to shake hands with all the other men in the room.

Rosa
In Peru, if you go visit your friends, you never arrive on time. No one arrives on time. It's perfectly okay to arrive an hour late, nobody cares – it's expected! If you really want people to be punctual, you have to say 'hora inglesa' which means 'English time'!

Ian
These days fewer and fewer people smoke, and generally nowadays it's not really acceptable to smoke in people's houses. I mean it would be okay if the hosts started smoking in the house themselves, but normally you go out into the garden, if you want to smoke, especially if there are young children in the house. Sometimes everyone is out in the garden smoking!

Dong-Min
If we're meeting friends, we normally meet at about 7.00, and eat at maybe 7.30. People usually go home at about 11.00. Most Korean people are home before 11.00.

Lee Kuan
When you go out here, people expect you to dress smartly. The way you dress is important. Your clothes can't be dirty or crumpled or old. And it's important to be fashionable, especially for women, with nice make-up and jewellery. It's what people expect.

Ramon
It's normal to go out late in Spain, really late. I mean I often don't meet my friends until ten, even eleven o'clock. If you want to eat in a restaurant, that's about the normal time, and if you want to go dancing or go to bars, in Madrid, you can stay up until five, six, seven in the morning. There are still lots of people out at that time.

Khalid
We normally eat together with the family every evening. My mother and my sisters cook it and we all eat together. It's not normal to go on dates with a girlfriend, you must be engaged first. After dinner I normally go for a drive around with my friends. Sometimes we go to the shopping mall and see our friends.

Recording 8

(answers only)

a Generally you
b always offer
c usually shake
d quite common
e It's perfectly okay to
f Generally nowadays; not really acceptable
g People expect you
h It's important
i It's normal to

Recording 9

R = ROGER; L = LAURENCE

R: Hello?

L: Hello, Roger, it's Laurence.

R: Laurence! I haven't heard from you for ages! How are you?

L: Fine. We've just got back from a few days away with some relatives down on the coast. Anyway, how are things with you and Millie?

R: Great, fine – everything's fine. We've got all Millie's sisters round for lunch at the moment.

L: Yes, I can hear you're busy! Listen, I won't keep you. I was just phoning to ask if you and Millie are doing anything next Saturday night. If not, would you like to come over for a meal? Patrick and Colin are coming over, and we thought it would be nice if you were there, too.

R: We can't, I'm afraid. An old mate of mine from college is getting married up in Scotland, and we're going up there for the wedding. What a shame! It'd be nice to see you all again.

L: Yeah, it is a shame. I know, how about the following Saturday instead? I don't think we've got anything planned that night.

R: Yeah, I think that should be fine. I'll check with Millie and call you back if there's any problem, but ... no ... that'd be great!

L: Great! We'll look forward to seeing you. I'll let you get back to the family now. Give me a ring in a week or so to arrange a time.

R: Okay, then. Thanks for calling. See you!

L: Yeah, see you!

Module 8

Recording 1

1 A: ... so if you need to play a section of the tape again, make sure you've set the counter to zero so you can rewind to the part you want ...

   B: Right.

   A: .... otherwise it can take you a while to find it. OK, so rewind, and once you're in the right place and use the pause button if you need to – that's the one on the end there.

   B: Yes, I do know that.

   A: Of course, yes.

   B: Where do I switch it off?

   A: Just press this button at the back there. There's also a little light there to tell you it's plugged in.

2 C: They told me it was the very latest model. Well, I've had nothing but trouble with it over the last week. It's driving me mad to be honest 'cos I need to use it, y'know, every day.

   D: So what's the problem exactly?

   C: Well, it just keeps crashing, without warning. The screen just ... just freezes. I've no idea why – usually when I'm in the middle of something important, actually.

   D: Yeah, it always happens, doesn't it?

   C: And I have to switch it off and restart it. I keep losing my work, losing things I've done. It's so frustrating and I've tried re-installing …

3 … and you should all be aware of a few basic safety measures. Firstly, if something gets stuck, or the machine breaks down at any time, don't just leave it and hope someone else'll fix it. Switch the machine off here at the wall. There's no need to unplug it. Just switch it off here, and you open it here, by holding down this button here. Now, it can get extremely hot inside, especially if you're making a large number of copies so do take care you don't touch anything. Oh, and by the way, if you ever see smoke …

4 F: Is that new?
G: Yeah, I just got it the other day. Nice, isn't it?
F: Mmm.
G: It's got these really cool features and it's got loads of games on it. And it's got some really funny ring tones … like that …
F: Nice.
G: And I've just recorded a really good message for my voicemail, I'll play it to you. Oh, hang on. The batteries are a bit low at the moment. I'll recharge it as soon as I get home.

Recording 2

a You should switch off your mobile phone when you're in class, or in a cinema.
b You can plug in the vacuum cleaner at the wall socket over here.
c Press this button to turn it on.
d You can rewind or fast forward the tape using this button.
e You should restart your computer if you're having problems.
f I love this song. Turn up the volume!
g Does your mobile phone company charge you to replay your messages?
h You should always shut down your computer when you've finished work.
i If you hold down this button, it will restart your computer.
j You can pause the tape while you fill in the gaps.
k My computer's crashed again. I think it's got a virus.
l Can I use your mobile phone? Mine needs recharging.
m My Walkman batteries must need replacing. It's playing very slow.

Recording 4

What you have to remember is that the desert – any true desert – is an amazingly beautiful, amazingly spiritual place. It's also an extremely dangerous place, and every year we have several cases where people, usually tourists have serious problems in the desert and have to be rescued. And if people just use a bit of common sense, and follow a few basic rules for survival, this could so easily be avoided.

I think the first thing is, if you decide to go into the desert for whatever reason, just let one or two people know where and when you're going, and when you expect to get back. That way if something does go wrong, people will know where to start looking. There's not really much chance of finding you if we don't where to look. And never ever go into the desert alone. As for things you should take, well there's just one word which is water. You must be sure to take plenty of water, and by plenty, I mean at least two litres per person per day. In the desert there really is no such thing as too much water. And definitely no alcohol, not even a cold beer – that will dry you out and make you even thirstier. Check you've enough spare fuel for your vehicle – at least twenty litres. As for the equipment you should take, well, of course, a map, and a compass … preferably a couple of maps, and be sure to take a small first-aid kit with a pair of scissors, some bandages and a sharp knife. And take some matches so you can start a fire if need be.

You can experience extremes of climate in the desert, so you'll need to have lots of sun screen if you don't want a bad case of sunburn. On the other hand the temperature drops dramatically at night. Actually, more people die from the cold than from the heat, and very often people don't take any warm clothes to put on at night … but you'll need them …

Recording 5

(answers only)

a several	f plenty of	k some
b a bit of	g too much	l lots of
c a few	h no	m any
d one or two	i enough	
e much	j some	

Recording 6

1 I couldn't live without my mobile phone. I've had this phone for about six months now and I use it to organise my social life. I'm always sending texts and calling people when I'm out and about. I'd be really lost without it.

2 One thing I couldn't live without is my alarm clock. Now I know you might think that that sounds strange, but this alarm clock has sentimental value. I've had it for about twelve years now and it was given to me by friends at university because I just couldn't get up in the morning. Um … it's battery-operated and it's actually in the shape of a soldier and he's gorgeous actually because he's wearing a uniform and he has a helmet … and to turn the alarm off, you have to press down his helmet which I think is fantastic … so it … it's not valuable at all, it's got purely sentimental value but actually I couldn't live without it.

3 One thing I'd hate to be without is my guitar. I've had it for over twenty years, and I play it most days and sometimes when I go on holiday I don't take it with me and after about two days I'm wishing I had. It's an acoustic guitar, um … six string acoustic guitar. It's old, but it's got a really good sound … and er … I love it.

4 One thing I'd hate to be without is my computer. I don't remember what life was like before. Basically, because I have all my bits and pieces of information about my life on the computer, including my phone book, addresses, um … I use the Internet quite a lot and I e-mail friends and family and I don't know if I could write a letter and communicate with them without e-mail.

5 Um, okay so something I would hate to be without um … would be my CD Walkman. Um … I use it on the train um … because it blocks out all the sound of people on their mobile phones and … er … children crying. Um … so yeah, it's really important to me … um … it's grey … um … I've had it for about six years. I bought it when I was living in Japan. Um … it's quite slim although I think you can buy slimmer ones nowadays.

6 One thing I'd hate to be without is my ring. It was given to me by my dad as a birthday present when I was around thirteen years old and um … I don't think I've actually taken it off since. It's made of silver and it has a heart in the middle of it and two hands which are kind of holding the heart. Um … it originates from Ireland and it has a lot of sort of sentimental value for me because um … my grandmother came from Ireland and unfortunately I didn't really know her but it reminds me of her sometimes when I look at it.

Recording 7

Conversation 1

A = ASSISTANT; C= CUSTOMER

A: Can I help you at all?

C: Yes, I'd like to buy a Toshiba 50 cm screen television.

A: I'll just check that we've got one in stock. Just a moment. Yes, that's fine. You can either pick it up from our customer collection point or we can deliver it for you.

C: Do I have to pay for delivery?

A: Yes, I'm afraid it's an extra €20.00.

C: No, I'll pick it up then, thank you. Where is the customer collection point?

A: It's just round the back of the shop, you can't miss it. It'll be ready for you in about ten minutes. How would you like to pay, sir?

C: By Mastercard, if that's okay.

A: Yes, that's fine, so that's €349.99, please. Okay. If you could just sign here. Okay. This is your copy, and here's your receipt. Keep your receipt sir, because it's also your guarantee.

A: Oh okay, and erm … how long is it guaranteed for?

C: Two years parts and labour.

A: Right, thanks then …

Conversation 2

O = OPERATOR; C = CUSTOMER

O: Hello, this is First Directory, Tania speaking. Do you want to make an enquiry or place an order?

C: Place an order, please.

O: Have you ordered from us before?

C: Yes, but it was quite a long time ago.

O: Okay, let's try. Can you give me your postcode?

C: BR5 8KS … S for sugar.

O: And your house number?

C: 25.

O: Is that Miss E Simpson?

C: That's right.

O: Okay, what would you like to order today?

C: Erm, it's a pair of trousers from page twenty-one of your catalogue.

O: Have you got the reference number?

C: Yes. It's RZ1 224BL.

O: Okay, black trousers at €39.99. And the size?

C: Twelve … long.

O: Yes, we've got those in stock. Anything else?

C: No, that's it, thanks.

O: Okay the total cost of your order including postage and packing is €42.49 and it should be with you within three to five working days.

C: And I can send them back if they don't fit?

O: Yes, that's fine. Phone us up within seven days and we'll collect them free.

C: Great.

O: Would you like to pay now by credit card, or shall we send you a statement?

C: Er, send a statement, please.

O: Okay the order will be added to your next statement. Thank you for your order.

C: Thanks, bye.

Consolidation Modules 5–8

Recording 1

a On 17th July, 1938, American aviator, Douglas Corrigan was given permission to take off from an airfield near New York. He became the first pilot to cross the Atlantic in a solo plane, by accident. Corrigan was given a hero's welcome on his return to New York. Since then he's been known as 'Wrong Way' Corrigan.

b Sirimavo Bandaranaike was the first woman to be elected Prime Minister of her country. Her husband had been Prime Minister of Sri Lanka in the 1950s, until he was murdered in 1959. After this, Bandaranaike decided to enter politics herself, and the following year she was elected as Prime Minister – the first female prime minister in the world. She died in 2000 at the age of 84.

c Almost fifty years ago, Laika became the most famous dog in the world – she was the first animal in space. She was on board the Russian Sputnik 2, which was launched in November 1957. Sadly, Laika could not be brought back to Earth, and she died in space about a week after the launch. The Laika Institute in Moscow, one of Russia's most important research institutes, is named after her.

Recording 2

Conversation 1

D = DAVE; J = JANE; F = FRAN

D: 761 4503?

J: Hi, Dave. It's Jane here.

D: Oh hi, Jane. How are you?

J: I'm fine. Is Fran there?

D: Yeah, just a minute. I'll get her. Fran, Jane on the phone!

F: Okay, I'll pick it up in the other room. Hi, Jane!

J: Hi, listen, this is just a real quick one. I've got a little favour to ask. Have you still got your tent by any chance?

F: Yeah, I think so.

J: It's just that we're going camping next weekend, and I've just opened our tent up and discovered it's got a great big hole in it!

F: Oh, no. That's no good!

J: So I was wondering if we could borrow yours if you're not using it.

F: Sure no problem. Oh, hang on, though. You know what, I think I lent it to my sister.

J: Oh, right.

F: Yeah, she borrowed it last summer, I think. I'm sure she's not using it now, though. I'm just wondering how I can get it back from her before next weekend.

J: Maybe I could go round and pick it up?

F: Yeah, or she might be coming over this way. I tell you what. I'll just phone her and check she's still got it. I'm sure we can sort something out.

J: Oh well, thanks. Don't ask her to come over specially though, will you? I can easily go round there one evening next week.

F: Okay, well I'll tell her that and I'll call you back in a few minutes, alright?

J: Yeah. Speak to you in a bit. Bye.

Conversation 2

D = DAD; B = BECKY

B: Dad?

D: Yeah?

B: You know Sam and I are going to France on Sunday?

D: Yeah.

B: Well, I was just wondering; it's just that we need to be at the station at seven in the morning.

D: Yes.

B: Well, the thing is – Sam's mum was gonna give us a lift down there, you know with all our stuff, but she's going away herself now, so I was just wondering …

D: You're not asking me to take you, I hope!

B: Well, it would be a real help. Our rucksacks are going to be ever so heavy and it's going to be really hard to get a bus at that time on a Sunday morning.

D: What time will I have to get up, about half past five? And aren't your mum and I going out somewhere on Saturday night, some dinner or something? I don't suppose we'll be in bed before one in the morning. I can't be up again at five!

B: Oh please, Dad!

D: Why don't you ask your mother? She's always saying she likes getting up early.

B: I have asked her. She said to ask you!

D: Did she? Well, I'll have to think about it, but I'm not promising anything.

B: Thanks, Dad. I'll go and ring Sam.

Module 9

Recording 1

1 According to the Health Minister, Alan Barnett, more than twenty hospitals have been opened during the last ten years. In addition, waiting lists for major operations are shorter than at any time in the last thirty years. 'The nation's health system has never been in better shape,' he claimed in a speech given to …

2 All the evidence suggests that English continues to grow as a world language. The latest estimates indicate that there are now more than a billion people currently learning English – far more than there were just twenty years ago.

3 The figures published today show that road deaths are twenty-seven percent below the figures for the previous year and that child deaths and serious injuries are thirty-eight percent down. Deaths and serious injuries are now at their lowest levels since records began more than fifty years ago. Even so, an average of six people died and 364 were injured …

4 Rail fares are set to rise by an average of five percent from January next year. This means that the price of a single ticket from London to Manchester will go up from …

5 Following the release of the latest statistics showing a jobless figure of six percent for October, Treasurer Peter Costello said that the result was the 'lowest in Australia since March 1990'. The unemployment rate has fallen this year from seven percent in January to 6.2 percent in September and six percent in October …

6 Our screens are filled with ridiculous reality shows, imported soap operas and cartoons that would insult the intelligence of a two-year-old. The quality of TV in this country has reached its lowest point ever. We can only hope that things improve when …

7 All the evidence is that people are generally optimistic about the economic situation. According to a recent telephone poll, eighty-six percent of people in the state believe their economic situation is as good (41%) or better (45%) than it was four years ago.

8 … and for longer than ever before. Travel figures from the Office for National Statistics show yet another year-on-year increase in the number of holidays taken abroad. Up by three percent, with spending up by eight percent which is all the more surprising against a background of …

9 A: We're discussing schools. Are they getting better, or are they getting worse? What do you the listeners think? Our next caller is James on line four. James, what's your view on this?

B: Well, I think it's about time people faced up to the fact that under this government, standards in our schools have fallen dramatically …

A: You think so?

B: I do, yes. I mean look at the way twenty years ago we had a school system to be proud of, but thanks to all these so-called reforms things just go from bad to worse. Let me give you an example, my daughter who is eleven years old …

10 Although it's true there are more people registered for exercise programmes at their local gym than ever before, almost sixty-five percent of people who sign up do not attend the gym after the first couple of weeks. Indeed, recent research gives a clear indication that increased car use, and the growth of home entertainment such as computer games, videos and DVDs mean that we actually get less exercise than we did twenty years ago.

Recording 3

1 I would definitely travel on a train without a ticket. I wouldn't feel bad about it at all. If I was in a hurry and if the ticket office was closed, or the machine didn't have any change or whatever. If the ticket inspectors came round I would offer to pay, of course. I mean I wouldn't hide in the toilets or anything, but if they didn't ask me, I wouldn't worry about it. I wouldn't make any special effort to pay at the end of the journey.

2 I'd never break the speed limit in an area with lots of people around because obviously it's very dangerous. If a child stepped in front of my car and I was speeding, I would never forgive myself. But I suppose I don't really worry so much about breaking the speed limit on the motorway. I wouldn't drive at a really crazy speed, but I would go a bit faster than the speed limit. I wouldn't really feel bad about that.

3 I have to admit that I would do a lot of the things here. I'm probably not very socially responsible, apart from one thing – I would never drop litter. I absolutely hate litter. I'd put my rubbish in my bag and take it home if there weren't any litter bins around.

Recording 4

1 I'll do something really special.
2 I'd move to a big house by the sea.
3 I'll probably buy a pair of jeans.
4 I'd go to live in California.
5 I'll probably stay at home.
6 I'll be famous one day.
7 I'd buy some new trainers.
8 I'll go on holiday with my parents.
9 I'd give up work.
10 I'd be a famous rock star.

Recording 6

1 President of the St Ambrosian Hotel and Tourism Association

… and as you know, plans were made last year for a new luxury hotel and golf course just outside the capital at Grand Bay. Unfortunately, the Foundation has not been able to get enough money from our foreign investors for the hotel project to continue. I am sorry to say that this project, which is of the greatest importance for all the people of St Ambrosia, will have to be abandoned if we do not receive money from the Lottery Committee. The benefits of the hotel project continuing are obvious. We believe it will bring an extra 50,000 tourists a year to St Ambrosia. Think of how this will help the economy of our island, and the hotel will also create hundreds of jobs for local people. I am sure that your committee will approve our application for SA$4 million so that this very impressive project …

2 President of the St Ambrosian Sports Association

… we've always encouraged all St Ambrosians to play sport, to make the people of our island healthy in mind and body. But because there are no modern sports facilities on the island, our national athletics and football teams have to train in the public park, and our young people must play sport in the street, and so cannot learn and develop as they should. For SA$6 million, we could build a National Sports Centre for all St Ambrosians, young and old. The Sports Centre would provide a social centre for our island, especially for young people, who often have nothing to do. Our dream is, one day, to send a team to the Olympic Games to represent St Ambrosia. The National Sports Centre is a necessary part of our dream. Please, help the dream become a reality.

3 Vice-chancellor of the University of St Ambrosia

… we all know that, because of the poor facilities at the university, St Ambrosia is losing its best and most intelligent young people, who are choosing to study abroad, and not returning to the island when they have completed their studies. The young people of this island, the young people who will go on to become engineers, doctors, lawyers, teachers must have the best possible education here in St Ambrosia, not in some other country. Without education, there is no future for us. We desperately need new equipment in our Computer Science and Technology Department. For SA$4.5 million, we could make the necessary improvements to make sure that young St Ambrosians no longer have to go abroad.

4 Director of the St Ambrosian Children's Hospital

My message to you is a very simple one. Our hospital, which helps the very poorest children of St Ambrosia, needs money for beds and medical equipment. We cannot continue without your help. We need SA$3.5 million to stay open for another year, and to care for the sick children of our island. Without us, many of these children will have no one to help them. If you care at all about the poor children of St Ambrosia, you must help us.

5 Chief-executive of International Petroleum Incorporated

This is really a simple business proposition. We believe that there is a possibility, a good possibility perhaps, that there are large oil deposits under the sea off the north coast of St Ambrosia. Obviously, looking for the oil will take several years, and there is a risk that we will find nothing. Therefore, we feel it is reasonable that the government of St Ambrosia shares this risk with International Petroleum Incorporated. SA$ 8 million seems a small amount if we consider that if we find oil, and I repeat, if we find oil – St Ambrosia could become one of the richest islands in the world.

Recording 8

1 The proportion of the world's surface which is covered in water is 71%.
2 The lowest temperature ever recorded was in Vostok, Antarctica and it was minus 89 degrees celsius.
3 The average cost of a wedding in the UK is 27,753.
4 The closest distance between Earth and the planet Mars is 55,680,000 kilometres.
5 The estimated population of the world in mid-2005 was 6.3 billion.
6 The speed of light is 300,000 kilometres per second.
7 The population of Japan is approximately 126 million.
8 The area of the world's largest shopping mall in Alberta, Canada, is 483,080 square metres.
9 The percentage of British people who are over sixty-five is 7%.
10 The largest ever crowd for a sporting event was 199,859 – at the World Cup Final between Brazil and Uruguay in 1950.

Module 10

Recording 1

A: So, there was a carrot, a scarf and some coal in the middle of some grass …
B: Yes.
A: … but no one had put them there.
B: That's right. No one had put them on the grass.
A: So how had they… how had these things got into the field?
B: Well, that's what you've got to find out, isn't it?
A: Hmm. Let me think. Had someone actually taken these things onto the grass? I mean they hadn't fallen from an aeroplane or something.
B: No, they hadn't fallen from an aeroplane. Someone had taken them into the field, but they didn't put them on the grass.
A: They didn't put them on the grass … so how had they …?
C: Had they put them somewhere else? Somewhere higher up, not on the grass? Is that right?
B: Yeah, you're getting there.
C: Yeah, I think I know this actually. Had there been snow on the ground at one stage, and that snow had melted?
B: Yeah, you've got it.
C: Yeah, and they'd made a snowman – y'know, carrot for the nose, coal for the eyes, scarf …
A: Oh, I see.
C: … and when the sun came out, the snowman melted and the things ended up on the grass even though no one had actually put them there.
B: That's it! Simple, eh?
A: Well, it is if you know the answer!
B: I've got another one. See if you can get this one …

Recording 2

1 She lived in Paris.
2 I'd left my umbrella at home.
3 I left my umbrella at home.
4 They sold all the tickets.
5 My uncle had reserved a table.
6 She'd lived in Paris.
7 They'd sold all the tickets.
8 My uncle reserved a table.

Recording 5

M = MICHAEL; W = WOMAN; S = SECRETARY

On the phone

M: Can I speak to Mr Bell?

W: I'm sorry, but I've only just started working here, and I don't know who Mr Bell is. Can you ring back later when my boss, Mr Findlater, is here?

M: Yes, I will. Is Mr Findlater's first name Harry?

W: Yes, it is.

M: Have you ever noticed a tattoo on the back of Mr Findlater's hand?

W: Yes, I have – a tattoo of an owl.

The following day

M: Who gave you my brother's number?

S: It's not a phone number. It's a bank account for Mr Bell, one of our customers.

Recording 7

One evening, a young man and his wife were on a trip to visit his mother. Usually, they arrived in time for supper, but they had had a late start, and now it was getting dark and the fog was getting thicker. So they decided to look for a place to stay overnight and go on in the morning.

Just off the road, they saw a small house in the woods. 'Maybe they rent rooms,' the wife said. So they stopped to ask. They knocked at the door and waited. Eventually, an elderly man and woman came to the door. They didn't rent rooms they said, but they would be glad to have them stay overnight as their guests. They had plenty of room, and they would enjoy the company.

The old woman made coffee and brought out some cake, and the four of them talked for a while. Then the young couple were taken to their room. They again offered to pay, but the old man said he would not think of accepting any money.

The couple got up early next morning, before their hosts had awakened. On the table in the kitchen, they left an envelope with some money in it for the room. Then they went on to the next town.

They stopped in a restaurant and had breakfast. When they told the owner where they had stayed, he was shocked. 'That can't be,' he said. 'That house burned to the ground about a month ago and the man and woman who lived there died in the fire. I kept the newspaper. Look, I'll show you.'

The owner disappeared around the back, and re-appeared a moment later with an old newspaper. The headline told its own story: COUPLE DIE IN TRAGIC HOUSE FIRE and there was a photo of the couple who had taken them in the previous night. The young couple could not believe their eyes. They drove back to the house … only now there was no house. Just a burned-out shell. They stood staring at the ruins trying to understand what had happened.

Suddenly, the woman screamed. There, on the badly-burned table, was the envelope they had left that morning.

Module 11

Recording 1

(answers only)

1	aren't allowed	6	shouldn't
2	are allowed	7	can't
3	don't have to; can	8	ought to
4	mustn't	9	shouldn't
5	should; don't have to	10	have to

Recording 2

1 aren't allowed to … the public aren't allowed to … the public aren't allowed to come in here

2 are allowed to … cyclists are allowed to … cyclists are allowed to use this path

3 don't have to … you don't have to cycle … you don't have to cycle on this path
can … you can walk … you can walk if you want

4 mustn't … you mustn't wear … you mustn't wear jeans or T-shirts

5 should … you should … you should dress smartly
don't have to … you don't have to wear … you don't have to wear a suit and a tie

6 shouldn't … you shouldn't … you shouldn't swim here

7 can't … you can't … you can't park your car here

8 ought to … you ought to … you ought to have your boarding card ready for inspection

9 shouldn't … you shouldn't … you shouldn't dive into the swimming pool

10 have to … you have to … you have to show your passport

Recording 3

a One rule I find really annoying is … um … when you get on an aeroplane and before it takes off they say that you have to listen to the safety announcement. I don't travel a lot, but I've been on loads of planes and they're always the same. They're always the same announcements, they're always the same demonstrations and I just find it … just really annoying to have to listen to it again. And what's really annoying is it's totally unnecessary because I've heard it a thousand times and I don't believe that it would save my life anyway.

b One … um … recent rule that's been introduced is having to pay before you board the buses. Um … I understand that this is supposed to speed up the process of getting on the bus, but I find this really annoying. I've seen people running for the bus with heavy shopping and they can't get on because they haven't paid. Also I think the problem is if you … if you haven't got the right change or … um … the ticket machine isn't working, it means you can't get on so I think um … the law needs to be looked at.

c Um … a rule that does annoy me is what you can and you can't wear at work. Um … if … in most offices men have to wear a tie and a suit and um … I mean, don't get me wrong, I think it's very important to look professional at work and it's important to give a good impression that you can do your job properly. It's just that if you go into any clothes shop um … suits are either black or they're grey or they're navy blue so the situation you have in an office is that everyone looks the same,

d One rule that really annoys me, but then again it's only an unwritten social rule these days, is the rule that you have to change your name when you get married in Britain. Um … in Italy, for example, you can keep your maiden name, but in Britain you've got to change it, which means so much inconvenience. I mean, for example, you've got to contact your bank, your friends, your … I mean even shops that you have accounts with and tell them that you're now somebody else. I think I'm going through a bit of an identity crisis with it.

e What really annoys me in a hotel is that you sometimes have to check out at a ridiculously early time, perhaps even eight o'clock in the morning. I'm not even awake at that time. If you've paid for a room you should be able to keep it till midday.

f D'you know, one thing I find really annoying is when you're in a railway station and you really need to go to the ladies' room, you know what I mean, and unfortunately you have to pay 20p to go. Well, usually you don't have 20p in your bag so you're running around trying to get change from shops. Why on earth do they ask you to pay in public places? I mean, they must know you're in a hurry.

Recording 4

(answers only)

a weren't allowed to; had to
b couldn't; had to
c weren't allowed to
d couldn't; were allowed to
e could; didn't have to; had to

Recording 5

1 Who does most of the housework in your house?
2 Did you do well in your last exam?
3 Do you ever do the washing up in your house?
4 Do you ever do the ironing?
5 Are you planning to do any exercise later today?
6 Where do you usually do your homework?
7 Do people have to do military service in your country?
8 Write the names of any languages you did, or are doing, at secondary school.
9 Have you ever done any aerobics or yoga?
10 Do you like doing grammar exercises?
11 Have you done any shopping today?
12 Are you planning to do any work today?

Module 12

Recording 1

Andrew, who was thirty-five, was an experienced rower who had won international competitions. However Debra, who was twenty-seven and a physical education teacher, had only learned to row the year before the competition. But she soon found she enjoyed life on board the tiny seven-metre boat.

From early on, however, it was clear that Andrew was suffering from acute anxiety, and had developed an irrational fear of the ocean – something he had never experienced before. At first, Debra and Andrew tried to overcome this and they continued their journey. Then one day, the boat was caught in a violent storm. Debra found Andrew in the cabin shaking and unable to even talk to her.

It was clear that Andrew could not continue. With the nearest rescue boat five days away, Debra and Andrew had to make the toughest decision of their lives. Should Debra abandon the race in order to return home with her husband, or continue to Barbados, knowing that she would have to face the dangers of the Atlantic alone?

Recording 2

At this stage, Debra could easily have given up and gone back to England with her husband. But she passionately believed she could complete the journey alone and become only the tenth woman ever to cross the Atlantic by rowing boat. Andrew supported her 100% in her decision. They spent the five days needed for the rescue vessel to reach their boat preparing for the solo journey.

When the boat finally arrived and Andrew departed, she wrote in her diary: 'I couldn't help thinking that if anything went wrong we might never see each other again.'

Once she was alone, Debra could only sleep for short periods due to the danger of a collision with the huge oil tankers, which would have sunk a tiny boat like hers. Sharks, extreme weather conditions and the lack of fresh food all added to the dangers. Apart from the physical hardships, Debra suffered from severe loneliness, particularly around Christmas after more than three months at sea alone. The only human contact she had – apart from messages of advice and support from her husband – was on day seventy-four of the journey when she unexpectedly met a yacht called 'Seventh Heaven'. The people on board gave her a loaf of fresh bread, some biscuits, and more importantly she says, ten minutes of talking face to face with some other human beings.

To the rapturous applause of hundreds of well-wishers and a large number of press, Debra finally rowed into Port St Charles in Barbados on 26th January 2002. Her husband was among those waiting to congratulate her.

Although the official winners of the race had crossed the finishing line seventy days before, The Times wrote that 'The real winner of the race is the girl that came last.'

Recording 3

(answers only)

1 should have learned
2 wouldn't have entered
3 shouldn't have entered
4 could have died
5 wouldn't have survived
6 shouldn't have taken
7 would've found
8 would've given
9 could have attacked
10 should have given

Recording 4

could have, could've, she could've given up
should have, should've, he should've persuaded her
should not have, shouldn't've, he shouldn't've left her
would have, would've, he would've been responsible

Recording 5

1 I had worked really hard ever since leaving university. I worked for a big travel company and by the age of thirty I had reached the position of company director, which was really something for a woman of my age. I spent my whole life travelling the world. It was a great job! When I had my first baby, I decided to go back to work and leave the baby with a nanny, but after a couple of months I just hated it. I hated leaving her. I just couldn't do it any more. So in the end I decided to give up my job and become a full-time mother, and that's what I've been doing ever since. I've got two children now, and of course, we've got far less money than before, but I've never regretted it for a moment. The last five years have been absolutely great.

2 I always dreamed of being a professional footballer. I just wanted to play all the time, and I was doing pretty well. I got a place in the junior team of a big football club. Then when I was nineteen I broke my leg really badly and couldn't play for about six months. I tried to return, but I had lots of problems with my leg and I realised that I would never be able to play for a big club again. I had offers to play for small clubs, but that wasn't what I wanted, so I decided to give up my career and retrain as a coach, and that's what I've done. Mind you, this is definitely second best. I'd rather be a player.

3 I met Nikos while I was on holiday in Greece. It was a typical holiday romance, I suppose, except that we really, really liked each other. So basically after I came home Nikos followed me back to England, and persuaded me to go and live with him in Greece. I never thought I could leave my family and my friends and my job as a nurse and everything, but that's what I did, and here I am. We run a restaurant together on this beautiful island, and basically, it's all worked out really well.

Recording 6

(answers only)

I was stupid for a while
And now I feel like a fool
Was I ever loved by you?
I never had your heart
We were never meant to be
I could drown if I stay here
I know I will be okay
Was I ever loved by you?
So much hurt, so much pain
And I hope that in time, you'll
Was I ever loved by you?
You never gave your heart
There's a life out there for me.

Recording 7

far, heart	mind, sign
bruised, confused	okay, pain
fool, you	reach, see

Recording 8

1 A: OK, come on. It's time your light was out.
   B: But Dad …
   A: No, no. It's school tomorrow. Come on.
   B: But it's only ten o'clock. Mum always lets me stay up till …
   A: Well, I'm not mum, am I? So come on – lights out now. Come on, give me a kiss. OK. Good night, sweet dreams.
   B: Night night.
   A: See you in the morning.
   B: See you in the morning. Oh, Dad?
   A: Yes, what is it?
   B: Can I get a glass of water before I put the light out? It's just that I get ever so thirsty.

2 C: Right, well I'd better be going. My train is about to leave, any time now.
   D: Right …
   C: Well, it was nice meeting you. Thanks for coming to see me off. There was really no need.
   D: Oh, that's all right. It was nice meeting you too. I really enjoyed the concert. I think it went really well.
   C: Oh good, thank you. I enjoyed it, too. Um … thanks again. You've really been a great help. Thanks for arranging everything and er … being so helpful … booking the hotel and everything.
   D: It was my pleasure, really.
   C: Well, I'll be off, then. I'll see you around, maybe.
   D: I hope so.
   C: Yeah.
   D: Right, safe journey.
   C: Bye.
   D: Bye. Take care.
   C: I will.
   D: Keep in touch.
   C: Oh yes! But you haven't given me your e-mail …
   D: Oh, I'll write it down for you.
   C: Right, I wonder … would you like a cup of coffee? I think there's another train in about an hour and I'm not in such a hurry. There are one or two points about the concert I'd like to go through with you …

3 E: … for everything you've done, and we'd like you to accept this small gift from all of us on the course, with our very best wishes.
   F: Oh, thank you, thank you. That's very kind of you. Thanks, they're lovely. Thank you. … Well, oh dear … um … gosh. I'm not very good at speeches. Let me see. Well, first of all, thank you for the lovely flowers and the wonderful gift. It's really very touching. I'd like to thank you all for being such a nice group to work with. You've all worked really hard during the course. … No, no, really It's been great working with you; even you, Adam! Em, … I know you're all going off to various exciting places and do come and see me if ever you come back this way. You know where to find me. You've all got my e-mail address. … Oh thank you. Well, that's it really, and I wish you all the very best of luck … and do keep in touch.

Consolidation modules 9–12

Recording 1

1 Well, of course, looking back, it's all too easy to see the mistakes you've made. At the time it seemed like a great idea – the city's first Brazilian music club, fantastic, and we thought: 'Yeah, let's go for it!' So Dino – that's my ex-partner, my ex-business partner – we borrowed money from the bank; too much really. I think I borrowed far too much money. We owed so much, you know we were always in debt, I couldn't pay the staff some weeks, never mind myself. And, well, after we'd opened we didn't get as many people in the club as we'd hoped. The place was empty a lot of nights, the atmosphere wasn't right, and the club just didn't take off. And of course it didn't help when my dear friend Dino disappeared one day with most of what money we did have … and we never saw him again! So we had all kinds of problems, really. We closed about … um … six months later, and I lost everything – my house, everything! So here I am, still looking for a job, you know, but maybe if I'd thought about it a bit more …

2 Tennis now, and Florida-born teenager Patsy Kapinski has reached the final of her first major pro-tournament, the Australian Open Championships, by beating South African Lotte de Kuyper 6–1, 6–1 in the semi-final. It's Kapinski's first season on the pro-circuit, and she'll be the youngest player ever to play in the finals of the Australian Open. Victory in the final would bring Ms Kapinski approximately $800,000 in prize money. The beaten finalist will receive approximately $200,000. In the final, she is due to play fellow American Carine Mendel, the number one seed, who beat the French woman Béatrice Garros 6–4, 4–6, 6–2 in the other semi-final. Mendel has already played Kapinski twice this season, winning both matches comfortably. If Kapinski wins this final …

3 I find it so hard to imagine really. I'm the kind of person who likes to be outside, you know, to be active. Here, where I live now, I have the beach very close. I can go to the beach every day, I can see my friends there, go swimming – you know it's very nice, very sociable. But I think in Britain you can't do this. I think maybe you don't have the beaches like we have in my country. People live in another way, the weather is cloudy, often raining. I suppose, I don't know, but I can imagine. Also, someone like me, I'm the kind of person, really I need the sun every day. I really miss the sunshine, the warm weather. I don't like dark, winter. And of course all my friends are here. My friends are very important to me. Maybe I could find new friends, I don't know. I think if I lived in Britain …

Pearson Education Limited
Edinburgh Gate
Harlow
Essex CM20 2JE
England
And Associated Companies throughout the world.

www.longman.com/cuttingedge

First published 2005

ISBN 0582 825172

Set in 9/12.5pt ITS Stone Informal and 10/13pt Congress Sans.

Printed in Spain by Mateu Cromo, S.A. Pinto (Madrid)

Author acknowledgements

We would like to thank the following people for their help and contribution: Helen Barker, Sean Burke, Jonathan Bygrave, Vince Desmond, David Evans, Brenda Lynch, Lisa Manklow, Heather Morris, Dennis Murphy, Carrie Priestley, Jacqui Robinson, Glenn Taylor, Catherine Timothy, David Todd, Clare Tyrer, Justin Vollmer and Penny Reid (Producer) for making the unscripted recordings. We would also like to thank the publishing team for their support and encouragement, in particular Jenny Colley (Senior Publisher), Lindsay White (Project Manager), Shona Rodger and Rhona Snelling (Editors), Jonathan Barnard (Senior Designer), Andy Thorpe (Mac Artist) and Alma Gray (Producer).

The publishers and authors are very grateful to the following people and institutions for keeping user diaries:
Natalie Beach, Noreen Bannigan, St Giles College, London; Allie Charlwood, St Giles College, Brighton; Lynn Dunlop, EF Int. School of Language, Cambridge; Andrew Mitchell, Kirsten Holt, Oxford House College, London; Nalini Malhotra, Jenny Hardacre, Anglia Polytechnic University, Cambridge; Juan Antonio Rico, Eurostudy, Bilbao; Christine Pace, Avila Centro de Ingles , Avila; Johnathan Green, Eurolog Idiomas, Barcelona; Dawn Main, English Teachers Collective, Madrid; Yolanda Marzal, Globe Centre, Gandia, Valencia; Christina Barrio de la Fuente, EOI de Vigo; Rosa Maria Garcia Canton, Centro de Estudios UVE, Santander; Elżbieta Jodłowska, SJO Uniwersytet Opolski, Opole; Szymon Wach, SJo Politechnika Opolska, Opole; Stoyanka Georgieva Juleva, Panayot Volov Secondary School, Byala; Galia Papzikova, Pharos, Sofia; Mariana Niekolova, Pharos, Sofia; Janete Galvau Pinto, Cultura Inglesa, Ribeirao Preto; Solange Moras, Cultura Inglesa, Sao Carlos; Asiya Ilyasova, Golnar Sosnovskaya, Kazan State University, Kazan; Tatyana Polyanskaya, Kolosova Victoria, Big Ben, Moscow; Natalia Sorokina, Megapolis, Moscow; S. Shevchenko, I. Nuzha, St Petersburg University; Polina Beliniova, Language Centre Institute of Foreign Languages, St Petersburg; John Cahill, Ras Al Khaimah Women's College, UAE; Simon Gallivan, Napoleon Mannering, Kanda Gaigo Gakven, Tokyo; David B Stewart, Tokyo Institute of Technology; John Cargill, The British Council, Tokyo; Luciano Di Maio, Liceo Rosmini – Rovereto Trento, Corso Bettini; Joy Etty, Bernadette Gilmore, Catania University, Sicily; Clare Powell, British Council, Naples; Gemma Dawkes, IH Prato, Prato; Samantha Hayden, Alpha & Beta, Bolzano; Charlotte Bowler, Tracey Sinclair, The British School of Verona; Chris Powell, International House, Pisa; Ryan Johnstone, Elicos Centre, Northbridge WA; Heidi Wodzak, ITESL – Redcliff, Olivos; Marcela Jalo, Escuela de Lenguas UNLP, Calle; Cirtia Dottesi, Redcliffe, Caspar Campos, Paia de BS; Phil Hanham, Instituto CEDI, Salto; Nancy Maria Varesi Bossio, Gral pagola; David Hill, International House, Istanbul; Osmangazi University, Turkey.

and the following people for reporting on the manuscript:
Leslie Hendra, International House, London; Frances Traynor, International House, Sydney; Drew Hyde, Frances King School of English, London; Sally Parry, United Int College, London; Mike Carter, International House, Seville; Amanda Bailey, St Giles School of English, London; Tracey Sinclair, The British School, Verona; Alicia Cauregli, Universidad Siglo XXI, Cordoba; Bożena Fijałkowska, Liceum Ogólnoksztalcące IX im M. Konopnickiej, Lublin; Claire Nichols, BKC-International House, Moscow; Edyta Frelik, Linguaton, Lublin.

We are grateful to the following for permission to reproduce copyright material:
Curtis Brown Limited and HarperCollins Publishers for an extract adapted from 'The Guests' by Alvin Schwartz published in *Scary Stories to Tell in the Dark*, 1981; and John Wiley & Sons Limited for an extract adapted from *Psychometric Testing* by Philip Carter and Ken Russell, 2001.

We are also grateful to the following for permission to reproduce copyright song lyrics:
Music Sales Limited for the lyrics to 'Manic Monday', Words and Music by Prince © 1985 Controversy Music, USA and Universal/MCA Music Limited. All rights reserved. International copyright secured; Music Sales Limited for the lyrics to '(Remember the Days of the) Old Schoolyard', Words and Music by

Cat Stevens © 1977 Cat Music Limited and Sony Music Publishing (UK) Limited. All rights reserved. International copyright secured; Music Sales Limited and Perfect Songs for the lyrics to 'Out of Reach', Words and Music by Gabrielle and Jonathan Shorten © 2001 Universal Music Publishing Limited. All rights reserved. International copyright secured.

Illustrations by:
Adrian Barclay (Beehive) pp19, 62–63, 124; Barbara Bellingham (*début art*) p21; David Atkinson pp74, 98, 137, 138; Flatliner (*début art*) p26; Fred van Deelan (The Organisation) p103; Jerry Tapscott pp14, 24, 34, 58, 61, 68, 78, 97, 100, 110, 120; Mark Dickson (Folio) pp10–11, 72, 126–127, 131, 134; Melanie Barnes pp48–49; Michael Ogden (The Inkshed) p7; Mickey Finn (The Organisation) p27; Paul Burgess pp86–87; Peter Richardson pp108–109; Renee Mansfield (3 in-a-box) pp20, 115; Stuart Robertson (The Inkshed) p106; Yane Christensen (Sylvie Poggio) pp17, 56, 73.

Photo acknowledgements

We are grateful to the following for permission to reproduce copyright photographs:
Alamy/RubberBall Productions for p24 (royalty free), /Janine Wiedel Photolibrary, Jacky Chapman 45 top, /Image State/Pictor International 95 right, /David Hoffman 116 centre left, /Banana Stock 125 bottom left (royalty free); Arcaid/John Edward Linden for p99 bottom centre; Corbis 76 centre left (royalty free) Corbis/Dave Bartruff for p6 left, /Steve Prezant 7 top, /Norbert Schaefer 12, /David Katzenstein 16a, /Michael Keller 23 (Saara), 136, /Sygma/Durand Patrick 36 bottom, /David Turnley 43 bottom right, /Rob Lewine 50 (Dino), /Jim Craigmyle 52 top, /Sygma/Keline Howard 66 top left, /Robert Holmes 76 bottom, /Underwood & Underwood 91 top, /Hulton 91 centre, /Sygma 91 bottom, /Bettmann 93 bottom, /Nik Wheeler 113e, /Dennis Wilson 113d, /Matthias Kulka 112(3), /Adam Woolfitt 114; James David Photography for p99 centre right; Dominic Photography/Catherine Ashmore for p66 top right; Eye Ubiquitous/Sue Passmore for p54 right, /Paul Sehault 74 bottom left, /Hugh Rooney 80a, /Tim Hawkins 99 top right, /Michael George 100, /Sean Aidan 105; Getty /Kevin Horan 51 top right, /Ken Fisher 55 centre left, /The Image Bank 118, /Nicolas Russell for p14, /Bob Thomas 23 (Robin), 134, /Britt Erlanson 71 right, /Chronoscope 130, /Stone/Stephen Schauer 16(3), /Dale Durfee 23 (Daniel),/Bruce Ayers 30 left above, 51 top left, /Hugh Sitton 30 left below, /Andreas Kuehn 55 centre, /Kevin Mackintosh 70, /J.P. Williams 76 top left, /Jeff Zaruba 88 bottom, /Nick Dolding 120, /Taxi/Justin Pumfrey 16b, 60 bottom, /Bavaria 29 bottom left, /Derek Richards 29 top right, /Barry Willis 61, /Josef Beck 74 bottom right; Ronald Grant Archive for p39 bottom, 39 centre below, 39 top, 102a, 102b; Hutchison Library/Michael Macintyre for p23 (Chang),/Nancy Durrell McKenna 50 (Oliver), 125 top left; Image State for p30 right above, 55 left, /Age Fotostock, Pedro Coll 50 (Zak); First Light 50 (Caroline), 77, /Age Fotostock/Stuart Pearce 54 left, /Image Source 80d (royalty free), 116 top right (royalty free), /StockImage 84 top, /Neill & Dilys King 93 centre below, /Index Stock 94 right, /Age Fotostock, Glamour International 112(5), /Age Fotostock, Ken Welsh 113f, /Age Fotostock, Claver Carroll 113c, /Mimi Cotter 116 bottom right; Impact Photos /Brian Rybolt for p28, /Mark Henley 31, /David Slimings 33 top, /Alan Keohane 52 centre, /Simon Shepheard 58, /Robin Laurence 76 top right, /G. Deichmann 84 bottom, /Ray Roberts 112(2); Kobal Collection for p64 bottom, 102d; Life File 76 centre bottom; Jeff Moore (jeff@jmal.co.uk) for p52 bottom, 80b, 88 top, 112(1), 113a, 113g; Moviestore Collection/Warner Brothers for p67 right; Panos Pictures/Giacomo Pirozzi for p42 bottom right; Pearson Education for p16c, 85 all, 113(4); Penguin Books Ltd; cover photograph by Jamie Thompson, Reprinted by permission of , for p67; Photodisc Green/Mel Curtis (royalty free) for p139; Photos For Books for p34, 40, 50 (Alice), 50 (Nora), 55 right, 74 top, 80e, 88 centre above; Pictures Colour Library for p30 right below, 33 bottom, 99 bottom left; /Clive Sawyer 45 bottom; Popperfoto/DGL for p42 top left; Punchstock/Photodisc/Steve Mason for p6 right (royalty free), /BananaStock 43 top right, (royalty free); Redferns/Somon Ritter for p66 centre right, /David Redfern 93 top; Rex Features/Mark Pain for p42 bottom left, /Ron C. Angle/BEI 42 top right, /Seamus Murphy 43 bottom Left, /Richard Young 43 top left, Ken McKay 60 top, /Dennis Stone 119 top, /David Crichlow 122-123 all, /Stockbyte 125 bottom right (royalty free); Luke Rheinhart/Ann Cockcroft, poet for 124 top; Sony Computer Entertainment Inc. © Electronic Arts, EA SPORTS for p67 left; Topham Picturepoint for p18, 29 bottom right, 32 top, 33 left, 39 centre above, 64 centre, 71 left, 99 top left, 102e, /The Image Works/Arnold Gold/New Haven Register 7 bottom, /The Images Works 32 bottom, 94 left, 95 left, 119 bottom, /Dion Ogust 23 (Nadine), /Kent Meireis 29 top right, /Bob Daemmrich 42 centre right, /Esbin-Anderson 51 bottom left, 55 centre right, /Randi Anglin 51 bottom right, /Mike Greenlar 75, /Boyd Norton 116 top left, /Empics 16(1), /AP 16(2), 93 centre, /UPPA 38, /HIP/Science Museum 64 top, /Geoff Caddick 66 bottom, /Photri 80c, 88 centre below, 116 bottom left, /PA 93 centre above, /Charles Walker 102f, /Novosti 117 top.

The cover photograph has been kindly supplied by Getty Images/Image Bank

Picture Researcher: Liz Moore

Every effort has been made to trace the copyright holders and we apologise in advance for any unintentional omissions. We would be pleased to insert the appropriate acknowledgement in any subsequent edition of this publication.

This book is dedicated to Joseph, Jessica and Isabel.